What the reviewers said …

"*One Woman's War*, by Gladys Arnold, demonstrates that genuine Canadian Heroes do exist. … This book is lively and witty, filled with anecdotes about famous people."

— *Alberta Report*

"powerful and poignant"

— *The Montreal Gazette*

"*One Woman's War* is both compelling and highly informative."

— *Saskatoon Star-Phoenix*

"Her recollections are crystal-clear, and her story adds an interesting footnote to the larger histories of the time."

— *Globe and Mail*

"Not only an absorbing account of her wartime experiences, but an exploration of what it means to be Canadian."

— *Canadian Press*

"… a remarkable, endearing work, which brings to life the drama of World War Two in France"

— *Ottawa Woman*

"She evokes the excitement, the pain and heroism of an entire generation."

— *Hamilton Spectator*

Presenting Goodread Biographies

The Goodread Biographies imprint was established in 1983 to reprint the best of Candian biography, autobiography, diaries, memoirs and letters in paperback format.

Books in this series are chosen from the hardcover list of all of Canada's publishing houses. By selecting a wide range of interesting books that have been well received in the bookstores and well reviewed in the press, we aim to give readers inexpensive and easy access to titles they missed in hardcover.

You'll probably find other books in the Goodread Biographies series that you will enjoy. Check the back pages of this book for details on other titles in the series. You'll find our books on the paperback shelves of your local bookstore. If you have difficulty obtaining any of our titles, get in touch with us and we'll give you the name of a bookstore near you which stocks our complete list.

ONE WOMAN'S WAR

A Canadian Reporter with the Free French

GLADYS ARNOLD

1988
Goodread Biographies

Published in hardcover in 1987
by James Lorimer and Company

First published in paperback in 1988
by Goodread Biographies

Canadian Cataloguing in Publication Data

Arnold, Gladys, 1905-
One Woman's War
(Goodread Biographies)
ISBN 0-88780-154-4

1. Arnold, Gladys, 1905-.   2. France combattante.
3. World war, 1939-1945 -- personal narratives, Canadian.
4. France -- History -- German occupation, 1940-1945.
5. War correspondents -- Canada -- Biography. 6. War correspondents -- France -- Biography. I. Title.

D811.5A76 1988   940.54'86'440924   C88-098592-5

Goodread Biographies is the paperback imprint of
Formac Publishing Company Limited
5359 Inglis Street
Halifax, Nova Scotia B3H 1J4

Printed and bound in Canada

Acknowledgments

Without the help and patience of many people both in Canada and in France, this book could not have been written. In Canada the author warmly thanks the Canada Council for the Explorations Grant that made my final research in France possible; thanks also to I. Norman Smith, Dr. John Robbins and the late Dr. Wilfrid Eggleston for their aid and confidence. Grateful acknowledgment goes especially to my editor, Heather Robertson, and to Edna F. Hunt, without whose encouragement and skills I would have been lost. I also wish to thank Yousuf Karsh, Dr. Ronald Trites and Dr. Christina Fiedorowicz, Wladyslaw Henoch, Naomi Lang, Harriet Werry and Mme Odile Echeverri at the French Embassy in Ottawa.

In France I wish to express my appreciation to Ambassadors Gabriel Bonneau and Jean Basdevant, to Professor André and Charlotte Labaste, the late Irène Lézine, Elisabeth de Miribel, Nellita Geoffroy-Duchaume, Blanche Boëtte, Henri Martin-Prèvel, the Archives of the Ministry of Foreign Affairs, Paris, and Professor J. E. Duroselle, University of Paris.

Readers will meet many of my Canadian colleagues and friends within this book, but there were others who participated in our war effort to whom I would like to pay tribute. They include Andrée Leduc, Claire Charpentier, Marjorie Stowell, Cyrille Felteau, Marjorie Gray, Barbara Thompson, Phyllis Wilson, Denise Ouimet, Suzanne Cloutier and Jacques Carisse.

Thanks go to the following for permission to make brief quotations from other publications: Constable Publishers (London, England) and Plon-Perrin Editions (Paris), the Canadian Institute of International Affairs, the late Cecil Lingard and Professor Douglas G. Anglin.

To the people who endured occupation in Europe, and the civilians who manned the homefront in Britain, Canada and the Commonwealth, without whose dedication and sacrifice our Armed Forces could not have attained victory.

PART ONE

The Fall of France

one

The day Canada entered the Second World War, on September 10, 1939, Canadian civilians were no longer allowed to leave the country without special permission, except to visit the United States. Luckily I had my passage to France already booked and needed only a ticket to New York. I had to get back to work.

I was Paris correspondent for Canadian Press and, in fact, the only accredited Canadian reporter in France. For four years I had been sending stories with a "Canadian angle" to the CP office in Toronto, as well as contributing regularly to the Sifton papers in the West.

Knowing war was imminent, I had returned to Canada early in August to visit my parents in Victoria and to return to Saskatchewan, where I was born. I had been homesick for the sight of the big night sky and the golden haze of windborne chaff, and for the smell of wheat baking in the sun. But I had expected to be back in Paris before the war broke out.

As a young reporter with the Regina *Leader-Post,* I had gone to Europe in 1935, intending to stay for a year or so. My reason for going can be boiled down to two words: political curiosity. Living through the drought and unemployment of the Depression in Saskatchewan, those of us in our twenties passionately debated the pros and cons of socialism, communism, fascism and democracy, searching for answers to why more than a million Canadians could not find a job. In Saskatchewan it was difficult to examine these isms firsthand. But in Europe surely we would find some answers.

With my life savings of $500 in my belt, I sailed out of Fort Churchill,

Manitoba, at the end of July 1935 in one of the first freighters to carry wheat to Europe. After several months in London I arrived in Paris on December 28, not knowing a word of French. Language courses at the Alliance Française and new friends at my pension helped me pick up the language fairly quickly. I soon realized, however, that in the year I had allowed myself I could not learn enough about the isms I had come to study. And I was going broke.

During a brief visit to London in February 1936 I saw Clifford Sifton of the Sifton papers, who told me that Canadian Press did not have a correspondent in Paris. Immediately I sent off articles to CP in Toronto, but for three months there was no response although I posted articles every week. When my assets were about to enter the two-figure range, I wrote to CP serving notice that, unless I had some commitment soon, these articles would be my last. Shortly after a letter arrived from CP editor Gillis Purcell. "You're our Paris correspondent," he announced. "We're paying you $15 a week." A cheque was enclosed.

Now that war had come I had to get back to Paris. I wanted to see firsthand the conflict between fascism and democracy. And I expected to be Canada's first war correspondent on the Continent. "We can't be responsible for you if you go back," Gil Purcell warned. "Better think it over."

I could not imagine *not* going — staying home would be like leaving a theatre just after the curtain rises and the main characters are identified. I told Gil I would be responsible for myself. After grumbling a lot he gave me a raise of $5 a week and wished me well.

My passport now contained a visa that was good for an "unlimited" stay in France, furnished by Comte Jean de Dampierre, French minister to Canada in Ottawa. After stamping my passport he asked me if I would deliver a diplomatic pouch to the Ministry of Foreign Affairs in Paris. "Our Legation here has just opened," he told me. "Usually we send a courier but I have no one to send."

I sailed in mid-October. My passenger ship, the *Washington*, was being sent from New York to pick up Americans assembling in Irish, British and French ports. Along the rails stood elderly couples returning home to Europe and members of a Scottish girl's pipe band which had performed at the New York World's Fair. But the majority of the passengers were men. The ship moved out with no fluttering ribbons or coloured confetti, no music and excited laughter, no waving scarves or shouted last-minute messages. There were no smiles. On deck I was surrounded by anxious faces; below, on the dock, those being left behind were huddled in groups, many of them crying.

Along the railings men leaned out to catch a last glimpse of the Statue of Liberty. They were men from Britain, France and other European countries returning home to join the army. That is, all but the Poles. Poland had fallen to Hitler, so the few Poles aboard hoped to fight in the armies of their Western allies.

As we left the harbour I took a long last look as others were doing, and wondered how long it would be before I would see Canada again. Although most, if not all, the other passengers were going home while I was leaving mine, we shared the same sense that our destiny was unknown.

The first reality of war came as the continent disappeared into a blazing sunset and darkness fell. Suddenly our ship was awash with light. Painted on each side and brightly illuminated was an enormous Stars and Stripes. From the upper deck spotlights focused on American flags. We radiated light, yet as I saw the men hunched, usually alone at the rail and gazing into the night in silent contemplation, there was something obscene about that light. Out there, in the dangerous dark without a spark of light to mark their presence, Allied ships were creeping along cautiously. To the men on board those ships, the *Washington* must have looked like the biggest pleasure craft in the world.

Almost the entire crew of the *Washington* were Germans from Hamburg. One of the officers, an American, appeared at the door of my cabin and said, "Please don't unpack. All passengers are being moved up to First Class. Be very careful of what you say within hearing of the personnel of the ship." Looking around my new cabin, which was twice the size of the one I could afford and had clothes cupboards that made my bits of wardrobe look woefully inadequate, I realized how comfortable it must be to be rich, and that this was an uncommon way to be setting off for a war.

The atmosphere aboard ship was anything but holiday-like. Instinctively people of each nation drifted together as if for mutual comfort. As far as I knew there was only one other Canadian, a university student who had received a scholarship for a year's study in France. She was cheerfully making her way to Grenoble or Montpellier, having beaten down the objections of her parents.

There were about 300 passengers. My first encounter was with four Poles — Wscislaw Wroblewski, Ludwig Walasik, Julien Ramotowski and Wladyslaw Henoch. They were young oceanographers returning from an eighteen-month scientific expedition which had taken them in a small ketch from Gdynia, Poland, down the coasts of Europe and

Africa to Dakar, Senegal, across the South Atlantic to Rio and up the coasts of the Americas to the end of their mission in Chicago via the St. Lawrence. Our days and evenings were spent in the luxurious lounges, watching movies, eating fabulous meals, or on deck at night watching the phosphorescent glow in the water as the waves broke against the side of the ship. We talked about everything except the war. We discussed their expedition, talked about Canada, about books and music, and played bridge interminably. I have never felt like playing bridge since.

Tossing in my berth at night, I relived evenings I had spent in Canada with friends, especially remembering two who told me they shared the views of a group at Oxford who had declared that if war broke out they would not enlist. These friends in Regina, Stuart Thom and Robbie Robertson, spent one whole evening scoffing at me and calling me a romantic. Remember the First World War? There had been no moral basis for war in 1914. It had been like wars in Europe for hundreds of years — waged for influence, power and territory. They angrily argued that thousands of young Canadians had died for nothing, and they did not intend to do the same. (By June 1940 both were volunteers in uniform — Stuart in the navy where he became a corvette captain and Robbie in the army educational services.)

Two French friends, Suzette Provost and Hélène Compérot, who had accompanied me to Canada, had returned to France safely in late September, but I had had no word since. What was happening in Paris? In Europe? Who among my friends were in camps or at the Front? How soon would the Germans start their push west and why had they not already begun? During my wakeful nights I shuddered at what had happened in Poland and in the Munich fiasco in September 1938, when Neville Chamberlain had proclaimed "Peace in our time." Suspicious, as all journalists in Paris and London were, about our state of preparedness, my crossing of the Atlantic was full of foreboding.

The unreality of that trip still troubles me. Every day the sun shone. There were no clouds and the ocean was smooth. We fed the gulls, watched a whale blow and strained our eyes to see if any other ships were out there. But in the six days it took to reach the port of Cobh, Ireland, we seemed to be absolutely alone in that vast expanse of sea and sky.

We had no sooner docked in Cobh before the ship was surrounded by swarms of small craft filled with men and women holding up their lace and linen handiwork. They waved and shouted, urging us to buy their doilies, tea cloths and shawls, as the soldiers-to-be on deck looked down in disbelief. Other hawkers were selling feverishly to Americans now beginning to come aboard. The crowd waiting on the dock was happy to make last-minute purchases, but the vendors in the boats soon realized they were in the wrong market and rapidly rowed back to shore. A voice near me muttered bitterly, "Laces and linens! Have they no imagination? No feeling?"

The following day we berthed at Southampton. In the meantime the whole ship had been converted into one big bed. Lounges, library, theatre, writing-rooms and all available cabins were filled with narrow cots. More were stacked in corridors and on the decks. While the *Washington* was taking on American passengers, my Polish friends and I went off to see the city. When I had left Southampton three months earlier, it had been a festive place with tourists everywhere in the streets and the harbour full of ships. The German *Bremen* had docked ahead of my ship, the *Aurania* to one side, the *Berengaria* was about to sail, and another great, white sea queen on the horizon was off to the Orient. Everywhere the harbour was gay with flags of many nations, gleaming white decks and red funnels.

What a different Southampton my friends and I were seeing that day. Dark troopships lined the quays; the merchantmen were painted dull gray, their portholes sealed. Billows of canvas concealed the snouts of guns. On the streets most people carried a small, square box which they had strapped on their backs, slung from their shoulders or tied to the handlebars of their bicycles. At four o'clock children streamed into streets carrying their boxes. They contained gas-masks.

In a Canadian Press article I wrote at the time: "Little by little the shadows eat into the streets. The sun sinks, the twilight grows, and no lights come on. Now the whole city is swallowed in obscurity. Double-decked trams crawl along packed with human beings. Almost complete blackout now. A dimmed red globe illuminates the interior of the tram ... all windows are painted over; it takes courage to force one's way into the gloom. The motorman examines your fare with his flashlight. Inside you suffocate among strange odours, pressing bodies, the touch of damp cloth or a hand. In time your nose takes on a new intelligence. Among the clammy human odours it picks out the acrid smell of Harris tweed and the horsey scent of leather and a soldier's moist uniform. A sudden breath tells you your neighbour to the left has been eating fish. Whiffs of beer, tobacco, onion and menthol waft back and forth until you can't bear it another moment and are glad to stumble out into the thick, black night. One by one the shop doors have closed; the word 'Open' in dimly glowing metallic paint indicates a pharmacy or a restaurant. It is now totally black, but quickly eyes and ears become accustomed. After colliding with several even blacker spots you realize these are other people and slowly you begin to detect their approach in time to dodge...."

With my Polish friends I entered a restaurant through three layers of dark curtains. Not a glimmer of light announced its presence from the street. Inside, life flowed on busy and light-hearted. Excellent food was being served and we quite forgot the circumstances. Other diners were friendly and more ready to talk with us than I had ever found the English to be before. We exchanged toasts and drank too much, and finally groped our way back to the ship somewhat more than merry.

Fortunately, my posh cabin had a table and chair so I could use my portable Underwood. This was my chance to put together my Southampton article and post it, along with other impressions of the crossing, to Gil Purcell. As I wrote in the early morning I could hear the rattle of chains and thumps of trunks, crates and baggage. Shouts and curses of the sailors mingled with the sounds of crying children, irate parents and the stern voices of the ship's officers trying to bring some order and satisfy questions of nearly two thousand Americans who had come aboard the previous day and during the night.

We had lost the British passengers and some other nationals; only the Europeans remained. Instinctively the French, Poles, Belgians and others drew away from the mobs of excited tourists, most of them fleeing Europe. Children raced along the decks and through the lounges, upsetting cots and causing the stewards to raise their fists in the air. The Americans tried to settle into the cramped quarters; some wanted all their luggage and made nuisances of themselves until they were told sharply that they could keep only overnight bags because the rest was being stored below. Those of us who had made the crossing from New York were segregated in a small corner of the dining-room, for which we were thankful.

We left Southampton the next afternoon, stuffed to the "gunnels" with our human cargo. I wondered what would happen when we reached our French port, although we had no inkling which one it would be. Surely the ship could not carry many more passengers. The purser dismissed my doubts. "We'll bed'em down on the floors. We've a thousand mattresses below."

As the *Washington* drew alongside the French dock we leaned over the railings and eagerly observed the crowd, the French soldiers and officials. Suddenly we heard a tinny but familiar tune, one I recognized faintly but whose lyrics I could not remember. An elderly American standing behind me whooped with joy. "It must be that same old record," he cried.

"What is it?"

"'Land of Hope and Glory,'" he said. "I've been hoping our port would be Le Verdon.... This is where we Americans landed in France in 1918. When we came in they were playing that record to welcome us. It's so scratched I didn't recognize it at first."

Le Verdon, the ocean port of the ancient city of Bordeaux, is nearly sixty miles inland on the wide Garonne River. The river and city's harbour could accommodate all but the largest ocean-going vessels, so hundreds of Americans had to come to the coast by train. They stood on the dock surrounded by mountains of luggage and watched closely as we disembarked.

We all boarded the train and at Bordeaux parted for our various destinations. I was remaining in the city with friends for a few days so arranged to meet my Polish friends at a Paris restaurant a week later.

I was astonished to find Bordeaux, on the surface at least, calm and unchanged. My hostess, Mme Compérot, and her daughter, my friend Hélène who taught philosophy in a Bordeaux lycée, told me how Périgueux and other small cities some ninety kilometres from Bordeaux had become the wartime home of the civilian population of Strasbourg, Alsace.

"The evacuation took place in forty-eight hours and each person was allowed only forty kilos of personal effects," Mme Compérot said. "It must have been dreadful for them. Still, nothing could be worse than occupation," she shuddered. "We know from the last war."

I decided to stop over in Périgueux on my way to Paris. The evacuation of more than 200,000 urban people into mainly farming areas was worth writing about. In Périgueux I met the mayor, and he took the time to show me around.

How, I wondered, could these small cities and the countryside cope with such a sudden influx of so many people? "How could you decide to accept them?" I asked the mayor innocently.

"We had no choice, Mademoiselle," he told me. "We were just ordered to prepare for them. It's war you know." He shrugged his shoulders.

I discovered that the policeman on the beat or directing traffic had a Strasbourg policeman at his side. In stores, behind counters, in bars, restaurants, offices, the post office and railway station, there were double staffs. Every home had its Strasbourg individual or family and the overflow was billeted on farms and in villages throughout the countryside.

Knowing the Alsatian dialect must be a problem because of its resemblance to German, I wondered how the host families had reacted. How were they treating their "guests"? How were the teachers in the schools managing?

"It's a big problem," admitted the mayor. "But we've held large public meetings to explain to our own people how important this inconvenience is. Some complain that the 'guests' are German. We remind them of the Paris tourists and their funny accent. We remind them how happy we were to get our Alsace back, and of their own good fortune. They do not have to leave their homes for who knows how long. We ask if they can deny hospitality to our own unfortunate people. Now, after two months of this extraordinary war, our people are beginning to understand."

I visited a school. The class was mixed, with equal numbers of children from each city. For my benefit the teacher asked some of the children from Strasbourg to tell us what was different in Périgueux. Already these children were speaking a barely accented French. "It's queer here," answered one small boy who was billeted on a farm. "They have no water in the houses. We must go outside to get water out of a deep hole in the ground. At home on our farm we had hot and cold water coming out of taps in our kitchen and bathroom."

Another child jumped up. "It's not true. Everybody knows that on farms water comes from wells. Who ever heard of hot water coming out of taps on a farm? He lies."

The teacher smiled at me and quieted her class. "If you double that many times you will understand our problems," she said.

"Some charitable organizations in Paris are helping us," the mayor told me. "We are planning to have evergreen trees brought here for Christmas to make the people feel more at home. It is not our custom, but in Alsace they have Christmas trees. The ladies of the charity are sending us the decorations, and toys and books for gifts."

As I left Périgueux I realized that war has many faces we never see.

After travelling through old towns and a countryside that seemed strangely peaceful, I stepped off the train in Paris and felt for the first time a change in atmosphere. The quiet was audible. There was none of the noise and confusion I associated with French stations, no quick-tapping heels and nervous, high-pitched voices. Now travellers silently picked up their valises and moved off. There were no blue-bloused porters. The station employees were very elderly men in shabby, ill-fitting uniforms that dated back to the First World War and smelled of mothballs. Tired-looking women, dressed mostly in black and wearing worn felt slippers, pushed brooms around the cavernous *salle des pas perdus*. The atmosphere was lugubrious and chilling.

I had already begun to worry about finding a place to live. Had my friend Irène Lézine received my telegram asking her to reserve a room for me in the American residence at the Cité Universitaire? After leaving Paris in August, I had not heard from Irène. She had a Russian background, and I wondered about her wartime status, especially after Russia and Germany had signed a friendship pact.

What a relief it was to see her blonde head emerge from the crowd. I noticed, as I always did, the graceful movement of her walk, which again reminded me of full-skirted Russian dancers gliding across the stage. After embracing me she seized the larger of my suitcases and announced, "You're staying with me until you find accommodation. The Cité Universitaire has been requisitioned. All the residences including the American House are barracks now."

We dragged the suitcases down to the metro, tripping over each other's questions. Her brother and brother-in-law were both at the Front. Had I seen Hélène and her mother in Bordeaux? Yes. Had she been able to get her naturalization papers? No.

Irène had been in Paris since she was two years old; her mother, brother and sister were all French citizens. Several times in the past I had accompanied her to police headquarters where she regularly inquired about her request for naturalization. But always without results. I asked her what the problem was this time.

"The same old thing, only worse than ever now the war's on. I'm a single female. Of course, my brother did his military service, my sister married a Frenchman and Mother got her papers before the First World War, when she had some influence. They know me at that desk and keep on joking and telling me to marry a Frenchman," she laughed, half angry and half rueful about French bureaucracy. "Remember the one I saw when you came with me in the spring? Well he offered to marry me himself if that would help."

"But being Russian . . .?"

"No, I'm French even if I'm not yet naturalized. I have a Nansen Pass [issued to stateless persons by the League of Nations]. And there isn't any more Russia, only the USSR. Besides, my director at the lab told me not to worry. He'll look out for me if I'm bothered."

Irène was a child psychologist and had been conducting a special study of children under two years of age. I asked her about the babies.

"No babies for the duration," she replied somewhat mischievously. "My babies now are pilots. We are testing would-be pilots for their speed of reaction under stress of various forms, and old ones from the First War to see if they are still up to it. I suppose you'd call us the scientific side of the air force."

Irène took my hand and squeezed it. "I'm so glad you're back. I was afraid you wouldn't come but Hélène and Suzette told me you'd be back for sure. We'll have some fun in spite of the war." Her clear, gray eyes twinkled.

At midnight the air-raid sirens sounded and I found myself being hurried down several flights of stairs. To save electricity elevators in apartment buildings were not in use. We wound up in a dark underground cellar with other tenants. Everyone wore night clothes and robes; some women had scarves tied hastily over rubber curlers. We settled ourselves on long, wooden benches. People stared at one another.

Suddenly an old lady gazed sharply at Irène and asked, "My dear, are you not Mademoiselle Lézine? The last time we spoke, I remember, you were a child and we were down here in the shelter, in the last war." For the most part we sat in silence, listening to the distant rumble of guns. With almost a note of relief someone remarked that at last the war was beginning.

Suddenly we began sniffing the air. Nothing in the world smells better than oven-fresh bread. We were next to a bakery, and the door into the corridor between us was open. Irène and I got up and walked into the hall. As we did the smell of bread was joined by delicious fragrances of warm pastries and fruit tarts. The baker, a white-haired man with an enormous floury apron over an ample paunch, beamed at us. "Just like the the last war Mam'iselle Lézine, n'est-ce pas? So you are all down in the shelter again. Here, take back something to eat." He took down a plate and filled it with pastries and handed us two baguettes of bread, fresh from the oven.

When the "all clear" sounded we spent the next ten minutes shaking hands all around before climbing back upstairs. Apparently no situation is complete without a vigorous arm pump.

After returning to Irène's I began to worry about finding living quarters in the city. "Try the Foyer International on the Boulevard St. Michel," advised Irène. "The hotels and pensions around the Sorbonne are freezing. The Foyer has heat. Miss Watson has seen to that. You know how good the meals are and it's cheap."

Sarah Watson was an American who had been a student in Paris before the First World War. During the war she remained in the city doing volunteer work, and opened the Foyer in 1920 to make a homelike residence for female students from the United States. It overlooked the Luxembourg Gardens, a location that appealed to me.

When I arrived at the Foyer, Mme Marcelle Fournier, a charming, soft-voiced Frenchwoman and Sarah Watson's partner, showed me into the sitting-room. Miss Watson sailed in. "Sailed" is the right word. I remember a former resident saying that in any army Miss Watson would be a drill sergeant. Of medium height and thick-set, Miss Watson stood ruler straight. Her strong, square-jawed, almost masculine face was softened by twinkling, bright blue eyes and an unruly cowlick. Her smile was enveloping. In spite of twenty-five years in France, she had a heavy American accent. She defended herself by saying, "Well I *am* an American," and went merrily on her way pronouncing *soeur* as "soor" and *lieu* as "loo."

I learned that Miss Watson loved Paris passionately and that her maternal instinct had turned itself to attending to the needs and comforting the broken hearts of the girls boarding at the Foyer. When the Americans left, Miss Watson had opened her doors to girls from the French provinces, a few Greeks, Egyptians and Romanians. I explained that the Cité was no longer available. "I'm only taking one course at the Sorbonne," I told her. "My job is writing for the Canadian Press."

"Don't worry. Several residents now aren't students," she replied. "One is a secretary at our Embassy. I'll have to put you on the seventh floor. All the lower rooms are taken. Your typewriter won't disturb anyone. Sorry you can't use the elevator but I'll have a chair placed at the fourth floor landing in case you need a rest." She grinned.

The room was large and clinically white because it had been used as quarantine quarters. The bright-flowered curtains at the windows had heavy, dark over-drapes to black-out any light at night. Lamps and wall fixtures were equipped with dark blue bulbs. From my window I looked out on roofs and the trees of the Luxembourg Gardens, the golden dome of Les Invalides was to the left, Sacré Coeur floated above Montmartre far to the right, and the spires of Notre Dame marked the course of the invisible Seine.

In the bathroom was an enormous sunken tub, a luxury I used frequently during the winter and spring of the "phony" war. Miss Watson sent up a desk and comfortable arm-chairs to make my room at the Foyer the most pleasant accommodation I enjoyed in my five years in Paris.

This certainly is a preposterous war, I mused as I looked around the room. For a struggling young journalist trying to exist on the dubious bounty of the Canadian Press and precarious freelancing at a cent a word, the war was certainly treating me well. So far, except for a few false air alerts, no war was visible from Paris.

Soon after moving in, I went around to the police station of the Fifth Arrondissement (the Latin Quarter). Long lines of foreigners edged slowly towards two policemen who stood behind the counter in a dingy, gray, dimly lit room. Identity cards were being issued and each person was being fingerprinted. When I showed my passport the young policeman eyed me disapprovingly and asked what I was doing in Paris with a war on. Shouldn't I be at home with my parents?

I dug out my press card and the card that gave me permission to circulate anywhere in France. I told him I had a job to do, and dutifully placed my hands on the counter to be fingerprinted. The older policeman leaned over and handed me an identity card to sign and said tartly, "We don't fingerprint British subjects. The British are our allies. Besides they feel insulted if asked for fingerprints." He waved me away with half a smile.

A few minutes later I was walking down the Boulevard St. Michel towards my favourite café. There were fewer students about but otherwise it looked the same as it had in the early summer. Some students were gathered around the sidewalk bins of books in front of the Librarie Gibert; others sipped coffee or apéritifs at sidewalk tables; still others had their heads together over books or were engaged in earnest conversation. Aged waiters lounged in doorways. Overhead the sun shone warmly for late October, and those students living in unheated rooms were taking full advantage of it.

I found a table and sat down. It was time to take stock. I had a place to live and my identity card; now I needed to register for a course at the Sorbonne, visit the Canadian Legation, find out where the Information and Censorship offices were, and deliver that diplomatic mail pouch to the Ministry of Foreign Affairs.

two

The arrival of a foreigner carrying a French diplomatic pouch caused something of a sensation at the Ministry of Foreign Affairs. Thanks to my Canadian passport I got by the guard at the courtyard entrance of Quai d'Orsay. Two French-style Black Marias were parked in the shadows, ready to disgorge policemen or guardsmen at a moment's notice. I had time to inhale the stale air of the bare and grim gray corridors hidden behind the sumptuous foyer while being passed from hand to hand, through three guards and two officials, before a distinguished-looking, middle-aged man hurried towards me.

Comte Serge de Fleury had been forewarned of my presence. I introduced myself.

"Now what is this about a diplomatic pouch?" he exclaimed, eyeing my overnight bag suspiciously. I opened it and drew out a thin bag. He seized it and quickly examined the seals. They were intact.

"But I don't understand." He stared at me uncertainly. "It's irregular, most irregular. How did you obtain this bag, Miss?"

"Your Minister in Ottawa, M. de Dampierre, entrusted it to me. He hadn't a courier to send."

Assured that my credentials were genuine, de Fleury relaxed and became gracious and helpful. He took me to the Hôtel Continental in the rue de Castiglione, an unlikely place to find the Commissariat (later Ministry) of Information and the Censorship offices. There we met Pierre Comert, the government's Chief Press Officer for the Anglo-American press. I realized I had met him; he had been handling press relations when I was writing an article on Quai d'Orsay. It was good to see him again, for a more knowledgeable and competent journalist would be hard to find. As I was the only Canadian journalist in Paris, I received the new wartime accreditation at once. He introduced me to Mme Leleu, Chief Liaison Officer. She was to become a friend and an excellent guide, and gave me invaluable help arranging interviews and unearthing stories for Canadian Press.

I remember walking out of the Continental thinking how incongruous it was to see the hurly-burly of the press in this setting of bedroom-offices, dainty wallpapers, crystal chandeliers and ballroom typing pools.

Time was interminable for all the frustrated journalists haunting the Hôtel Continental and the Ministry of War, pulling strings wherever we could to get permission to visit the Front, the Maginot Line or the naval bases. We were all scratching for war-related stories or trying to arrange interviews at headquarters with generals — maybe, with luck, interviews with Gamelin or Weygand who must know the real situation.

I knew I was not part of the small charmed circle of the Big League, but I was happy to be in the league at all. "Stick to human interest stories," I had been ordered. "The boys in the London Bureau will look after political and military stuff." In retrospect, I believe our bureau in London actually thought all politically newsworthy reporting could only emanate from London.

My membership in the Union Internationale des Associations de Presse gave me access to press conferences at the Hôtel Continental and at Quai d'Orsay, though my credentials did not rate the briefings at the War Office. This was not because I was a female reporter but because I was only a *Canadian* reporter. The correspondents of the British and American press were the ones that counted.

Though I was convinced it was more important for Canadians who were at war to know what was happening than the Americans who were not in the war, I soon discovered that Canada figured far down on the list of important countries in the eyes of those doing the news briefing. I suspected I owed my accreditation and passes less to my impressive CP credentials than to French sentimentality about Canada. In the eyes of most, Canada was still a British colony, and every French person knew the status of colonies. Where else could we expect to be except under the wing of Great Brtitain?

I did, however, get a chance to encounter journalists whose names I knew and whom I regarded with awe. I kept hoping that the Canadian Press would one day send instructions for me to interview Edouard

Daladier, prime minister until March 1940, or Paul Reynaud, who succeeded him, and authorize me to send press telegrams by the bushel — as Percy Philip of the *New York Times,* Harold King of Reuters and Alexander Werth of the *New Statesman* did. Gil Purcell had impressed upon me that Canadian Press had a scanty budget and did not run to frills.

One morning the newspapers announced the arrival of the first contingent of Canadians in Britain. The headline read, "Indians arrive from Canada!" Pictures of Indians both in native dress and in uniform were splashed all over the front pages. A number of Indians had been among the first arrivals, and French reporters in London, who as children had dreamed of meeting a Canadian Indian, gave them an effusive welcome and all the headlines. Other Canadians did not stand a chance.

Canadian Press, perhaps unwittingly, gave me the real story to write. Had I been chasing military and political stories I would never have had time to talk to and live with the people who gave me faith in the successful outcome of the war. Thanks to Mme Leleu, who saw me almost every day, and Pierre Comert whose briefings I attended, I was able to obtain feature stories and interviews peripheral to the non-war.

How is an army of millions fed? I joined a busload of mostly Americans to visit one of the food supply stations scattered all over France. We arrived at a group of long, nondescript sheds on the outskirts of a small town. "You handle the food for 200,000 men in these old shacks?" one American asked. "In America we'd have all new, modern buildings with the latest equipment for packaging and refrigeration."

"I doubt it," our colonel guide answered. "That would make the commissariat instantly visible from the air, and an easy target."

Bread for 200,000 men in the front lines was made in enormous stone bake-ovens by mobilized bakers. The dough was hand-kneaded. The loaves were round, about nine inches deep and sixteen inches in diameter, and encased in an inch of golden crust. The heavy crust preserved the bread for shipping and for use over a period of at least ten days. The baker cut a twelve-day-old loaf and showed us the interior. It had the same soft texture as a fresh loaf baked that morning. The aroma of the warm, fresh loaves sent us drooling to the colonel, who went in turn with a hungry look to find the baker. Beaming with pride the baker cut large slabs of a new loaf for us to wash down with red wine. Coffee was being roasted nearby in high iron kettles, and each kettle was being constantly stirred by two soldiers. The fragrance of the coffee was almost strong enough to tantalize enemy pilots. Weathered sheds at the edge of the village housed walls of canned preserves, dried beans, split peas, lentils, spaghetti, onions, dried fruits and sugar, while a constant stream of wine barrels rolled along a rack out into railway cars. Twice a day two long trains slid out, packed to bursting, and headed for innumerable, smaller distribution points closer to the Front. It all went on so quietly that even the villagers were hardly aware of it.

"It's quite true that an army fights on its stomach," the colonel declared. "For the French soldier the essentials are bread, cheese and wine. It's a big job to keep millions of soldiers supplied but we've had experience."

Eve Curie, journalist and daughter of Marie Curie of radium fame, was officially in charge of women's auxiliary services in war industries and related jobs. I accompanied her on some expeditions to see French women at work.

With over five million men mobilized, I began to understand that France could not have carried on had not wives, sisters, daughters and even mothers taken their places in civilian life by the hundreds of thousands. They had stepped into jobs on farms and in factories, businesses, offices, restaurants and all the service industries. Women were driving buses and working in metro stations, bars and shops as well as handling professional jobs as teachers, nurses, lawyers and doctors. The retired also were back on the job.

All physically fit men between eighteen and sixty were expected to do their duty. Vast numbers were mobilized *sur place*, in essential war industries and other ancillary activities where their skills were necessary to back up the nearly three million men in uniform. With Eve I visited an armament factory where almost all the workers were women. They were making shell cases. Everywhere, neatly stacked, were large brass cases, standing two or three feet high.

"Our main problem is to persuade the women that the cases don't have to shine like looking-glasses," grumbled a supervisor. "Some actually stay after hours to put on an extra shine. They say to me, 'But these are *French* shells. No German can make a shell that looks like ours!' We explain they must work faster and turn out greater quantities, not more beautiful cases." He sighed. "It's no use, they want them looking like their own brass *jardinières*."

Mme Leleu arranged an interview for me with Mme Albert Lebrun, wife of the President of France. After touring the magnificent Elysées palace, we had tea and Mme Lebrun described some of the difficulties of running such an establishment after having lived a very simple life. I mentioned that I had seen her in Les Halles, the great, central market of Paris. In the background a limousine and chauffeur waited. "Yes," she said seriously, "my husband has a delicate stomach so I always shop for meat and vegetables for his meals myself."

The Chief of the new Press and Propaganda Commissariat was, to the astonishment of most of the foreign press, France's foremost playwright, Jean Giraudoux. *Ondine*, his latest production, was playing at the Théâtre Athénée. I had not missed any of his plays in five years and could not help wondering what experience had prepared him for his new post.

Giraudoux's staff was composed of such press and information experts as novelists Colette and Georges Duhamel, as well as other writers and poets of note. They were reinforced by a battery of literary intellectuals from the Collège de France; none of them, as far as I could find out, had ever had anything to do with popular journalism. Some of the releases and documentation we correspondents received might have been suitable for the *Queen's Quarterly* or the University of Montreal's *l'Inter*. Much of it had to do with aspects of French culture and was no doubt welcomed by French departments of Canadian universities. But for hometown folk in Regina, Victoria, Halifax and the rest of Canada, who were hungry to know where and what the action was, there was not much I could use.

I had looked into the morgues of a number of newspapers in Canada to find that they contained little or nothing about France. Other than the Toronto *Star*, their dossiers consisted of a few clippings, mostly Associated Press coverage of sensational love or crime stories. Were Canadians to see France and the war only through American eyes? Innocently, I thought an interview with Giraudoux might set things straight.

Commissaire Giraudoux received me with distant, unsmiling politeness. "And what can we do for you, Mademoiselle?"

I launched into an explanation of the difference between the needs of Canadian and American readers. "Just because we are North Americans too that doesn't mean our interests are the same," I declared. "People here never seem to understand that we are *not* Americans; we're an independent country, part of the British Commonwealth and, most of all, your allies. Why, the United States is not even in the war!"

"You think we should be sending to Canada the documentation we send to Britain?"

"Certainly not," I told him. "There should be a special service for Canada. Hundreds of thousands of Canadian soldiers are in training and will come over here as their fathers did before them. They are your allies. Their families want to know everything about France and French life. They want to know how their men will be received on leave. A few broadcasts by Françoise Rosay won't do it, though that was a good idea. People want to know about the food situation. What are the medical services, the hospitals and nursing services? How are you going to get enough blood for transfusions once the real war starts? What do the French think is behind this 'phony' war." I hurried on excitedly with my final, devastating shot. "And of course you know that more than one-quarter of the Canadians in the forces are French-speaking!"

As I talked, Giraudoux's face grew longer. "Mademoiselle," he said, "to tell the truth I know nothing about press and information matters, or what I am doing here. I'm a writer, not a journalist. I'm mobilized here. Why, I can't think." His voice grew grumpier. "I'm sure you are right. Something should be done about Canada but . . ." He shrugged his shoulders. "I promise you I'll speak to somebody."

When I started to thank him he suddenly settled back in his chair and said with a sparkle in his eyes, "Ah, Canada. Tell me, Mademoiselle, how is the theatre doing over there? How many Canadians speak French, did you say?"

"About three million. I'm sorry, I've never lived in Quebec so I can't tell you about their theatres, but in Winnipeg they have a fine French-speaking theatre company."

We talked a few minutes more about the theatre, the one subject that did arouse his enthusiasm. As I left, he said, "I'll do what I can, Mademoiselle, but I can't promise anything." Nothing ever came of it.

My friendships among the journalists grew as we gossiped about the military stalemate. Russia invaded Finland and we wondered if this had been part of the Russo-German non-aggression pact. Arved Arenstam, a Latvian journalist who wrote for European papers, was the best informed. He assured me the Finns would fight. One day Arved appeared at the Hôtel Continental, handsome in a well-cut uniform complete with great coat and swagger stick. We went out for coffee. "War correspondents" had to be in uniform, and they had to buy them themselves, he told me grinning. "I haven't been able to get anywhere with the 'brass' so I went to the best tailor in town. This outfit cost me a fortune. Maybe I'll make an impression now and get to the Maginot Line."

Arved was easily the most experienced of the foreign journalists, and popular with most. He spoke six or so languages, and had attended every European and international conference on military and foreign affairs for the past dozen years. The League of Nations was an open book to him and he was ready to give information or a tip even to the fringe reporters. I wished him luck in getting to the Maginot Line, but I did not feel too hopeful.

Several times a month Mme Madeleine LeVerrier, editor of the prestigious political revue *l'Europe Nouvelle,* held receptions in the journal's offices, which gave foreign journalists opportunities to meet and talk informally with French generals and politicians. In a relaxed wine and cheese setting, we could ask questions of Socialist leader Leon Blum, Pierre Cot, leader of the Radical Socialist Party and former Minister for Air, and other prominent political figures such as Daladier and Reynaud. One thread running through all these conversations was the complete confidence these men had in the French Army, the Franco-British Entente and the Maginot Line. If there were doubts during those winter and early spring months, they were well hidden. It was inconceivable that Hitler could win. Whatever venal ambitions may have lain behind the First World War, this war was being waged for different reasons. It was perceived as a struggle to safeguard our values, our human dignity and freedom. Hitler and his Nazis symbolized evil, a threat to a system of values built up painfully over centuries. We believed that, if ever there was a just cause to fight for, it was this one.

One aspect of our conversation during these receptions still surprises me. When the mechanics of the war were under discussion, the speculation was all about "holding the line," war in depth, trenches and superior manpower. Air and mechanized warfare was spoken of as useful adjuncts to the real army on the ground. Obviously few, if any, thought in terms other than those of the First World War.

After one of these meetings Arved told me he had asked Mme LeVerrier why, no matter how many times he applied, he was never invited to accompany other journalists, almost all of whom were British or American, to see the Maginot Line.

"My dear friend," she said, "you will never go."

"And why not? I'm well qualified, better than most of them and you see I'm properly uniformed!"

"Dear Arved, you represent Latvia. It is of no importance to the powers that decide these things. France needs arms and you know where they must come from…"

I tackled Pierre Comert on the same subject. "Canada's in this war too," I said. "Why shouldn't I visit the Maginot Line? Canadians want to know about it too. They have heard about nothing else, but they have no idea what it is or what it is like. They want an eyewitness account."

"Mademoiselle, it's impossible. There's no place for a woman on these trips. We can't be responsible. Get one of the others to give you a story. I'm sorry."

I was furious and went to our Legation to see if someone could help me. Fortunately I ran into General Georges Vanier, our Minister to France (later Ambassador and eventually Governor-General of Canada). He was sympathetic as always, and told me that Major General Léo LaFlêche, Military Attaché at the Legation, was at the moment visiting the Line. "Why don't you interview him when he gets back instead?"

It was obvious to me that if newsmen like Arenstam or Karel Mazel, who represented the foremost newspaper in Prague, were unable to go, I did not stand a chance. So I settled for General LaFlêche.

General LaFlêche was enthusiastic in his praise of what he had seen of the Maginot Line and the morale of the officers and men manning it. "You cannot imagine such fortifications. We were greatly impressed. Men or tanks could never cross that barrier of steel — rows and rows of steel rail protuding from the ground in series and unending rows — like powerful teeth that tear the heart out of an engine. Jungles of barbed-wire. The men are comfortable, warm, well-provisioned. Nothing like the old days in the trenches and bivouacs. It's an underground fortress stretching from the Swiss border to Belgium; plenty of ammunition and the latest in guns. May we thank God it's impenetrable!"

Unfortunately, the Germans never did try to penetrate it.

Eve Curie suggested I visit the clean-up posts set up in the Paris railway stations by the Women's Voluntary Services with the help of the Boy Scouts and Eclaireuses (Girl Guides). Baths, shaves, hair-cuts and uniform cleaning gave soldiers on leave or on their way home an opportunity to tidy up, so they reached their families looking as though they had been away on a business trip instead of at the Front.

At the Garé Montparnasse an elderly, crippled veteran was in charge. When he realized who my readers were, he broke into smiles. "Canadians!" he said. "During the First World War I was a liaison officer. How many friends I made among the Canadians! They used to come over to our mess sometimes. Said the food was better. When are they arriving in Paris?"

"I don't know, but some contingents are already in England."

"Oh, I know," he said and we both laughed, remembering the

headlines about the Indians. "Mademoiselle, you must let me know. You must tell me when they are arriving," the old veteran urged, shaking my hand vigorously. "I must be at the station to welcome them, to shake the hands of the sons of my old friends. I saw them at Ypres and Arras. Fighting like devils they were. You mustn't forget Mam-zelle."

At the Legation I was told that a large hotel had been requisitioned for Canadian soldiers on leave. When I visited it, a Canadian doctor who was in charge took me on the grand tour. In one of the hotel bedrooms, I looked around taking in the view, punched the mattress and then pulled out a drawer in the bedside table. In it I saw a Gideon Bible and a small package. When I picked up the package my crimson-faced guide gasped. "I ... I'm sorry. You see ... some of them are bound to ... we want to take precautions. I'm responsible for their health and have to see that the boys are ... are ... safe." Suddenly I realized I was holding a package of condoms.

At times there did indeed seem to be a war on. There was action at sea, ships were lost, a passenger ship was sunk. But the newspapers downplayed these events. The capture of a German submarine entangled in a steel defence net in the North Sea, however, hit all the headlines. Our sense of proportion suffered. The German attack on Norway brought the war closer yet. *Narvik* was on everyone's lips. Patriotic fervour rose to fever pitch as soldiers, among them Czechs and Poles — including two of my ship companions — left for Norway. Some journalists disappeared along with them.

I lunched one day with General and Mme Vanier and we discussed the war. General Vanier was not as optimistic about the situation as General LaFlêche had been. He emphasized that he did not believe negotiations were going on behind the scenes between the Allies and Germany, and that he doubted the Germans would be foolish enough to attack the Maginot Line. I could see he was worried. "All these stories about negotiations and a frontal attack on the Line are just Fifth Column propaganda," he said moodily.

He asked me if I would have time to give English lessons to two Frenchmen, a submarine commander and an economist with the Franco-British Commission for Economic Warfare. The submarine commander spoke no English but he had a list of submarine jargon in both English and French; this was the minimum vocabulary he needed to communicate with the crews of other Allied submarines. In only two weeks I had to teach him how to pronounce the English words, so we met daily and worked frantically.

The economist, I discovered, was engaged in the exchange of

foodstuffs between France and the United Kingdom. No money was to be exchanged; all purchases were merely book entries, he told me. Butter, eggs, milk and strawberries were going to England from Normandy and Brittany. Arrangements were under way for some beef. With Denmark cut off, the British increased their supplies of dairy products from France. According to my student, butter from Normandy was the best. "It's the sweetest, but the most expensive butter in the world. The cows aren't animals in Normandy, they're family. Farmers often take better care of them then they do of their wives."

Although the economist had studied English he had had little chance to speak it. Now it was a matter of learning his specialized vocabulary and polishing his pronunciation. Often I went to his home for dinner and he and I had an evening session which was frequently interrupted by his teenaged children who eagerly asked questions about Canada. In the eight weeks we worked together, I not only expanded my French vocabulary but had an intimate look at French family life.

three

A t the same time I was playing the role of English teacher, I was exploring Paris to see what changes the war had brought. Nothing was immediately visible, but my trips soon revealed that the sombreness I had detected at the railway station lurked just below the city's surface. Hidden among the trees in the president's pear orchard in the Luxembourg Gardens, just opposite the Foyer, were anti-aircraft guns. Netting and barbed wire kept away the children who were playing and sailing their boats in the basin behind the Senate. More anti-aircraft guns were hidden away in the Bois de Boulogne and in other city parks. At Versailles the palace grounds bristled with defensive hardware.

At Place Denfert-Rochereau, the Lion of Belfort glared over pillowy anti-blast covering; the bas-relief on the Arc de Triomphe, especially Rude's famous *Le Départ* (better known as *La Marseillaise*), was muffled; at the Place de la Concorde the central obelisk rose out of a huge pile of sandbags. Carpeaux's lovely "Dance" at the Opéra was shrouded. The thirteenth-century stained glass of Ste Chapelle had been taken down within hours of the declaration of war and replaced with clear glass. The sight of all this had the stagey feel of a giant movie set.

After the sudden, brutal crushing of Poland in September, tens of thousands of families had fled Paris and gone to relatives in the country or in ancestral villages. They had jammed the trains or departed in mattress-topped cars stuffed with children, grandmothers and household goods. Tourists scattered to the seaports. "We expected to be bombed at once like Warsaw was," Irène said, "but nothing happened. There were a few alerts, then almost nothing more."

The waiting had begun. As the weeks passed, the numbing fear and tension began to drain away. By the time I returned to Paris, families were drifting back. Restaurants, bars, cafés, theatres, the opera, cabarets, *chansonniers* and the *boîtes* of Montmartre and Montparnasse were in full swing. On the streets were many uniforms, some with the shoulder flashes of Poland and Czechoslovakia. Judging by my glimpse of Southampton and reports of London, the black-out in Paris was more like a blue-out. The glass in the hooded street lights, the car lamps, even flashlights were painted dark blue. In the middle of each glass a tiny cross was scratched to let out a sliver of light. At night the traffic policemen prudently retreated to sidewalk corners as cars and buses made their way along the streets. In the midnight blue, people bumped into one another. Shoulder straps of purses or gas-masks got entangled, and bursts of laughter followed. Such laughter and apologies I had never heard before in Paris streets. Somehow the darkened city had developed an unusual and unforgettable humour and gentleness.

Almost all my friends were French and I found their lives torn apart. Compulsory service had called up their fathers, husbands, fiancés and brothers.

My best friend Paul Tchernia, an oceanographer I had met in 1935 when we were the sole passengers aboard the French freighter sailing from Fort Churchill, Manitoba, had joined the navy. Albert Vernier was somewhere near the Maginot Line. I had introduced him to his fiancée, Madeleine LeMoal. René Gilbert, an artist, and the husbands of several friends were in the army somewhere and I was never to see them again. Ricki Mounier was in the air force. He was eight years younger than I but we were exchanging language lessons and shared a passion for American movies. His mother had proposed that a marriage be arranged between us because I would be a good influence and Ricki was the sort of young man who needed an *"older woman."* He was rich, as well, but I had the common sense of a Saskatchewan girl and gracefully declined.

The few journalists I knew well were nearly all foreigners, except Jean Piot. He was an art buff and his "penthouse" on the Ile St. Louis was a fascinating small art gallery. Thanks to him I had a number of articles published in his paper, *l'Oeuvre*. Another friend, Karel Mazel, who represented the largest newspaper in Prague, had translated a series of my articles about Canada for his paper. Karel had a romantic

Slovak temperament and kept very unconventional hours. We met as early as 7 a.m. (in Prague people were at work at 7) and as late as 11 p.m. Devastated by what had happened to his country, Karel was already writing for small underground papers.

Meanwhile my Polish shipmates were in residence in a military barracks. All of them came down with colds and one or two with pneumonia, a clear sign that their quarters were not up to the standards of the *Washington*. When they were better we gathered into our company a female Polish colonel who had been in charge of an anti-aircraft battery in Warsaw before the city fell. She had fled through Romania and eventually arrived in Paris where she joined the staff of General Wladyslaw Sikorski, the man in command of the Poles who had escaped to fight with the Allies. (I was amazed when she told me that women in Poland could attend military college and have the same training as young men.)

One memorable evening in Montmartre, we found a reasonable place to eat where they served Polish food. Besides a huge platter of various kinds of smoked and pickled meats, another of cheese, and large baskets of bread, the Poles demolished a number of bottles of wine. As tongues loosened, they burst into song and entertained us with tunes that should have been joyful but sounded more like a dirge.

From time to time they remembered me and demanded some Canadian songs. While I am no Maureen Forrester, I can carry a tune, so I obliged with "The Maple Leaf Forever," "Barney Google," "Yes, We Have No Bananas" and "The Prisoner's Song" (I did not mention that three of my selections were probably American). The last choice was unfortunate; however, by this time my Polish companions were no longer aware of the lyrics. Being gentlemen of the first order, they did not mumble, stutter or stumble when we left but walked out stiff as boards while the Colonel (whose intake had been moderate) and I giggled our way after them.

The city was in total darkness, but we had our blue-painted flashlights with their sliver of light. With no vehicles in sight, we took the middle of the road down the hill to the steep flight of steps to the boulevards below. As we got into step, arm in arm, the men began singing again, loud and clear. Suddenly we were confronted by two policemen who materialized out of the shadows and demanded that we stop and show our papers.

A beam from their flashlights travelled over our faces and downward. They caught the Polish flashes on the shoulders of my cohorts.

When they saw my Canadian passport, they exclaimed, "Canada, Mademoiselle! And what are you doing here?"

In a moment everybody was smiling and shaking hands all around, while the policemen cautioned us to keep our voices down. They accompanied us to the head of the long staircase and bid us good night, having decided, I suspect, that we could make it to the bottom intact.

On moonlit evenings my Yugoslav friend Tonscek frequently joined our party in the crowded outdoor cafés. A teacher at the School of Oriental Languages in Paris, Tonscek was a former pupil of mine, and had insisted that we begin our English lessons with *Hamlet*. Some of the most memorable evenings of my life were spent at those sidewalk tables, especially at Les Deux Magots, as we watched the play of moonlight on the old stones of St.-Germain-des-Prés.

The old edifice took on a soft-glowing sheen and must have looked as it did to Henry James and Oscar Wilde, both of whom had taken pre-dinner apéritifs at these tables before electricity blotted out the stars. When eyes became accustomed to the darkened city, it seemed to be bathed in translucent deep blue light. The waiters, old men called out of retirement, had the courtly manner of another age and would often exclaim, "Regardez Mam-zelle, est-ce-qu'elle n'est pas belle, la nuit? Et puis, Saint Germain, et Paris. Quelle belle ville, quelle beauté." And Parisians at other tables, forgetting the reason for it, would nod and smile.

In the evenings or early mornings a single reconnaissance plane would fly over Paris. No bombs. As winter passed and spring came, occasionally showers of propaganda were dropped to warn Parisians about the British. "Britain will fight to the last Frenchman." "Why fight? We have a common enemy." Or simply, "Can you trust the English? How many divisions are in France?" The reaction among almost all I spoke to was one of indignation. Exchanging views with waiters, people in buses and cafés, with friends, I found most of them scornful of such a futile exercise. "Sales Boches, how stupid and naive do they think we are? Do they think we don't know what they did to Poland? They can try to turn us against Britain, but they won't succeed!"

The newspapers during that winter reported light brushes with the enemy. More serious were reports about the war at sea, but the French were intensely proud of their navy and everybody seemed to believe that the British fleet was unbeatable. Radio and newspapers fed us great quantities of reassurances and optimism. It was becoming an inconvenient and rather boring war.

Like most people, I no longer sought the shelters or got out of bed at night. The lone reconnaissance plane on its nightly visit rarely lifted an eye. In the cafés and bars everyone speculated with a puzzled or knowing air about what was "really" going on. Obviously something *must* be going on behind the scenes. Negotiations? Rumours spread. Undoubtedly negotiations. Was a deal being worked out? After Munich anything could be believed. Germany must be short of fuel. Germany had lost enormous amounts of war material in concquering Poland. How could so much steel be replaced? These and a hundred other theories were discussed. What happened to Poland was a tragedy, but Poland was a small country and the attack so swift, massive and unexpected that it was all over before the Allies could get there. Now the West was another story.

I tried to look up some American and Canadian friends but most had gone to England or returned home. Gabrielle Roy, then still trying to make up her mind whether to be a writer or an actress, had gone home to write *The Tin Flute.* Jules Leger, I heard, was marrying a girl named Gaby, and had returned home. Kay Moore of Winnipeg had dropped her studies and taken a job at the British Embassy. Gabrielle, Kay and I had lived at the same pension in the home of an extraordinary woman, the wife of a celebrated poet, Pierre-Jean Jouve. Mme Jouve had been a pacifist in the First World War. She and novelist Georges Duhamel, as well as other internationally known French writers, had been exiled to Switzerland for their anti-war activities, which had culminated in the hair-brained scheme of dropping leaflets over Allied and German trenches urging the soldiers on both sides to throw away their guns, go home and let the generals and politicians fight it out. They worked with an English group, which was not so lucky. Instead of being exiled as their French cohorts were, members of the English group went to jail.

While we lived at Madame Jouve's we discovered that she kept two rooms in her apartment free for refugees from Germany. Thus we met Thomas Mann and his daughter, who paused there before leaving for the United States. They took their meals in their rooms and slipped in and out like shadows. It was only when they were leaving that by chance some of us were introduced to the Nobel-prize-winning novelist.

War-related stories became more and more difficult to find as winter turned into spring and our fears dissipated. The metro and buses and suburban trains were filled on Sundays with people coming back from the country with arms filled with wild hyacinths and daffodils. The flower stalls displayed masses of colour and on

May 1, as usual, everyone carried bouquets of lily-of-the-valley, the symbol of peace. The chestnuts along the Champs-Elysées were in full bloom and the avenue was alive with strollers in the evenings. Every sidewalk table had its quota of French families and men in uniform watching the high coiffured girls in spring dresses. The skirts were fashionably short, with an underfrill of white eyelet embroidery or a lace petticoat showing an inch below.

One evening old General Goulet, his granddaughter Lizette and I sat at a sidewalk café enjoying the parade of French fashion. "I knew war was inevitable when the skirts shortened," General Goulet informed me. "It was the same in 1914. Not as short as they are now, but short enough to turn our heads." He rolled his eyes and lifted his cognac.

Most people carried their gas-mask containers; however, the contents usually turned out to be anything except gas-masks. Cartoonists and humourists were full of advice on how the gas-mask container could be transformed into a chic and attractive accessory for afternoon or evening wear, which spoke volumes about the general sense of reality. "Especially designed slip-on covers make elegant containers with added compartments to carry identity cards, tickets, cosmetics, cigarettes…"; "suede or leather is smart for the 'sportif,' and will turn those ugly tin containers into accessories of class," joked *Le Canard Enchainé* and the comedians of Les Deux Anes. I had only just received mine; foreigners were the last to be equipped with gas-masks.

Meanwhile the newspapers were filled with a hodge-podge of contradictory stories. The waiting for visible signs of war had gone on for almost eight months. I saw Albert and Paul during their leave, and we spent hours analysing the situation. They were as puzzled as the rest of us. Germany had occupied Denmark and successfully invaded Norway. Russia and Finland were at war. Though we thought we were deeply involved, only later did it become evident that our involvement was academic. It had not yet touched us. Paul had seen some action as a naval officer and did not believe negotiations were going on secretly. "They mean business. We're losing a lot of tonnage," was his only indiscreet comment. All he wanted to do was see a Fred Astaire movie. He was as puzzled as we were about the inaction of the army.

"There's almost nothing going on at the Front," Albert remarked to reassure his fiancée Madeleine. "In fact we're bored to death. I don't know what it was like in the last war, but we've seen some of the best shows. Gracie Fields, Maurice Chevalier, Mistinguet, orchestras, theatre groups, all to entertain us. I've seen more shows in the past months than I saw all the years I was studying at l'Ecole Coloniale."

On the last day of Albert's leave, Madeleine, Irène, Tonscek, Karel and I went to a Sunday concert at the Chatelet. The orchestra was being conducted by Paul Paray. The big hall was crowded, probably because the concerts were free. To open, the orchestra began to play a Wagner overture. In the audience someone hissed and shouted, "We don't want Nazi music — no Nazi music." The conductor stopped and turned to face the audience. In a thunderous voice that could be heard in every corner he shouted, "There may be a war on with Germany but it has nothing to do with music. Music has no nationality and whoever said that will either leave this hall at once or make an effort to be civilized." The whole audience and the orchestra stood up and cheered.

"You see," Irène enthused, "we are becoming more civilized. In the last war German music was forbidden."

After dinner we sat sipping coffee and a liqueur in front of a café. It was a magnificent night. The moonlight was so bright I felt sure that Paris must lay naked and wholly exposed to the eyes in the sky in spite of the "blue-out." The evening was warm and every chair was filled. There was laughter and lively discussion going on all around us. Albert and Madeleine held hands under the table (in those days serious French couples were discreet about exhibiting their affection in public). Around about ten o'clock we became conscious of the whine of a plane, and soon it was directly over our heads. No one moved or even paused in conversation. A moment or two later we heard the ack-ack of guns off to the west. So accustomed had we become to these visits that no one even thought of moving.

That evening was the last time I saw Albert or Paul until the war was almost over.

Early May 1940: magnificent weather. The submerged apprehension and the boredom of waiting turned my thoughts to the country. Prairie-born, from people of the land, I found the call of the scents on the spring wind, the sunny skies and bursting growth irresistible. Why not visit the châteaux of the Loire? In five years I had not taken the time to visit these jewels, which were usually among the first tourist targets. Perhaps, subconsciously, I knew something was about to happen.

May 10, 1940: Atop the château of Chinon, a decrepit old guide was explaining how, down below, Jeanne d'Arc had picked out King

Charles VII from among his courtiers and had persuaded him to allow her to command his armies. Suddenly we heard the roar of planes. A squadron swept in low over our heads, and as we gazed up, there on the wings we saw the unmistakable swastika. Then came several earth-shaking explosions. We stared at one another speechless. The half-crippled guide exclaimed, "The war has started! They're after the bridges over the Loire." Hélène and I were expected in Bordeaux and hurried off to the bus station.

May 13, 1940: On my return trip to Paris, I saw the first, devastating signs of war. Our train pulled into sidings three times to allow munitions trains to pass. At one siding we were stopped for an hour alongside a second passenger train that had been machine-gunned. Its windows were smashed; bullet-holes, like ropes of beads, had pierced the sides of the passenger coaches. The passengers were refugees from Holland and Belgium travelling to the towns and cities where the French government had ordered them to be billeted. Red Cross, local medical and social service personnel had taken off the dead and wounded.

I walked through the train. It had been carrying whole school classes of children, hospital patients from Belgium, old people, women. On top of the cars and along the sides were painted large red crosses and the words "hôpital" and "enfants." Obviously these messages had been ignored by pilots following their orders to terrorize the civilian population. Blood was spattered everywhere, broken glass and tufts of hair were partially embedded in the back of a seat. The silence was awesome and the eyes of the remaining, untouched passengers and children were blank. I rushed to a washroom and retched. It was the first and only time I vomited. Such scenes were to become familiar.

Back in Paris I moved quickly to get this story through the censors at the Continental. There were few journalists around and those I saw were in a hurry. I remembered how it had looked a week before — disgruntled newsmen lounging about and wondering where to look next.

From the Continental I went to the Red Cross office to offer my services. I was told I could be useful at the North Station where refugee trains were arriving. In addition to taking names, addresses and messages, I had crying or stunned children to comfort while trying to get details of where they had come from. Many were alone. It was necessary to conduct groups of bewildered refugees across the city to other stations, from which they were being sent to villages;

towns and cities all over southern France. Mayors had been notified that they would receive a quota of refugees and must designate families to house them.

The refugee trains that had been machine-gunned paused in the Paris suburbs where the dead and wounded were removed by police, firemen and Boy Scouts. On one occasion a Red Cross worker and I took a little girl of three to several hospitals and walked the wards until we found her mother who had been wounded. It was a heart-warming moment in the midst of so much tragedy.

In those days portable radios were rare. If I were in the Foyer at news-time, I could listen to Miss Watson's, but like most people I depended upon the newspapers. They were filled with optimistic and reassuring reports about the might of the Allied forces and the Maginot Line, as well as tirades against the barbarism of German attacks on Holland, Belgium and Luxembourg. (Months later I looked up coverage for May 10 to June 17, and discovered that people in Ottawa, Toronto and other Canadian cities and towns knew more about what was actually happening in the war zone than we did in Paris.)

One day my old friend Gabriel Christol, a Paris architect, asked me to lunch with the director of the Louvre. All through the meal I wondered why I had been invited, but with the arrival of coffee the director came to the point. He explained that he was the president of an unusual organization. When official word came that a soldier had been killed at the Front, women of the organization delivered the telegrams to the families and broke the news as gently as possible.

"As you know, most of our women are working long hours, but those who have some free time help us. Would you be willing to volunteer?"

I hesitated. How could I handle so much grief? What comfort could I, a stranger, be to these stricken families?

"I know it's difficult," my friend said. "I think it could be comforting to a bereaved woman to know her grief is shared by someone representing our Allies, especially a Canadian. There will be many Canadian wives and mothers facing the same loss, the same grief. Please accept, our women will understand and be grateful." I agreed.

The pace of the German invasion was so rapid and created so much confusion that I doubt if there were many telegrams delivered. At any rate, I was not called upon.

The tempo of Paris life quickened only slightly. Children were no longer allowed to play in Luxembourg Gardens and other parks. Once again families were crowding the trains and returning to relatives in the country. Miss Watson had told the Foyer residents from Egypt, the south of France and other places that she could not be responsible for their safety and advised them to return home. At the same time my journalist friends, the waiters, the people in buses and the metro, at lunch counters and the bistros scoffed at the idea that the "Boches" could ever reach Paris. "We stopped them less than fifty kilometres from Paris last time after nearly five years of fighting," they said. "The French and British armies are the best in the world. Soon the Boches will find out. They lost a lot in Poland and Norway. Soon we'll cut their supply lines. Just watch!"

Everyone protested angrily about the unprovoked and brutal attack on neutral Rotterdam and the way the Dutch refugees had been strafed on the roads. News came that Princess Juliana and her children were safe in London, and were soon followed by the Netherlands government and Queen Wilhelmina. Fighting was going on in Belgium, but it was impossible to find out where the various armies were involved.

At about this time I ran into Arved Arenstam. He, unlike many others, was pessimistic. Though he praised the calibre and morale of the Allied armies, he commented soberly, "Not even the military seems to realize there is *no* Maginot Line between Belgium and France — only a series of cement block houses and blinds scattered along the frontier." He complained, as others did, about the lack of solid information. But he became more cheerful when talking about the French air force and the RAF. He was anticipating an interview with General Weygand.

"But how were you able to get up to the war zone?" I asked. "How did you finally get permission?"

"This uniform came in handy," he grinned. "I'm working with a French photographer and so far nobody has said a word."

"Next time you're back will you give me your impressions?"

In his usual generous way he promised, but it was the last time I ever saw him.

The war correspondents had disappeared. My pleas to go north fell on deaf ears.

June 1, 1940: A day never to be forgotten. I lost my briefcase with every piece of identification I needed.

Irène and I met for an apéritif at Chez Dupont on the Boulevard St. Michel, then went to a small restaurant in the rue de la Harpe, and finally on to the local cinema where a foreign picture was playing. After the show we dropped into a café for hot wine. Irène's metro station was only a few steps from the Foyer. As I bid her good night, I suddenly realized that I was missing my briefcase.

"Catastrophe!" Irène screamed. "We must go back. With your fair hair you could be in jail as a Fifth Columnist with the first *flic* [policeman] we meet."

We retraced our steps. My heart was doing a triple rhythm, for I had already been stopped on the streets a number of times and asked to show my papers. Back to Chez Dupont. Nothing there. The restaurant in the rue de la Harpe was closed, but a man closing the shutters next door told us the owner lived on the third floor of a building down the street. He eyed us with great concern.

We felt our way up the stairs in the darkness because the *veilleuse* (a kind of night-light that lasts fifteen seconds between floors) was out of order. Hoping we had found the right place, we knocked. The door was opened and a man, wearing a night-cap and silhouetted against faint light, peered out at us. I told him I had lost my papers and they might still be in his restaurant. He dressed quickly and we ran to the restaurant, but no briefcase. The restaurateur looked under all tables, ran to the kitchen and came back wringing his hands. "It is not here, Mam-zelle. To the police! Go at once to the police."

If I had not been too worried before, I was now. We still had the cinema and the café, but I had a premonition that we would not find it in either place. The cinema manager was just closing, but he hurried us to the gallery and we looked under every seat while he muttered and scolded. How could I possibly be so careless as to lose all my personal papers at such a time? Did I not know how dangerous it was to be without papers, especially now with the Fifth Columnists everywhere? See the police at once, he urged. By now my stomach was a big knot of panic.

The café was closed. I was now truly alarmed. At last we went to the police station, only to find it full of policemen congratulating one of their colleagues on the birth of his first son. They pushed us through to the desk and I was happy to recognize the elderly sergeant who had refused to have me fingerprinted the autumn before. His smile was replaced by a frown when I explained my predicament. Such utter recklessness! Such heedless stupidity, especially at this time! Meekly, trying to shrink into myself while he scolded, I stood there while he made out a paper explaining who I was, took down the number of my passport which, luckily, I had memorized, and stamped it with a large red stamp. He called over another officer who added a big blue stamp and then ordered me to return on Monday morning.

We were on our way out when glasses of wine were thrust into our hands and we were asked to drink a toast to the newborn. Then with much hand-shaking we left. I had exactly seven francs (about twenty five cents then) left in my change purse so Irène lent me fifty francs and a scarf to cover my hair. I relaxed when the Foyer door closed behind me.

Sunday morning I remembered that before meeting Irène I had mailed a letter to my mother at the nearby post office. Clutching my *laissez-passer*, I raced to the post office, knowing it closed at noon. The elderly woman and young girl behind the counter were alarmed by my story and looked behind the counter and wickets. But no briefcase. I was now thoroughly aware of how dangerous it was to be in Europe without all the proper papers. Perhaps on Monday the Canadian Legation could help. Maybe General Vanier could get another passport for me?

That night I again thought of the post office. It must be there. On Monday morning I returned to the post office. The man behind the wicket had been there on Saturday. After listening to my breathless explanation, he walked over to a broom closet and beckoned to me. There, sitting on top of a scrub pail among mops and brooms, sat my precious *vache*.

"I put it there Saturday night. I'm sure everything is in order." Then I got a lecture. "Especially with that blonde hair!" he said. "You should be home in Canada. Quelle idiote."

There were still no bombs in Paris. Refugees arriving by trains had been joined by those in cars. First came the chauffeur-driven, but within days all kinds of vehicles were moving across Paris and down the boulevard St. Michel, past the Foyer and on towards the Porte d'Orleans and Versailles. Soon they were arriving on foot. These growing columns of Belgians and Netherlanders passed under our windows at the Foyer, and Miss Watson began to take in as many as she had beds for. Their stories were horrifying. One woman in her sixties, who had never been on a bicycle in her life, rode from Antwerp to Paris. Another woman who was almost mad with grief told me how she had buried two of her children by the roadside after a raid on the column. Their villages had been bombed and strafed; the bombing had continued as they struggled along the roads. They were in shock, their stories disjointed and jumbled. Our minds were not equipped for the tales they poured out, in spite of what we were seeing and hearing with our eyes and ears.

One morning I wakened to the sound of an army marching out of step. Looking out, I saw our boulevard filled with people and every kind of vehicle. The human river stretched across the road, across the sidewalks and hugged the fence of Luxembourg Gardens. In addition to cars, vans and trucks, there were wagons, horse-drawn carts, bicycles, push carts, baby carriages, children's wagons. But the great majority were on foot — old people, young people, women of all ages, boys and girls lugging baskets, suitcases, bedrolls, and babies or smaller children too exhausted to walk. They were locked together in the common, gray weariness of their faces and shocked eyes. Among them, goats, the occasional cow and donkey, and an entire flock of sheep munched along the boulevard. In the carts and wagons were piles of clothing, bits of furniture and cooking pots, cages of pigeons, hens and rabbits, bedding and often, riding on top, small children, a pregnant woman or an aged man or woman. One woman I spoke to had come from the Belgian border carrying a seven-day-old baby.

The people struggling along the avenues, asking for water at cafés, bedding down for the night on the streets, sidewalks and in doorways, represented every class of society. What will remain forever in my memory, however, was the slow, uneven, shuffling of feet and the awful silence.

There is something strange about the human mind. While it can be aroused to emotions of indignation and horror in reaction to the news and pictures of atrocities and brutal attacks on the helpless, it seems unable to grasp total reality until it is made to confront the horrors firsthand. Today my memory of the military events in the battles of Flanders and France is murky and blurred, but what remains vivid and alive is the sight of those refugees and the behaviour of the civilian population.

Each day planes flew high over Paris. We heard the anti-aircraft guns, but no bombs fell. Rumours circulated. German parachutists in Dutch or Belgian uniforms, aided by squads of motorcyclists, had preceded the German tanks and troops in taking The Hague, Rotterdam, Ghent, Courtrai and other cities. Security in Paris tightened. Irène and I, thanks to our fair complexions, were asked almost daily for identification, and each time my heart nearly stopped as I remembered my briefcase. "Your papers, please" is engraved on my mind.

June 3, 1940: Bright and sunny without a cloud. I took my article about the refugees to the Continental but did not see anyone I knew to talk to. Walking back along the Seine, I could hardly believe that a war was on, that the Germans were already somewhere in northern France.

Bombing was reported from Nancy, Calais, Namur and other cities to the north and even to the west and south, yet still no bombs in Paris. The bombing seemed haphazard, almost frivolous. We did not realize at the time that it was a tactic to disrupt communications and transportation and to sow panic. That the civilian population could be used deliberately to impede Allied troop movements never occurred to us. The attacks were played down.

We were shocked and horrified by the brief accounts in the newspapers, but It was an intellectual, not a visceral, reaction. We did not know that German armoured columns were moving rapidly towards cities with names we had learned at school — Amiens, Arras, Lille — nor that German motorized columns were moving along the coast of the North Sea and the Channel, while others were heading towards Paris from the east. A few words on the radio told us motorized vehicles were far ahead of the German armies. "They'll be cut off. They're crazy, they'll run out of gas and supplies and we'll finish them off," people in the cafés predicted confidently. There was no understanding of the modern warfare military tactics that employed masses of machines rather than armies of men.

I was puzzling over these things when the sirens sounded. People crossing the square in front of Notre Dame did not seem inclined to hurry. As I joined them I noticed a long line of little girls walking in pairs with one nun in the lead and two behind. The nuns were almost running as they urged, "Vite, vite!" I realized that the alert was unusually long. Following the girls to the Cathedral, I could not help pausing outside to scan the sky. An enormous number of planes — they looked like a great swarm of silver dragonflies — were crossing the sky above the city. Then came the sound of guns. The planes circled and dived like gulls. Around and among them appeared snowy puffs of smoke and bursts of orange-red flame. Against the unclouded blue of the June sky, it looked so innocent. The planes flew high, dipping and darting, sparkling with silvery flashes, seemingly as harmless as a show of fireworks. I could not grasp that this meant death for someone.

A woman clutched my arm. "Come inside Mademoiselle. Quickly. Ils sont sérieux, ces Boches." She pulled at me and I followed her into the Cathedral and down into the crypt. There, in orderly rows, sat the children and the nuns. The woman beside me kept muttering, "Ces Boches, ces Boches, ces sales Boches...encore...."

Emerging later, I found that at least this part of Paris looked unchanged. The same magnificent sun and sky. The flower market a blaze of colour on the Left Bank, students again settled in front of cafés on the Boulevard St. Michel poring over books and flirting. The old waiters in the doorways talked to one another in low tones. They looked worried. I got home and called Irène. We decided to meet for dinner at the Crèperie Bretonne in rue Monsieur le Prince before going to see what damage had been done. Miss Watson had told me she heard that the Citroën plant had been bombed and some people wounded.

Irène and I walked along the Seine until we came to the Pont Mirabeau. Policemen stood around while workmen and soldiers were cleaning up the debris. The bridge had been damaged. In the side streets a number of buildings appeared to have crumbled on one side or the other. Glass was being swept up everywhere. The shock was not what I had expected. When the policeman told us that several people had been killed, I only felt numb. The crowds were extremely curious and were trying to go closer to the Citroën plant, but the police turned us all back with a stern warning. We listened as a soldier told us that as far as he knew, nobody at the plant had been killed or injured, but perhaps there were casualties in some other part of the city. We realized then that Citroën had not been the only target.

By the time we had reached the Citroën complex all the ambulances had disappeared. No one was making a fuss. Even the damage we saw did not register. It was as though all of us, including the policemen and soldiers at the site, had lost all feeling. Just as in a cyclone on the Saskatchewan prairies, in war bombs are expected and people can only become very still and wait. I learned then, and in the next weeks, that in moments of great danger people do not panic. They accept.

On the late-night news, casualties were placed at about 240 with 20 dead. By the next morning, the casualty list stood at 2,000 with more than 200 dead. It was strange. Whether one or two hundred, the numbness was the same. It could not be deepened, heightened, or changed. The next few days of June were filled with confusion and contradiction. Rumours swept through the city and sent the foreign press hurrying to the Continental where we hoped for official information. The situation was serious, but not out of hand. We could expect a massive Allied counter-attack at any moment. The Germans had crossed the Aisne. Report denied. They were approaching Rheims. Untrue — Nazis propaganda. King Leopold of Belgium had asked for an armistice. Denied. Confirmed. The papers and radio lulled us with stories of the heroism of our armies and of how they were "holding" the enemy. The Maginot Line was intact.

Rumour after rumour circulated and had to be checked out. But how? Officials were tight-lipped. At the Ministry of Information officials spoke reassuringly but their eyes were worried. In my naiveté I cabled our London bureau and asked for credentials as a "war" correspondent so I could leave Paris to find out what was happening. I never received an answer.

Even the catastrophe at Dunkirk did not seem to penetrate our consciousness; we discussed it merely as a "victory" because so many thousands of British and French soldiers had been evacuated. Factual information was scanty. "Our armies are holding back the Germans in order to let the British Expeditionary Forces escape," blared the radio. "Some thousands of French have been taken off."* Bitterness and pride echoed in the announcers' voices. We heard nothing about the total loss of guns, tanks and other military equipment in northern France. The utter faith of the civilian population was impenetrable. We simply could not envisage defeat.

Early in December 1939, I had teamed up with Suzanne Wunder, a correspondent for the *Christian Science Monitor* who was later supplanted by a male journalist posted to cover the military side of the war. Suzanne and I exchanged information and co-operated in the "leg work" for our human-interest stories. Suzanne now told me that a friend of hers who worked for the Paris edition of the *Herald-Tribune* had warned her that the government was planning to leave Paris. That afternoon I met Percy Philip of the *New York Times*. He, of course, had "sources." Was the government planning to move? He told me he had heard the same rumour but had been assured at the War Office that it was probably "Fifth Column propaganda spread to panic the people." "I've been told the British and French have just begun the counter-attack. I hope it is true," he said.

"Where *is* the Front? Where are they counter-attacked?" I asked.

"God knows, that's what *I'm* trying to find out."

On Saturday morning the tone on the radio reports suddenly

---

* Professor J.E. Duroselle, distinguished war historian and member of the French Institute, states in his book *l'Abime* (1982) that 200,000 British and 140,000 French were evacuated.

changed. The commentator's voice was laboured. "The French are holding... they have shortened the line at the Bresle River." Mme Fournier's news was equally disquieting. "I heard a story at the baker's that the Germans are in Normandy — *Normandy!* It can't be possible!"

During lunch Irène told me that she and her colleagues had been warned that, should it be expedient, their laboratory and staff would move to quarters being prepared outside Bordeaux. "We're still testing pilots so things can't be as bad as it sounds," she said. "We've been told, however, that we have to find our own way there. The lab has only enough transportation for the equipment and documentation."

It began to dawn on us that we might have to leave Paris. If we had to leave, we were determined to leave together. "I passed the Montparnasse station this morning," Irène said. "Hundreds of people were trying to get on trains but only the sick and women with children were allowed on. I don't think we can count on trains, though maybe my *laissez-passer* and your press card will work. Still, probably things aren't that bad. These commentators are so sensational."

On Sunday I took the bus to l'Etoile and sauntered down the Champs-Elysées. It was still crowded, though the people at the tables were usually quiet. There was a strange feeling in the air as I sat and watched the crowd around me, the kind of feeling that permeates a crowd gathered outside a tall building where someone is standing at the top, deciding whether or not to jump.

Back at the Foyer, Miss Watson told me that she had decided to tell her refugee boarders to move in the morning. "I'm beseiged by French students, girls from the provinces. Many were boarding in private homes but the people are leaving. I must take them in."

"What about me? Do you want my room?"

"Oh no, you've a job to do."

"Do you really think the Germans will reach Paris?"

"No, of course not, but we have to consider that they might. Then we'll have a street-by-street fight of a lifetime!"

June 10, 1940: At 10 a.m. I entered the courtyard of the Continental. Not a car in sight, only a huge pile of mailbags in the middle on the cobblestones, a soldier sitting on top with a rifle across his knees.

"No need to go in," he said. "They've all gone. I'm waiting for a van to pick up this mail."

"Gone! Gone where? How am I to get my articles censored?"

He shrugged his shoulders. "They've gone to Tours. The government's gone too. Tours."

The world seemed to be falling apart. Paris? What was going to happen to Paris?

"They say the Germans may be in Paris tomorrow. I hear they are near Beauvais," he continued.

"Beauvais? But Beauvais is just outside Paris!"

"Yes, but that's what they say, and I have to stay here and guard mailbags."

I ran all the way to the nearest café and telephoned Irène.

"Yes, I know," she answered as I blurted out the news. "I got my slip to go to our lab outside Bordeaux this morning. They are loading equipment right now. The staff has to find its own way there."

"I'll go to the Canadian Legation and find out what they advise, and then to the bank and get whatever money I have. Meet you this afternoon."

The old French doorman at the Legation seized my hands. "Mademoiselle, why are you still here? You must leave at once, at once. Everyone has gone. It is dangerous for you Mademoiselle . . . ."

Where had the Legation gone? He named a château somewhere near Tours, but I knew it would be hopeless to try to get in touch. I had not a clue where it was. At the bank the calm was ludicrous. A few people were at the wickets. I found I had less than a hundred dollars. At the next wicket I recognized a young woman named Eleanor who I had met once or twice at Legation receptions.

"I bought an old Ford from a soldier this morning," Eleanor announced, "but I can't get gas for it. You have to get it from the military and they won't give me any. Say they aren't allowed to. But I bet you could get some with your press card. I've only about a gallon left. If you're leaving town I could take you with me — if you can get gas."

It was a heaven-sent chance. "I have to go to Tours," I told her. "The censorship and information staffs are there, and I must get my stuff censored. But I've promised to go with a friend. You'd have to take her too."

"It's only a two-seater with a rumble seat and it's at least ten years old," she protested. "I'll need the rumble seat for my clothes and things. I have a friend at the *Herald-Tribune*. If he's in town I think I can get him to drive me."

"I promised Irène we would leave together, so that's that. But if your friend doesn't turn up, call me. If you'll take us both, I know I can get the gas."

We left it at that. Within an hour she called the Foyer and left word that she could not find her journalist friend and was prepared to make an arrangement with me. She would take Irène.

When I got back to the Foyer I called Irène and told her not to worry about trains; we had a surer way out of Paris.

I had to choose what I could take with me in the one suitcase Eleanor had stipulated. So I packed a nightgown, toilet articles and the tools of the trade: notebooks, manuscripts, thesaurus, Oxford Dictionary, *Nouveau Petit Larousse*, the Canadian Almanac. Eleanor had suggested that Irène and I meet her after dinner to discuss our departure plans. Emerging from the metro, Irène and I noticed that the sky was a sooty gray and darkening rapidly. It was several blocks to Eleanor's apartment, and as we walked we noticed a peculiar smell. The streets were filling with dark smoke and a strong, acrid smell that caught at our throats. The eerie quiet sent a nightmarish fear up our spines. A woman grabbed Irène's arm and gasped, "It's the Germans. They're sending poison gas over Paris. What can we do?" She let go and raced down the street.

Poison gas? Our eyes were watering and the smell was foul. The dirty cloud was settling everywhere in a fine, grimy film. We found Eleanor in a state of panic, thinking she had been poisoned by gas. Irène rubbed a finger down her cheek. "It's oily. It can't be gas. I think poison gas is supposed to be yellow, and we'd be choking. Anyway, we've walked blocks in it and, though it stinks, I'm sure I'm not poisoned."

Eleanor turned on the radio but got nothing but static. She tried the telephone but the line was dead. Though uneasy, we decided there was nothing to be done but to endure whatever it was and make our plans to leave. "It's probably a smoke screen to hide the war plants," Irène suggested. "Or maybe the Germans are trying to frighten us."

It was agreed that Irène and I would buy food so we could picnic along the way. With so many people on the roads, restaurants with anything left to eat would be hard to find. "Besides," Eleanor said, "I don't want to leave the car. Somebody might steal it." We had lots of things to do, but thought we could be ready by the following evening.

Miss Watson warned me that I had better go as soon as I could. "I don't know how soon *they* will get here, but you will be interned. And I'm expecting a terrible battle for the city. I'm filling the Foyer with French girls so it can't be taken over by the Germans."

"So you're staying?" I need not have asked.

"Certainly. They aren't going to occupy *this* building. Besides, I'm an American and we aren't at war — yet." Her voice was grim.

Irène met me in the morning on the Avenue d'Orléans (now Avenue General Leclerc), where we shopped at the sidewalk food stalls. At one point, Irène said, "I think we should buy enough for several days. Tours must be overcrowded and..." A shopkeeper overheard us and we blushed crimson with embarrassment when he announced in a voice for all the nearby shopkeepers to hear. "So you're running away too! Poltroons! Cowards! Nothing will move *me*. If *they* get into Paris, well, I have this." He picked up a huge cleaver, waved it at us and spat.

We slunk away full of guilt, for we knew that nothing would budge those sidewalk merchants. No war or occupation has ever moved them; not in 1870 nor in 1914-1918, not even during the French Revolution. They are the *people* of Paris!

I wondered whether other Canadians had been able to leave. We left the food at Irène's flat and took the metro to Sevres/Babylone and went around to the Hôtel Lenox where I knew Frank Pickersgill had been living. The concierge told me he had left. At Shakespeare and Company, the American bookstore, Sylvia Beach told me that she had persuaded Ruth Camp, a Canadian student who had worked for her, to leave a few days earlier. I telephoned Helen Kirkwood but got no answer at Quaker headquarters; nor was I able to reach Suzanne Wunder.

At Les Deux Magots, Irène and I stopped for a sandwich. It was there that I suddenly realized that I was leaving Paris. I was leaving not of my own free will; I was being pushed out. Pushed out by the Germans. It made me furious, but I was also broken-hearted. "Let's walk through the Tuileries and the Place de la Concorde," I said. "I want to look down the Champs-Elysées and buy some postcards of Paris."

As we passed the Ministry of Marine, we noticed a number of military trucks and vans. Men in naval uniform were carrying out boxes. It was hard for Irène and me to exchange words, the lumps in our throats were so big. How could it be possible that this beautiful city was about to become a battleground? How could we imagine it in heaps of rubble such as we had seen in the newsreels of Warsaw? This lovely city, beloved all over the world. I thought of the old saying: "Each of us has two loves, our hometown and Paris."

Many stores in the rue de Rivoli were closed. The woman who sold postcards declared, "I don't believe they can take Paris. We stopped them the last time and our army will do it again. Besides, I hear the Americans have sent us 2,000 airplanes. Our pilots will bomb the *merde* out of them!"

"Then you are not leaving the city?"

"Leave! Leave Paris and my shop to thóse . . . Boches. Naturally not. They won't drive me out."

We had agreed to meet Eleanor at her apartment at 5:30. Although the air had cleared a little, the skies were still muddy gray and the silence eerie. Eleanor was not home, so we walked around the neighbourhood. Everything — the streets, the walls, the surfaces of the buildings — was covered with this dark, oily film. By this time we had heard that the film had come from oil storage dumps at the edge of the city. They had been destroyed to keep the oil out of the hands of the enemy.

Eleanor arrived in a flurry. She had come from the newspaper and told us that her friend Don Brigham had not turned up. No one knew where he was or when he would be back. Outside her door sat the old Ford. "I don't think I've more than a couple of quarts left," she said anxiously. "The first thing we have to do is get it filled."

At Military Headquarters I produced my press card and explained that I had to get to Tours to have my news dispatches censored. The young officer understood and, after checking our passports and identity cards, he had the tank filled to the brim. "If you need more you'll probably have to get it at a military post. I can't tell you where they are. I'm sure you won't find any filling stations open."

Back at the apartment, in growing panic Eleanor began to choose what she would take. Irène and I vetoed evening dresses, pictures and other non-essentials in favour of more useful clothing. She insisted on loading three kilos of coffee and a large bag of sugar into the rumble seat. "You can't bring more than one suitcase each," she insisted. "I absolutely refuse to leave my furs and hats behind." She stuffed two fur coats in on top of the sugar and brought out an enormous hatbox into which we had watched her cram nearly a dozen hats — all magnificent confections with famous labels. In went her two suitcases. Irène and I wondered just how we were going to get ours in. Eleanor tied down the hatbox with her long silk scarves. "I may as well use them as string," she said, "and I have to put in at least one evening dress. Who knows how long it will be before we get back and I may need it in Tours." She ran inside and brought out a leather shopping bag with some boxes of jewelry and an evening dress crushed in on top of them.

We looked around the apartment. "I hate leaving my things to the Germans," Eleanor exclaimed. "Well, at least they won't be drinking my coffee. Now I want to go around to the *Herald-Tribune*. Don may have come back and I'd feel safer with a man."

Irène and I exchanged glances and digested this. "Not until we've packed in our suitcases and picked up the food at Irène's," I said firmly. "We mustn't waste one drop of the gas."

Finally Eleanor agreed and we went to the Foyer where my suitcase and typewriter were waiting. Unable to speak, Irène and I hugged Miss Watson and Mme Fournier. My last, blurred view of Miss Watson, that solid, strong-chinned veteran, her short white hair standing on end, her blue eyes snapping, was of her standing four-square in the doorway. "Write," she cried. "And don't worry about me. The whole Nazi army can't drive me out of here!"

Irène went into her apartment for her suitcase and the food — small French loaves, cheese, fruit, hard-boiled eggs, a few slices of ham, tinned fruit, a can opener, cups and table napkins rolled in a heavy woolen blanket. Covering this with Irène's raincoat, we tied the whole bundle firmly on top of the suitcases in the loaded rumble seat. Eleanor insisted that her hatbox be tied on top so her precious hats would not be crushed. While Irène was inside, Eleanor kept insisting we could not take her. Three in the front seat would be too crowded, she argued, especially since I had to put my typewriter against the seat behind my knees. "No Irène — no gas," I said, sounding and feeling vicious.

At the *Herald-Tribune* Eleanor ran inside. In a few minutes she was back, our prayers rewarded. "He hasn't come in," she wailed, "and they haven't heard a thing. What shall we do now?"

"Dinner," said Irène. "A good one, because though we should reach Tours by tomorrow afternoon, with the roads crowded, we might not get into a restaurant."

On the Boulevard St. Germain we found the Vagenende open. It was old, full of worn red leather, plush, red lamp-shades, gleaming brass fittings and bevelled mirrors of Victorian vintage. Two or three ancient waiters were dolefully serving a few late dinners. The waiters did not believe the Germans could take Paris. The city would be damaged but it would never give up. Had not Monsieur Reynaud said so the night before? Had not he said, "We will fight before Paris, we will fight in Paris, street by street..."?

Unknown to us, Paris had already been declared an "open city."

Emerging from the restaurant, we found the streets dark and deserted. The oily smoke, still settling, had destroyed the "blue-out." Reluctantly we packed ourselves into the car again and decided that the Porte d'Orléans might be our best route. We drove along the Boulevard Raspail and the Avenue d'Orléans, and took a last look at the muffled Lion de Belfort looming in the darkness. At the Porte soldiers and two policemen waved us to a stop. One policeman turned a flashlight into our faces and ordered us out of the car. Quickly we produced our passports and identity cards as a soldier approached. I showed my press card. Eleanor's papers were handed back immediately. They took longer over Irène's. "Russian origin," they said. "A Nansen Pass." A long pause followed as we held our breath. Then they began to smile and we all relaxed. "Well, well," said one policeman, handing back my papers. "With your hair [he looked at Irène and me], you'd better not lose your papers."

As we prepared to proceed, he stopped us while he consulted the soldiers. "You'll never get more than a kilometre before you'll run into the refugees and the road is impassable. You'd be wiser to stay here for the night where we can keep an eye on you. Safer. Wait until daylight."

We thanked him and drew up to the curb. "Why don't we go back and have a good night's sleep in our own beds and start early in the morning," Eleanor suggested. "I'll drop you off and pick you up in the morning."

Irène dug me in the ribs and we both shook our heads, sharing one thought. What if Don had returned? "We can't waste a drop of gas," I protested again. "We'd better stay here. It's safer even if it is uncomfortable. Who knows how soon the Germans will begin to bomb the city?"

At first light we bid goodbye to the policemen and the soldiers with whom we had talked intermittently during the night. They were as ignorant of the situation as we were and were prepared for a street-by-street battle. All night long, motorized vehicles passed us, hauling guns into the city. We heard the sounds of planes to the west and muffled explosions followed by the sharp ack-ack of anti-aircraft guns. Most of the time we walked or sat and said nothing, each of us deep in her own thoughts.

four

We left Paris in the gray dawn of June 12; the shabby and shuttered buildings seemed to draw back within themselves as we passed. Mixed with my feelings of rage and helplessness at being forced to leave was a sense of guilt. I felt that the blind windows had closed their eyes to me with reproach and disdain.

It was as the policemen had said. Within a kilometre we ran into a solid wall of refugees. Though we had passed many bedded down along the avenues, it was impossible to imagine what we were seeing now. An endless river of people on foot, in carts, wagons and cars; animals and bicycles so tightly packed across the road and sidewalks that no one could move more than a step or two at a time. The traffic had thickened as we approached this mass and suddenly it closed in behind us, making it impossible to back up and try some other route. We dared not move the slightest distance or someone would instantly move into the space. Eleanor began to show her ingenuity. Her foot on the brake became numb as hour after hour we inched forward. Long after noon we took out some sandwiches and opened a bottle of Evian water. Our dream of a picnic vanished. Eleanor produced a bottle of brandy and we laced the Evian with it.

The day crawled by. I got out and talked to people. I could send an article from Tours. Most of the people were from northern France and Paris, but a few Belgians were among them and I took down their incredible stories. One story was repeated over and over again; it was the same one I had heard at the Foyer and the North Station.

"They came into our village on motorcycles. They told the mayor that our village was a military target and would be bombed in twenty minutes, so if he wanted to save the people he should get them out of the place at once. The town-crier rode his bicycle around shouting this message and, of course, we left. The Germans said that they were our friends and, being humane, were saving us. They said the Nazis would take care of us if we didn't leave. So, what could we do? We put the children on the train or in a bus if we could and then started walking."

Everywhere these motorcycle squads, racing many kilometres ahead of the army, repeated this operation. The sudden, unexpected arrival of helmeted young men bewildered the villagers and the word "Nazi" was enough to cause panic. At the same time no one thought or said anything about defeat or losing the war. When I asked if our armies could hold them back, the people stared at me and said. "But, of course. That is why we must go south and not get in the way of our own troops. The war has barely started." It was true that armies of men were trying to pass us in the fields on the way to Paris.

Parisians on the road with whom I spoke kept talking about the coming battle of Paris. Over and over again, we heard of the arrival of American planes, anywhere from two to five thousand. While we pressed forward on the road, we could see the military vehicles, trucks, tanks, carriers and guns struggling to pass us, sometimes through us. Officers were shouting until they were so hoarse they could not speak above a whisper. "Let us pass, we must pass, we must reach Paris . . . ," they kept repeating as they urged the people to move aside and let them through. Where possible, the people moved. In other places, caught between buildings, the mass was so packed that even a bicycle could not get through and the armed vehicles tried to detour. And so it went, all day and evening and into the night. When I stood on the hood of the car, I longed for a camera. As far ahead as I could see, as far back as I could see, stretched the shifting flow of people. Behind us the city was there, so close. By nightfall, when everyone had stopped, we had travelled less than five miles. We were still well within the suburbs of Paris.

Eleanor was exhausted from moving the car a few inches at a time. She decided she would try to work her way to the edge of the road and try to turn into the first sideroad. By taking country roads, perhaps we could work our way past the flood. Slowly, as some of the people at the edges moved into doorways or open spaces to bed down, the road opened up a little and we eased our way slightly to the right. Meanwhile the soldiers with equipment squeezing past kept asking what was happening in Paris? Had we seen the Germans? Where were they? Had we seen any American planes?

No one I spoke to had heard any news for several days. While the column was rife with rumours, no one had a portable radio or a newspaper. Even the soldiers shared our ignorance.

Just before midnight a great wave of German planes came over. They were dropping flares. Everywhere along the line people shouted hoarsely, "Put out that cigarette, you fool." "Mother of God, turn off that flashlight. Lights out. Lights out. *Idiot*, turn off that light. Imbecile, put out that match!" Voices screamed. There were sounds of people fighting, of smashing blows. It was bedlam in the dark. People somehow found space to cower by the road or against the walls. A space opened before us as people moved aside to seek shelter. Eleanor immediately started the engine while people swore and shouted, "Stop! Stop that noise!" as though they imagined the pilots of the planes overhead could hear us. It seemed like hours though it was only a few moments.

Eleanor stopped and ordered us out of the car. "Get out and get under the car. If we get a bomb nearby it will protect us from the flack at least." She proceeded to do that, but first put on her coat. Irène and I did not move. It seemed utterly useless. "I'm darned if I want to be squashed under a Tin Lizzie," I muttered. Irène agreed.

The planes passed over us and a very short distance beyond we saw the bright flashes as the bombs found their mark. The explosions shook the earth. "The're bombing the Versailles road I think," Irène said. "Lucky we didn't go that way, they missed us."

At the first light the column began moving again, this time at a slightly faster pace. During the night Eleanor kept edging to the right. I still see the gray and weary faces of the people. Here and there someone sat down suddenly, unable to go on. People offered water or help. Some simply refused to try another step. I wondered how far they had come. How many days had they been on the road? They looked so weary and forlorn that it would have been indecent to ask. The three of us all shared waves of guilt as we rode in the car and passed women with children. Their looks showed no resentment, only hopeless fatigue.

By late afternoon we were at the edge of the column, and the lovely countryside began opening up on both sides. At last, as our river flowed through Etampes, we found the sideroad and turned off. Other vehicles were ahead of us, but the people walking continued down the main road. Soon we were moving more rapidly, but even our secondary road was filling with people who had come by other routes and sideroads. All were moving towards Orléans. Elements of the French army passed us. An officer stopped us to ask about the situation in Paris. Had we heard anything? What was happening when we left? Had our column been bombed? He explained that communications had been cut. We told him how the bombers had missed us but we feared that Versailles road had been bombed. It was June 13, but we did not think that the Germans could be in Paris yet. In reality, the forward motorcycle squads of Germans were already in the Paris suburbs. The next morning at 6 a.m. the German army, headed by open limousines of high-ranking German officers and followed by tanks and guns, entered the city and paraded down the Champs-Elysées.

We stopped the car beside a woman sitting on the road. She had two small children beside her, a baby in her arms and a child's wagon with a large suitcase on it. Tied on top was a blanket and a large bundle of clothing. Another blanket was around her shoulders and she was crying. Eleanor argued that we had no room, but Irène and I insisted on stopping. The woman told us she had come all the way from Cambrai, just south of the Belgian border, and could go no further. She could not manage more than carrying the baby and pulling the wagon. The other children, girls of about four and six, were exhausted. They had simply sat down and refused to walk.

After giving them all a drink and some bread and cheese, we offered to take the older children as far as the post office in Orléans. We took Eleanor's hatbox off the loaded rumble seat, piled the woman's bundle on top, using the scarves to tie it down. We placed the six-year-old with her feet under the edge of the rumble seat rim, and told her to hold on tightly. Eleanor protested in no uncertain terms that she was not going to have her Paris hats crushed. Fortunately, the woman did not understand English. Irène said that she would take the smaller girl on her knees and I promised to hold the hatbox. The woman pinned the names and address on her daughters' nursery-school pinafores and kissed them goodbye. We told her not to worry, she would find them in the care of a post office employee in Orléans.

Orléans was jammed. Cars and vehicles of all kinds had simply come to a full stop in the crowds. Two or three elderly policemen were trying to sort things out. We left Eleanor with the car while Irène and I pushed and shoved our way through the crowd, carrying the blanket and bundle and moving the little girls ahead of us. Instinctively, the crowd opened before them as we explained over and over that they had to be left in the care of the post office until their mother arrived. I recall how instantly sympathetic the people were in spite of their own worries and predicament. "Poor children, poor children," they repeated, reaching out to touch them as we moved through. An obliging woman behind the parcel counter at the post office understood at once and took charge of the solemn-faced youngsters who had not uttered a word or dropped a tear since we had taken them from their mother.

There was no hope of getting into a restaurant or café. "Let's get out of town and picnic somewhere," Eleanor urged. We tried a secondary road, since the main road to Tours was almost as badly clogged as the one out of Paris. Unfortunately, the little tourist map we had did not show many sideroads. However we zig-zagged south. Now, very hungry, we pulled up and carried our blanket and food into a field. The countryside was beautiful; the fields were filled with scarlet poppies and white daisies. Around us were other groups, eating or sleeping, as though enjoying an outing on a bank holiday. We had reached a kind of numb tiredness that made our eyes feel gritty and sore. I knew I could not sleep so I drafted an article to send from Tours. An hour later we picked up our things and started down the road again.

Within a few minutes a boy peddled up beside us shouting, "Mesdames, Mesdames, you left your blanket on the ground. Here it is." He was clad only in a light shirt and short pants. He certainly needed it more than we did. We gave him two oranges.

It started to rain. "All the stopping and starting has used up most of our gas," Eleanor announced. "I hope we've enough to reach Tours." Thankfully, Blois came into sight. At every hotel the story was the same. "There isn't a free bed in Blois. Every sofa, every chair is occupied and people are sleeping on the floors and in corridors."

Now it was raining steadily, but we decided to drive on and watch for a military post until dark. Stopping in each village to ask for gas, beds and a meal, we were told by the townspeople who stood in front of their tiny restaurants and cafés waving us on that there was no food. "Nothing left, nothing left. All beds are full." At one place a farmer threatened us when we tried to enter his yard.

We moved out on a narrow sideroad. After a time I happened to look back and noticed that Eleanor's hatbox had disappeared. It might have been the speck I thought I saw on the road far behind. Irène caught my eye and turned her head. After a long look she turned back and grinned.

The clouds grew darker, and as night fell the rain turned into a cold and clammy mist. We crept along slowly until we saw what appeared to be a large barn. Perhaps there would be hay inside and we could rest. Eleanor parked the car and Irène and I approached the barn. From it came a sickly, stale smell of sweat, urine and rotting hay and the murmur and movement of many people. We realized that few odours are worse than the stench that comes from a mass of tired, dirty human bodies huddled together. We went back to the car, and Eleanor drove on until we found an open space. We urged her to curl up on the seat; we would find a place for ourselves. Instantly she fell asleep. It was an unforgettable night. No planes came near us, though we heard them in the distance. Irène and I walked up and down the road and talked. The mist became a drizzle and then stopped, but the night was so cold we needed to move to keep warm. Rarely in a lifetime does a moment arrive for two friends to walk and talk hour after hour under such circumstances. It was a shared experience that produced a lifelong friendship.

At dawn, of one accord, people rose out of the green grain and long grass like the dragon's teeth of Cadmus. Everywhere, as though by a common instinct, they rose to their feet and moved back to the road.

Our gas tank was almost empty, and Eleanor was becoming frantic. "It should have taken us just a few hours and here we are on the third day," she fidgeted. "We've got to find some." In the next village we luckily discovered that the nearest military post was close by. At first the officer stationed there refused to help. His gas was precious and needed for military vehicles. Finally, with my miraculous press card, I convinced him that we had to get to Tours. He softened and gave us four litres and pointed out a shortcut back to the main road. "It's enough to get you there. Good luck."

June 14 had dawned sunny and clear. As we entered the next village we saw an extraordinary sight in the central square. Long trestle tables had been set up under the trees, and upon them were heaped literally tons of ripe strawberries. A strawberry festival at such a moment was a pure existential experience. As the refugees moved down an avenue of dappled plane trees and across the square, women, old men and children urged them to fill anything they had with the luscious, fragrant fruit.

"Who could imagine such a scene?" I wrote in my notebook. "The long tables in the shade of the trees in their spring green; old women and children pouring berries into every kind of receptacle; women and older boys and girls staggering into the square with huge baskets of berries fresh from the fields; eager refugees sweeping the fruit from the tables into anything handy; toddlers running about, their faces and mouths bright red, their hands and lips dripping with the juice — a feeling of festivity and abundance. Yet we are here because we are at war and fleeing the Germans. In my wildest dreams I could never imagine a scene like this."

Seated on a chair on a low step before the Municipal Office was an elderly gentleman wearing his ribbon of office. Yes, he was the mayor. "There's no food left to spare here," he told me. "This is our strawberry crop and the farmers and villagers are picking it all. Take it, take it. There's no market for it now and it must not be wasted. If the Germans come we don't want them to have it."

The realization of how desperate the situation was came to us in Tours. The government had moved on. Apparently it had been housed for a day or two in a number of châteaux in the region. With some difficulty we located the Information and Censorship Services. Few people knew that the services had been there, housed in two grubby buildings in a side street. When we reached the buildings they were empty; just a few desks and chairs and papers scattered on the floors remained. Obviously those who had worked there had made a hasty exit, following the government to Bordeaux.

Eleanor was now so exhausted she felt she could not go on. Irène and I left her in the car and each made inquiries until Irène found a small hotel. A dishevelled woman told us that some people had just left and we could have the room, but warned that she could not do anything about clean bedding. There had been no time to wash or change sheets for days and her whole stock of linen had been used over and over again. We would have to leave very early because she intended to do a giant wash the next morning. We took the room and then found a restaurant. Back in the hotel again we turned the sheets (wondering how many times they had been turned) and fell on the bed, fully clothed. I remember nothing of that night except waking at the sound of explosions. They seemed far away. Irène shook me at six. "Shhh, let Eleanor sleep. Let's go to the end of the hall and get washed." I realized that we had not given a thought to washing the night before, once we had seen the bed.

After a breakfast of black coffee and hard, oven-toasted bread, we went to the post office where I sent cables to my mother in Victoria and to the Canadian Press bureau in London. My notes were on all sorts of scraps of paper; I had the rough draft I had written in the field and the two articles I had carried from Paris. It was a chance to post the articles and the draft, even though it was uncensored.

"The cables might get through," the post mistress said doubtfully, "but I can't promise for the letters. Paris is occupied."

We felt thunder-struck. Occupied! Occupied without a struggle? The post mistress nodded and then turned her face away, tears running down her cheeks. "Paris was declared an 'open city,' thank God. But now the battle will be here, on the Loire." She choked. We stared at one another, unable to speak.

"I'm going to post my articles anyway," I said. "They might get through, maybe via Nice or Marseilles." Later I learned that nothing had reached London, not even the cable.

Back on the main road to Poitiers, we found it impossible to talk. Memories, visions of our lives in Paris, flooded our minds. There were still thousands of people on the road, but spaced in a way that allowed us to move a little faster. We stopped to eat some stale bread and opened a can of fruit. Nearby was a young woman with a small boy. They had an old farm cart drawn by an old horse. In the back of the cart sat a very old lady and a girl of three or four. When I spoke to them, the young woman told me they had come all the way from the Ardennes. Then the old woman screamed at me. "This is the third time those Boches have occupied my home. In 1871, in the first big war and now. But I'll go back. We'll get them." Her voice dropped to a croak. "I'm eighty-three years old but I'll go back. I will die in my own home. Our soldiers will slaughter ces salauds, ces sauvages, ces barbares." Her eyes shone like black stones. "Our poor country. Three times in my life. My father killed, my husband died of wounds, two sons killed and now my grandsons . . . Where are they?" She suddenly hugged the little girl to her. "Now my great-grandchildren. What is to become of them?"

The young woman spoke. "Don't, Grandmother, you upset the children." She turned to me and began apologizing for the old lady, but the grandmother paid no attention. "Yes, these are my great-grandchildren. What will happen to them? Quelle vie, quelle vie!"

I asked her many questions. Her mind and memory were clear. "Yes, I'll live to go back. Heetlaire and his Nazies — they can't kill *me*." The face of her granddaughter was stony.

Black anger swelled my heart. Her spirit was the spirit of the five-day flight to Bordeaux. Everyone I spoke to talked of how the army would finish off the Germans. It was utterly impossible, unthinkable, that the Nazis could defeat the Allies. Who could accept that evil could triumph over good?

"The Americans will not let it happen," I was told. "They are sending planes. They will declare war ... maybe already? We know nothing. Hitler. Even the devil wouldn't let Hitler and the Gestapo win such a war. Besides there's our navy and the British navy." I had not the heart to tell them that I had heard that Paris was an "open city," and I can honestly say that I never heard a defeatist word among the ordinary people in all those five days. It was an experience that changed the course of my life. Whatever was happening in France, the people were not defeated. In the people, the true French spirit lived. Betrayed, misinformed, they were victims of the real defeatists, their trusted military and political leaders. But they were never afraid or defeated in spirit.

That night we parked the car by a wall. It was raining again and the night was pitch dark. Eleanor curled up in the car. Irène and I took the blanket and found a dry place in the doorway of a small, locked shed. By this time we were so used to the sound of planes and guns in the night that we barely listened. Perhaps we had something of the fatalism that sets in when a tornado or an earthquake strikes. At break of day, we found the car was parked against a huge gasoline storage tank.

Now the road was much clearer. Once again we were almost out of gas, even though we had obtained a little in Tours. At noon we ran into a long line of cars moving forward slowly and learned there actually was a gas station ahead. Eleanor fell into line. More than two hours later we were within a dozen cars of the station. Each driver was given two litres, which was considered enough to get to Angoulême. As we stood on the road exchanging rumours with other passengers, we heard that the Germans were in Paris and the fighting had been terrible. We explained that we had heard that Paris was an "open city" and there had not been any fighting. There were lots of bitter arguments, but most of us admitted that we should not believe anything. All these rumours were mere *bobards* spread by Fifth Columnists. One man declared that he had heard from an officer that the French armies had stopped the Germans just outside Paris where the battle of the century was in progress. What to believe? Was the post mistress in Poitiers right?

At that moment two motorcyclists, riding in perfect formation and wearing greenish-mustard uniforms and helmets with goggles that hid everything but their thrust-out chins, sped past us. Their equipment was neatly packaged and attached to the sides of the motorcycles and on their backs. They kept their eyes fixed in front of them and never risked a glance at us. A long, audible gasp ran the length of the column of cars as drivers and passengers stared after them.

"They're German! My God, they're German!" someone gasped. Yes, they were Germans, speeding south and paying not the slightest attention to us. Everybody began talking. "They're after our communications," exclaimed one man. "That equipment is to cut the lines. The Germans must be in Paris or how else could these two be away down here?" "They look like robots," said another. We realized that for days no one on the roads had heard a word of real news. As we were to learn later, there were some ten million people of France, Belgium and Holland displaced, and most of them on the roads of France. This was the exodus, the brilliant, if diabolic, idea of using a civilian population as a weapon against its own military protection.

Suddenly the talking stopped. We got our two litres and drove on silently.

As we approached Angoulême, the towers of a cathedral loomed above the city. Remembering that Angoulême had a magnificent, romanesque cathedral overlooking the Charente valley, I suggested we visit it. I think we all wanted to shake the vision of those motorcyclists out of our minds. We found a restaurant and had an excellent meal, our first in days. We ate like queens — oysters and paté de fois gras with truffles. Eleanor bought a bottle of special brandy, something I was to bless her for later. Then we set off and spent the next two hours enjoying the grandeur of the old cathedral, taking in the view along the escarpment and the Promenade des Remparts, and wandering through the old streets, some dating back to the twelfth century.

For a time the war was forgotten.

Finally we were on the last leg of our journey. The sun was low as we approached Bordeaux. Twice we were stopped at road blocks by soldiers who examined our papers and asked to see our *bons d'hébergement* indicating that someone in Bordeaux had rooms for us. Fortunately, my friend Andrée Chivallon (a Sorbonne student whose old-fashioned parents had asked me to keep an eye on her in Paris) had sent one to me, just in case. Irène had her official orders, and I told the soldiers that Eleanor was with me. We were given permission to enter the city.

Once in Bordeaux, we were lost in the masses. A city of 300,000 now held about two million people. We parted with Irène so she could find her way to the laboratory and her accommodation. When Eleanor and I reached the home of my friends we found them inundated with refugees. They took us to the home of Professor Daudin of Bordeaux University. There we were welcomed, fed and apologetically given a place to sleep on the porch floor. The Daudins questioned us eagerly for news, only to learn that since leaving Paris five days earlier we had heard only rumours. Bordeaux too was filled with conflicting stories. Professor Daudin believed that something was being worked out between the French and British governments. Churchill was rumoured to have spent a day in France. Might he even be there at the moment? Gratefully we accepted his family's hospitality. In spite of my professional instincts, I was too tired to try to seek information that night. I was to meet Irène the next day as soon as she was settled. Or so we thought at the time we parted that night. How could we have imagined that we were not to meet again for more than four years.

At midnight the drone of planes did not disturb our slumber, but the earth-shaking explosions jarred us awake. The harbour of Bordeaux on the Garonne River was being bombed. Ships waiting there to take refugees to Britain were sunk, blocking the harbour. We did not know that as we went back to sleep.

five

How could I find a way to remain in France? As a journalist did I not have an obligation to report the fate of these innocent victims whom I had come to admire so much? The government was in Bordeaux. How did it plan to look after these homeless people? Where were the armies? These and a hundred other questions filled my mind as I awoke on June 17.

Professor Daudin was as puzzled and anxious as I was. Paris, he said, was indeed an "open city." I was thankful. Were future generations to be deprived of the great cities built by their forebears? Was their visible history to be wiped out simply because Hitler had been loosed on the world? Whatever the faults and mistakes of the Allied nations, they were fighting for something other than greed and territorial expansion. Perhaps for the first time on a world scale, people were defending their spiritual ideals and values. Salvation lay in the people who shared these ideals. I knew it as a certainty. However black things appeared to be, Hitler could never triumph over that.

Officials, diplomats, wealthy Parisians and newsmen filled the hotels. Alexander Werth, Percy Philip, Jean Piot, André Giraud (Pertinax), Geneviève Tabouis and many British correspondents were there. We all looked alike, rumpled, haggard with fatigue and disillusionment. No one knew where the Canadian Legation was located, so I went to the American Consulate and, in my incredible naiveté, asked if officials there could give me some sort of credentials saying I was attached to an American newspaper. (I had written two or three articles for the *Christian Science Monitor*.) When the official who consented to see me learned the purpose of my visit, it was as though I had told him I was infected with the plague. "Journalist!" he yelled. "Definitely no! It's impossible. Have you any idea of the trouble you could cause us? We need three months to get permission from Washington for our own freelancers. The Department would never consent. In fact we wouldn't ask. Our own journalists are giving us enough trouble. No, I'm sorry." He rushed me out. Relenting at the door, he said, "Go around to the British and see what they can do."

At the British Embassy I joined a queue. The British Embassy had accepted responsiblity for Canadians, Australians and other Commonwealth or colonial citizens seeking help. I was told flatly that I could not remain in France, and was handed a ticket that allowed me to board any ship carrying British subjects, either from the Bordeaux harbour or the Atlantic port of Le Verdon. Ships were leaving for England, and I was told that I had better get on one.

At noon I entered the foyer of one of the big hotels, the Splendide. Many journalists were sitting around waiting for the radio newscast. I found my Czech friend Karel Mazel and we ordered apéritifs. He told me about his adventures on the road. Karel shared my view of the spirit of the people. Having arrived twenty-four hours earlier, he had been able to pick up the information that the government was in shambles and that the politicians had been trying all through the night to form another. An announcement was expected soon. With a crackle of static, the radio came on. We were startled to hear an announcement that Maréchal Pétain had become the new Premier of France. Then his voice came on, quavering with emotion, but his words put death into our hearts.

"I assume direction of the Government of France. I make to France the gift of my person. France no longer has the military power to continue the war against an enemy superior in number and in arms. We must cease to fight. I have asked . . . our opponent . . . if he will sign with us, as between soldiers, and in honour, the means to put an end to hostilities . . . an armistice."

"Armistice!" someone near me choked. It had come like a thunderclap. Who could conceive of it? Perhaps the most stunning psychological blow was that the announcement was made by the Maréchal of France, Philippe Pétain himself — Pétain, in 1918 the commander-in-chief of all French armies, the hero of Verdun, the field-marshal revered and honoured by the French nation and by military establishments the world over, the great military figure under whom French-speaking Canadians were proud to serve. Maréchal Pétain had asked for an armistice! I could not hold back the tears.

No one seemed capable of taking it in. In spite of what everyone knew about the swift and ruthless war machine that had swept across France like some mythical iron monster, forcing millions of civilians before it, no one, other than a segment of the upper echelons of government, the military and the chronic anglophobes, could accept it. Undoubtedly those exhausted millions, the bewildered and despairing soldiers (many cut off from their units and uncertain about what to do next), gave a sigh of relief at the thought of no more bombs. We were to learn that many units were completely unaware that the government had fallen, or that an armistice was being sought. They just went on fighting wherever they were. Many did not lay down their arms until twelve or thirteen days later.

People were weeping in the streets, cafés and hotel lobbies. The shock had paralyzed them.

I returned to Professor Daudin's home to find a despairing silence. Then came the sudden outpouring of accusations against the government. They, the people, had been betrayed. The Americans had not come to the rescue; those two or five thousand planes from the United States were an illusion. The British had not had sufficient air force left after the battles in Flanders and France. After that single outburst of wrath against the government, we could not talk even to one another. I could not bear to look at the naked pain in their faces.

Eleanor came in with the news that she had found Don Brigham, who had been in Bordeaux for several days. We told the Daudins that we would be leaving the next day and thanked them for the places at their table and on the floor of their porch.

On the morning of June 18, after a second bombing of the harbour in the night, I met Percy Philip in the square. He told me that the United States had declared that it would do everything in its power to help. Factories would be transformed to produce munitions; ships and planes were being built. The fact was that the United States did not have 5,000 or even 2,000 planes ready to send overseas. He had encountered the same rumour everywhere and was sure it had been spread by Fifth Columnists.

"Think what it has done to the morale," he said bitterly. "It's too late for France. Of course we will be in it, but will it be soon enough? What will the delay cost? Can Britian hold out long enough? Nothing like this German war machine has ever been seen in this world before."

"Are you staying on in France?" I asked.

"I suppose so. I don't know what the *Times* wants." He looked around at the hordes of people sleeping on benches and the ground.

"It's like something out of Dante's Inferno. What will you do?"

It was the first time I admitted, with resignation and despair, that I was leaving France.

"You know Don Brigham. He's American but his grandmother was English and his great-aunt has been living in France for years. Of course she has to leave or she'll be interned. He wants me to drive with him to Le Verdon. We can compare notes. He'll take my friend Hélène with us to say goodbye. Eleanor is driving his aunt."

I told him about my encounter with the officials at the American Consulate. He laughed. "They hate the sight of journalists, even our own," he said, and teased me about my naive expectations.

We said goodbye, and I wondered when, if ever, I would see him again. He was one of those tall, lanky Americans, soft-spoken and compassionate, with gray, western eyes that always seemed to be seeking distant horizons. Like the rest of us, he felt crushed.

Don, Hélène and I arrived at Le Verdon at about three o'clock. Eleanor and eighty-year-old Miss Robinson were right behind us. The verdant countryside along the way looked so peaceful as the vineyards gradually gave way to the pine forests. The smell of pine always makes me homesick. Bit by bit the forest sank into the golden sand dunes so typical of the Biscay coast.

The mouth of the Gironde River was a scene of utter chaos. Citroëns, Cadillacs, Fords, Renaults, Hillmans and jalopies of every make had been abandoned. Bicycles, carts and mountains of luggage lay scattered along the beach. People frantically clawed through trunks and boxes, tossing out the contents to find things they wanted to take with them. Some selections were comically pathetic — evening wear, hats, satin shoes. One woman carried an ornate clock. French officials, British officers and dock hands tried to keep order, and told us that when our turn came to embark we could take on board "only what we could carry." Women were throwing away valuable furs, gowns, coats and treasured trinkets. The fine cars and limousines were worthless. I learned the brutal truth about the ultimate value of material things, for all these discarded possessions had been "loved" by their owners only a few days before.

Hundreds of us were crowded together on the long quay. Tenders that usually ferried automobiles out to ships were now carrying human cargo, about 300 at a time. Finally our turn came. Eleanor, Miss Robinson and I stepped aboard, after saying an anxious farewell to Hélène and Don. I had two small suitcases; a boy offered to carry my typewriter.

The next four hours were spent on the tender, moving slowly around the harbour, approaching one ship after another, only to be signalled to back off. They were already overloaded. We stood on the flat surface of the tender, all 300 of us, jammed tight as toothpicks in a box. I was standing beside the captain and told him I was a journalist. Would he mind telling me what was going on? He explained that the planes overhead were Spitfires trying to drive off Messerschmitts, which were dropping magnetic mines into the bay.

Around us were freighters, corvettes, cruisers and one large British battleship signalling orders. Planes darted out from the mainland while the shore batteries fired in sudden bursts. The hours crawled by. Finally the captain said he thought we should return to shore. At that moment our tender was rocked violently and we clutched one another to remain upright as a loud explosion announced a plane hitting the water in a ball of fire and smoke. There was a muffled scream from a girl, but otherwise there was not a whisper on the tender. The girl's mother held her child's head close to her and said almost apologetically, "Please excuse her. It's the fourth raid we've been in since we left home."

Looking back now I realize I have seen panic, but it was not as I might have imagined it. There had been a moment of panic on the road the night the German bombers missed us, but it expressed itself as anger against those who lit cigarettes or turned on lights. People did not scatter but accepted the danger as an act of God. At Le Verdon there had been an element of panic in the way men and women abandoned their cars and searched frantically through their trunks, throwing their possessions in every direction. But on the tender, while the air battles went on, with the exception of the child, there was not a movement, not a cry was uttered.

The light was fading when a small cargo ship came puffing into the harbour and the big, gray battleship signalled to it to take us on board. Signal by signal our captain translated for me. The ship was Dutch, its name the *Stad Haarlem*. Its captain protested, saying he was almost out of food, had little water and there were only six cabins. The *Stad Haarlem* had come all the way from South America with a cargo of linseed. The warship fluttered its pennants and woofed its deep-throated growl, ordering the freighter to take us on board anyway.

We approached. When we touched the side, some of the men on the tender began throwing our suitcases up to the deck some ten feet above our heads. Every moment or so a gap opened between the vessels. I saw my suitcase rise in the air and then go down between the ships, as did others. Somehow I climbed the swaying rope ladder, clutching my seond valise and my typewriter. How, I will never know. I was on the tender one moment and somehow on the deck the next. Now I had only the clothing on my back because the valise I clung to contained the books and papers I had packed in Paris. The one in the sea contained my clothes.

Three hundred and some refugees crowded on the deck of that little ship. Women with babies were given the cabins. The captain gave up his own quarters. At the stern, a portion of the deck was covered. It had contained coal. This was the only shelter, and it became the sleeping quarters for most of the passengers for the next four nights.

Now, in the darkness, a small boat came alongside and twenty-three wounded British tommies were taken aboard. They were lowered through the hatch to a bed of linseed. Many people had retired under the sheltering roof of the coal hole, choosing to believe they had found the best places. The rest of us were scattered along the deck hoping for the signal to leave. More and more guns were firing and the tracer bullets arched overhead against the night sky. There were intermittent air battles as planes chased one another above the bay. Two planes came down in flames, one so close to our ship that some of us were thrown off our feet by the jolt of the explosion and the displacement of air. All the time we watched. It had the unreality of a final fireworks display before an exhibition stand. Suddenly a German plane came out of nowhere heading straight for us. We held our breath transfixed, and grasped the railings. It skimmed the water and fired a sudden burst of bullets. They left a string of bead-like holes across the deck. Miraculously, no one was injured but the attack unlocked a sudden flood of voices. Where before there had been almost no talk or mingling, now everybody was talking angrily.

Chilled, we reluctantly wiggled our way into the coal hole. After a few minutes Miss Robinson gasped, "I can't stand this fetid air. I'd rather freeze on the deck." Eleanor and I agreed. We found a canvas stretched over one of the big hatches, and Miss Robinson was game to try to sleep between us. Two charming young Irishmen we had been talking to earlier came along and offered to join us, sleeping on the outside. For three nights the five of us stretched out on the hatch. Our lifesaver was contained in Eleanor's bottles. She had clung to her Scotch and that precious Angoulême brandy. Regularly, during the night, they were passed back and forth.

At dawn the *Stad Haarlem* was well under way and everyone was asked to line up to receive a bowl of barley soup and one thick slice of bread. Tea and a second slice in the evening completed our daily ration.

The ship had come into Le Verdon for fresh food and water, since its last stop had been Buenos Aires, but the chaotic condition in the port prevented the loading of anything except water. Remnants in the ship's larder were set aside for the soldiers, the women with babies, children and several very old people. The captain appealed to passengers to give up any food they had brought aboard. I noted in my scribbler: "The rich on board demand and expect everything. They are unwilling to give up the food they have to the wounded lying below." Finally the captain used his authority to requisition supplies, promising a thorough search if they were not given willingly. A strange assortment appeared — bottles of wine, tins of sardines, smoked meat, paté de fois gras, cheese, some tinned fruit and chocolate. Eleanor handed over her coffee and sugar.

Even though it was clear that the food was for the soldiers, some passengers were rude and abusive, to the obvious disgust of everyone else. Sailors and a medical student took the food down and cared for the men. Each time the hatch was lifted clouds of moths rose out of the linseed and we wondered if the soldiers would be naked by the time we reached Britain.

There were only two toilets off deck and a third in the captain's quarters. The last was used by the cabin passengers and children. The captain joined us on deck and made a joke of it. Frequently the toilets broke down but the sailors were good-natured. From Le Verdon to Falmouth, England, four days and nights, there were always two queues halfway around the ship. At the time it did not seem funny.

Having spotted my typewriter, the captain asked me to take down the names and addresses of all passengers.

"What for?" I asked, witlessly.

"If the ship is torpedoed only a handful could be saved," he answered grimly. "We have only a few lifebelts and boats. The list will be placed in a waterproof bag that will float. It should be picked up eventually. If I send the names by wireless the message could be picked up by the enemy. We've several political figures on board as well as these soldiers. I can't take a chance."

Among the passengers were thirteen Canadian nuns from Quebec and a Canadian student, Robert Sproule, who for some reason was wearing ski boots. An Italian actress with a Pekinese played the grande dame, threatening the captain with the loss of his job because she had not been given a cabin nor milk for her dog. She would see to it that her "friends in high places in London" heard about it. Losing patience, the captain finally told her to take a jump in the sea — or words to that effect.

It was a relief to be busy taking the names of the people as they filed past my desk. Among the passengers was the leader of the Italian socialist party, Signor Sforza, and his daughter, who had been living in exile in France. Two young girls of twelve and fourteen had walked across France from a private school in Lausanne, dressed in light summer dresses and carrying only their purses. People along the way had given them food and they had slept in fields, ditches and once or twice in a farmhouse. During the walk they had crossed the German lines three times. The little money they had had been saved to buy tickets on a ship going to England once they reached the coast.

I heard a hundred stories about these people, most of whom were the wives and children of British, Belgian, French and other European diplomats and businessmen. They had all crossed France by one means or another; all had seen others killed in the bombing and were still marvelling that they had come through alive.

Everyone scanned the horizon for other ships, believing we were travelling in convoy, but the ocean landscape remained empty. Privately the captain told me we were alone, but he did not want to alarm the passengers. Apparently our ship had been too slow to keep up. Its top speed was eight knots.

We washed with sea water, something not to be recommended, especially without a towel. So the sun did the job, leaving a fine film of salt on our faces and hands. My skin, which never tans, burned and blistered. On the third day one of the cabin passengers offered the use of her cabin for a wash, though there was very little fresh water to spare. What a luxury. "Don't tell anyone," she whispered. "Or I'll be swamped."

The last night it rained and our luggage was soaked. Miss Robinson was taken into a cabin, and Eleanor and I were permitted to sit on a step leading below. Our clothing was clammy and cold, and we had run out of alcoholic comfort. It was that night the captain told me that we had been followed by a German submarine for about sixteen hours. "They probably decided it wasn't worth wasting a torpedo on us," he commented. "Or maybe they thought a corvette might come out to escort us, and make a better target. We'll reach Falmouth tomorrow afternoon if we don't attract any more bad company. Luckily we could keep the soldiers below. If a uniform had been seen, they would have let us have it."

The next morning a second freighter fell in behind us, and in the afternoon the coast of England loomed up out of the mist. We steamed into Falmouth harbour. Two nights before it had been heavily bombed, and masts and funnels were standing above the water everywhere. The *Stad Haarlem* could not thread its way through this tangled mess, so small boats came out to lead us through. When I last saw the Italian actress and her Pekinese, she was still uttering threats about her treatment.

Nearly everyone else, however, was filled with gratitude and admiration for the Dutch captain and crew who had brought us safely to England. They were all residents of Rotterdam and had received no word of what had happened to their families after the merciless German bombing. Someone went around with a pillow-slip collecting whatever money each passenger wanted to give. The two little English girls put in everything they had, keeping only enough to make a long-distance call to their parents in Yorkshire. The actress refused. We were deeply moved when the crew would not accept the money but asked that it be given to a refugee organization in London.

The quay was damaged but still in use. At the land end, a barrier had been erected. In it were two gates and signs directed us to one as British subjects; the other was for aliens. Miss Robinson, Eleanor and I joined our queue, shaking with cold. The skies were smoke gray and the rain was falling steadily. The town was invisible in a dense mist. The piles of luggage, a sorry mess, were becoming more soggy. In the other queue were a number of Polish and Czech soldiers from the other freighter. I wondered if my own Polish friends might be among them.

We moved towards the gates slowly. Our papers were being examined and those without papers were asked to stand aside. As we shuffled along, a dozen little Girl Guides appeared carrying cups, teapots and bags of sandwiches for us — the refugees.

From the time I had left Paris I had been taking notes, interviewing individuals and drafting rough paragraphs for articles. I had talked to dozens, maybe hundreds of people, listening to their stories and observing their behaviour. Though I had travelled with them, I had not, even for a second, thought of myself as one of them.

It had been the same in February 1939, when I had spent days at the Spanish frontier. Sleeping quarters had consisted of a parked, third-class railway carriage. In it the volunteer doctors, nurses and I had slept each night, fully dressed, on the wooden seats. At that time I was gathering the stories and observing the plight of Spanish refugees, hundreds of thousands of them swarming into France. With great difficulty, arrangements had been made by the French government to accept 10,000 a day. The area was a rather sparsely populated agricultural region and the refugees flowing in outnumbered the local French population. While I was there, between 20,000 and 30,000 crossed into France. Their trails through the Pyrenees to Puigcerda and Bourg-Madame were visible when the sunlight caught and flashed off the thousands of empty bottles and tin cans discarded along the way. Though deeply moved and enraged at the sight of those helpless victims of humanity's unwillingness to solve political problems in a civilized way, I was still the journalist, reporting their plight — but helpless to do anything about it.

It was at the moment a little Girl Guide offered me a cup of tea at the Falmouth quay that I realized that, in the eyes of everyone there, I was a refugee. In the past ten days I had suffered feelings of sadness, anger, frustration and outrage beyond anything I could have imagined, yet a part of me had been standing aside, observing, trying to analyse the situation and write down exactly what I saw and heard. The experience, to the point where I accepted a cup of tea, had been my job. Then I realized the difference. I was not a refugee like the others. Unlike those men and women in the queue for aliens, I could go home.

We were taken to a theatre in Falmouth. A town official, doctors, nurses and volunteers received us. Only British subjects, numbering about 200, were there. The foreigners had been taken somewhere else and we never saw them again.

Women with children were called to the platform first and taken backstage for a medical examination. Miss Robinson was called long before we were, so we had to bid her goodbye at the theatre. We hugged the gallant old lady who had been so cool and amusing, who had accepted the cold, wet and dirt on the cargo ship without a word of complaint. Once processed, the people were taken to hotels, private homes, or placed on trains for various parts of England.

By 2 a.m. everyone was exhausted, and yet our turn had not come. Given a space in a large dormitory, we dozed. We were beyond sleep. Back at the theatre, the doctors gave us a clean bill of health, and then we were taken to a sailors' "home" for breakfast — bacon, scrambled eggs, toast, jam, hot tea. Ambrosia!

Faces washed, hair combed, fed, we were not yet in a condition to realize the remarkable organization and care the volunteers of Falmouth had lavished upon us and other refugees, whatever their nationality. Looking back, I am amazed and again filled with gratitude, for the people of that city showed such kindness to us even though they themselves had lived through heavy bombings just before our arrival.

We found our luggage sitting in a big rain puddle. By this time, Eleanor and I had not changed our clothes for eleven days. Though Eleanor had some sodden clothing in her suitcase, I only had to worry about whether my *Petit Larousse* and other papers and books had survived.

We boarded a train for London. From somewhere I had heard that Canadians from the Continent were gathering at the Strand Palace, not far from Canada House in London. Luckily a double room was available, so Eleanor and I were heading there to have a bath and go to bed.

When we reached London, I telephoned the Canadian Press bureau to tell them I had arrived safely. I was told to report to the office immediately. In spite of my protests that I had to have some sleep, I got no sympathy. This was one of the times I cursed my profession. But I went.

Somehow I got to the bureau, thinking how Eleanor must be dead to the world after a luxurious hot bath. "Sit down and write the story," I was told. All the past days flooded through my mind and, no doubt, some of my recollections found their way to the pages. When I finally protested that I could not write another word, Sam Robertson, our superintendent, offered to take me out for something to eat. At that moment an alert sounded, and I was hurried along with the rest of the staff and others from Associated Press into the basement. The men put on hard hats. Looking around, I saw we were in a film library. Long chunks of film spewed out of wastepaper baskets; other films were lying on a counter, not even canned. Above our heads were thick glass blocks to let in a little light from the street. Wooden filing cabinets contained more film. If we were hit we would be burned alive in all that celluloid.

Not a sliver of light showed when we finally stepped out after the "all clear." Sam found a taxi. He wanted me to eat something but I could not think of food. "All I want is sleep," I mumbled. "I want to sleep, sleep. For God's sake, Sam, let me go to bed."

Back at the hotel, I found the foyer swarming with Canadians seeking news and greeting new arrivals. A hush fell when General

Georges and Mme Vanier stepped into the crowd. The tall, handsome couple caught every eye. General Vanier welcomed us and promised that Canada House and he and Mme Vanier would do everything possible to help solve problems and obtain news of missing Canadians. He spoke to us as to one big family, words of encouragement and comfort. Then he urged us all to get some sleep because we had much to face in the coming days. The warmth of the welcome was a balm to the soul.

six

Recalling those London days stirs up memories I have kept buried for more than four decades. Helpless anger and anxiety well up again and I recognize them as feelings I could not assimilate at the time. I was incapable of holding so much apprehension and grief.

Never had the streets of London been so colourful and noisy. Uniforms of many nations, a babel of French, Dutch, Norwegian, Polish and Czech mingled with London speech, as thousands of men and women poured into England from the Continent and overseas. The city had become a microcosm for half the world. The air was filled with joyful cries as pedestrians unexpectedly bumped into friends and relatives. Anxious questions followed about the missing. Though tense and fearful, the shifting crowds were euphoric.

Impulsively, refugees spoke to one another. A familiar accent in the street caused them to stop, stare and then begin sharing their common fears and bewilderment. The suddenness and speed of the German victory caused them — caused us all — to look for culprits, and the anger was turned to the top military and political leadership. Yet, looking back now, I wonder: Could they, those leaders, mostly hold-overs from the First World War, have anticipated the kind of war Hitler had loosed? Not even Britain had prepared its armies and civilians for the lightning of mechanized warfare. Britain too thought in terms of the Maginot Line, trenches, armies facing one another for long periods, gaining ground step by step.

Seeing the Londoners moving about doing their ordinary jobs, I and others arriving from the occupied countries were afraid. Our fear was engendered by their innocence, by the naiveté in their eyes.

Those of us who had seen the horrors of war firsthand now knew what people were capable of doing to one another. In five short weeks, my eyes had been opened by the blood and curly tufts of children's hair stuck to the backs of seats in railway carriages, by those teenaged youngsters calmly taking the dead from trains in Paris suburbs, by the mass of refugees shuffling along the French roads to the harbour of Le Verdon. Even more vividly I remember the faces of those slow-moving columns. The spirit I saw in their faces and hearts kept haunting me. All I could think of was that I was free. What must I do?

The Canadian Press put me to work at once. I seemed to move like an automaton, writing follow-up stories, giving talks over the BBC and CBC, handling assignments. Kay Moore was in London and told me that Frank Pickersgill and Ruth Camp had not arrived. Mary Harding at Canada House kept us all posted as others registered there. We were to discover, perhaps for the first time, how our common nationality gave us a special bond of comfort and warmth. Was it a dawning of nationalism we were experiencing?

Over London floated the big, silver sausage balloons. Otherwise, the skies were undefiled. It was Paris all over again — that unbearable waiting. Every moment, every day, we expected to hear the sirens announcing the first, massive waves of German bombers. They did not come. Meanwhile, London finally began to change. The lesson of what had happened in France had not been lost. Posters appeared on news stands, on underground walls and on the sides of buses. "Silence, someone may be listening!" "Beware of the Fifth Column."

A Canadian friend, Vera Welsh, invited me for the weekend to her home in the village of Warmington. It was in her cottage that Dickens wrote *Little Dorit*. On the train enroute I began to see the real change. To discourage enemy planes from landing, fields were dotted with agricultural machinery, tubs, pails, hayracks, plows, carts, anything and everything that could be hauled out of barns and scattered. Along roadsides were trestles, rolls of wire, the barriers used for jumping horses and anything else that could be pulled across the road quickly by the local people when they saw an enemy plane descending. At the edge of woods I saw elderly farmers walking slowly, carrying rifles. Then I noticed that all road signs, the names of stations and anything else that could reveal location had disappeared. Never having been to Banbury, where I had to change for Warmington, I naively asked the name of the town we were approaching. Instantly five pairs of eyes were fixed on me suspiciously and no one answered. I explained that

I had not travelled this road before and wondered how I would recognize it.

"Ask the conductor and he'll tell you when we get there," one man said gruffly. "Shouldn't ask questions."

Someone muttered something about Fifth Columnists.

I explained hastily that I was Canadian and produced my passport. Everyone relaxed a little and disappeared into their books or behind newspapers again. I felt better. Something was happening.

Back in London I read with anguish that the Germans now occupied more than half of France and the whole coast down to Spain. Bordeaux was occupied. I sent cable after cable, and waited. What had happened to my friends? For five years they had made me a member of their families.

June 30, 1940: "I hurt too much to feel," I wrote in my notebook. "People, laughter make me dizzy with pain. Where are my friends? Are they safe? I feel so much guilt for having left. It is like an arm torn from my body and the rest of me is left unattached to anything and bleeding . . . I can't cry. It is as if there are two of me; one senses a despair too deep for expression; the other sees everything but is impervious to feeling."

July 1, 1940: "Still no news. The waiting is unbearable and the stories others tell only increase my sense of guilt. It seems as though I have taken the easy way out. Yet what could I do? I'd be interned by now and could do nothing to help. I must find some way to serve better than this . . . .

"One lone plane over about four this morning. The whine of the German plane is different. Funny. I could hear it in my sleep before I could hear it awake . . . Eleanor wakened at the same moment . . . .

"I went to the Dominion Day ceremony at Westminster Abbey this morning. It turned out to have a bit of comic relief and provided a sidelight on our Canadian confusions. The congregation was made up of a few Canadian civilians and the rest were soldiers. A choir had been provided with a song sheet of 'O, Canada.' When the music began, we started to sing. Instead of the traditional lyrics, we struggled in bewilderment as we became aware that the choir was not singing the same words. Somehow we got through it and I inquired later to discover that the choir had been given the Helen Taylor version, until then unknown to most, if not all, of us. Further investigation turned up the fact that, at that time, there were no less than sixteen versions. Oh! Oh! O, Canada!"

My work with Canadian Press probably kept me sane. As usual, I was given stories that were neither political nor truly military. I interviewed arriving Canadian nurses, Victoria Order of Nurses and Salvation Army personnel. I wrote stories about voluntary services directed by Lady Peel, Lady Falmouth and Betty Asquith. Tens of thousands of women were flocking into the Land Army, becoming policewomen, bus drivers, cashiers, station agents and factory workers. To the astonishment of the authorities, more than 400 women could fly airplanes. Before the end of the war, some of them were ferrying bombers across the Atlantic.

Hundreds of ADC (Amazons Defence Corps) units were springing up all over the United Kingdom at the call of Mrs. Venetic Foster, an expert markswoman. Hand-grenade throwing and the care and use of weapons, from revolvers to submachine guns, became subjects for classes. The repercussions from the blitzkrieg on the Continent had torn wide open the doors for women to enter every kind of activity.

A drive for aluminium was described as aid for the "Tea Kettle Squadrons." Thousands of tons of aluminium utensils were gathered; including pots, sauce and frying pans from Buckingham, Sandringham, Windsor and St. James palaces. At an exhibition of these contributions a pair of Queen Elizabeth's shoe-trees and fragments of three airplanes shot down by "Cobber" Kain of New Zealand were prominently displayed. A large poster read:

> The stress of modern warfare brings,
> Glamour to unexpected things.
> The common kettle now contains,
> The stuff to fashion Hurricanes.
> And 'tis the shoe-tree not the oak,
> Defends us from the tyrant's yoke.

British humour was the best of all secret weapons. Said one woman, "I've always had an urge to throw a saucepan. Now I've got a splendid target." One cartoon showed a woman with her nose in the air passing by two of her neighbours. One neighbour whispers to the other, "Shhh, it's the stuck up thing she is since Lord Beaverbrook brought down two Dorniers with her frying pan."

Once work patterns were settled and I found a room in South Kensington, I began to think of others I knew in London. Miss MacDonald was the first to come to mind.

Miss MacDonald — I never addressed her by her first name — had been my first friend in London. She was a member of the Royal Institute of International Affairs. Through her I met Mme Pierre-Jean

Jouve, the pacifist in whose pension I had lived for a year in Paris and where I had met Kay Moore and Gabrielle Roy. Miss MacDonald had been Mme Jouve's English counterpart in the First World War, and a party to the scheme of dropping leaflets over the trenches urging soldiers on both sides to throw down their arms and go home. It seemed like a simple way to end the war. Now it was a terrible, wrenching decision for Miss MacDonald to accept the Second World War, but Hitler's fascist philosophy had forced her to abandon her pacifism.

Each time I was in London I saw Miss MacDonald, simply to enjoy her salty humour and wisdom. Now, knowing that she would be worried about me, I telephoned. She turned out to be my lady bountiful. After listening to my account of the turmoil in France and my escape, she said, "I'm going to buy an outfit of clothing for you. You can't live in those things forever." She took me to the shops she dealt with in Bond Street and began picking out clothing. Horrified at the debt she was building for me, I protested vigorously. But she insisted on an especially beautiful — and expensive — burgundy suit with matching blouse and a smart felt hat (all of which I kept for nearly twenty years).

"But I can never repay you. I simply can't afford these things," I stuttered. "I've never dared to even look into Bond Street!"

"You can't refuse," she insisted. "I'm an old woman and there is so little I can do now. But you are young and involved. Your clothing is in France, so this gives me a chance to participate a little." She smiled her beguiling smile. "I feel as though I'm arming a fighter — only I've always been a pacifist and I'd rather arm somebody who fights with a typewriter! You can't do your work without decent clothing. Perhaps some day you can do the same for someone else. I think of my dear friend, Mme Jouve. I am sure she is still in Paris. But where is her only son? Think of what she must be enduring under German occupation — and for how long? Think of her sacrifices. Let me do it for her."

Dear Miss MacDonald. I mustered up the grace to accept and wore the suit until it was threadbare. I was to learn later that Miss Mac-Donald and a grand-niece were killed during the blitz over London.

Day after day passed and still the unbearable waiting. Finally, a cable from Bordeaux. At least some of my friends were alive and had found a way to communicate. I sent more cables and ventured brief, innocuous letters, but there were no replies. The long silence had begun. Like so many others who were trying to reach friends and family in occupied countries, I feared that my cables and letters might betray friends sympathetic to the Allies. Dare we write or cable? Were we exposing helpless friends and relatives to reprisals? What a quandary!

At Lady Peel's invitation I went around to her reception centre to see the latest activities of her committee, the United Association of Britain and France in Aid of Refugees. More than 300 French schoolboys between the ages of ten and seventeen had crossed the Channel in open boats or with fishermen of the French Channel fleet. Some of the children had been in the Channel several days before being picked up. Now these schoolboys were in the charge of Lady Peel's committee. I talked to boys from Paris, Normandy, Brittany and St. Jean de Luz who had attended a school in Brittany. A group of the students had decided that they wanted to fight and took to the sea. Others along the coast begged fishermen to take them. Now they were pleading for uniforms, though some of them were not yet thirteen. Many were running around in female clothing, causing riots of laughter.

"We have gathered mostly clothing for women and very young children, as we did in the last war," I was told. "That's why the boys look so ridiculous. We were having their clothing washed or cleaned and had to give them something to wear after their baths."

The younger children were taken into private homes and boarding schools; the teenagers were enrolled in cadet corps. Most of those fourteen and over were fighting before the war ended, as pilots in the RAF, as members of the crews of mine-sweepers in the Channel or with the French fishing fleet which had arrived at southern England ports en masse. In all, more than 26,000 fishermen and their families as well as other civilians took refuge in England and participated in the war effort.

Early in July, I interviewed Canada's famous Yukon poet Robert Service. "His eyes were deep blue and below his white hair his face was as smooth and fresh as a child's," I wrote in my notebook. "He wore a pale blue suit with a beige-pink shirt and a deep red tie. Nervous. Perspiration on his forehead. He reminds me of a very cranky baby, complaining about the discomfort he had suffered in the 'appallingly dirty tramp steamer' that had saved him. He had lost his homes in Brittany and Nice, and an apartment in Paris. He grumbled that he hadn't had a chance to bring out his money. Concerned with the upheaval in his personal life, he seemed unaware of the tragedy he had left behind. What of his friends? I was disappointed and found it hard to equate him with Klondike bar-room ballads such as 'The Shooting of Dan McGrew'."

Shortly afterward, I received an unexpected note from Dr. Edith Summerskill, a Labour member of Parliament. She proposed that I take on some speaking engagements she would arrange in factories, women's organizations and so on. "The more that people are aware of what happened in France," she said, "the better prepared they will be. As an eyewitness of the confusion and how the civilians were used, you may have some advice to give. Please give it." While meeting with these audiences of working people in various parts of London, especially in the factories, I became aware of the one great quality they shared — compassion. I felt very defensive about the people of France (as opposed to their government) and I could not have suppressed my feelings had those English audiences expressed anger or criticism towards the ordinary people of France. To my astonishment I did not encounter, in even one meeting, a word of hostility or reproach. The audiences were stunned, as I was, by the fall of France. Their remarks revealed dismay, compassion and sorrow. Often tears were in their eyes. I mentioned this to the manager in one factory and he answered soberly, "It's all very well to criticize in peace time, but not now, not now." "We didn't know how close we were to the French people until this terrible tragedy," one woman said. "If we didn't have the Channel," another asked, "where would the Germans be now? This is what we ask ourselves."

I still think that there has never been enough attention paid to the great spiritual qualities exhibited in the attitude and understanding of these ordinary people. Not knowing exactly what they were facing but fully aware of the danger, they had hearts and minds large enough to show concern and sympathy for those locked in the European prison. It is only now, years later, that I become angry with those who examine the war with cynicism, write of the dead with scepticism, glide with the sophistication of ignorance over the behaviour and attitudes of the peoples who endured it, and dare to make so-called objective judgments. The people were human beings with all the human faults, but they rose to heights of courage and selflessness never since — or perhaps before — equalled. Who are the real heroes? And where are they honoured?

seven

I n London on Bastille Day (July 14), I was startled to
see a column of French soldiers and sailors, with a
few French air force and Zouave uniforms scattered
among them. Intrigued, I followed the procession to Grosvenor
Square and the statue of Marshal Ferdinand Foch (generalissimo of
Allied forces in France in 1918). A large crowd had gathered, and from
where I was standing I could not see who was addressing the soldiers,
but suddenly, swelling out of the throats of a few hundred men, came
"La Marseillaise." Many soldiers were without caps or jackets.
Wounded were sitting in troop-carriers, heads or arms swathed in
bandages. Others stood at attention or leaned on crutches. The British
public standing there joined in the singing, and then burst into cheers.
I could not stop the flow of tears that welled in my eyes.

Later that day I discovered that there were many French journalists
in London, and somebody at the BBC offered to take me to a reception
being held for them at the Carlton Club. There I encountered Geneviève Tabouis and was captivated by her enthusiasm for a young
unknown general, Charles de Gaulle. Back at the CP office, I scanned
the newspapers until I found de Gaulle's famous rallying call on the
day after I had left Bordeaux. It read:

TO ALL FRENCHMEN

France has lost a battle!
But France has not lost the war!

The governments of occasion have capitulated,
yielded to panic, forgotten honour, delivered the
country into servitude. Nevertheless, nothing is lost!

Nothing is lost because this war is a world war. In the universe immense forces have not yet been brought into play. One day these forces will crush the enemy. On that day France must be present at the victory. She will regain her liberty and her greatness. That is my goal, my only goal!

That is why I call upon all Frenchmen, wherever they may be, to unite with me in action, in sacrifice and in hope.

Our country is in peril of death
Let us all fight to save her.
VIVE LA FRANCE!

It was a message of prophetic vision. I wanted to meet this general. When I suggested an interview to my bureau chief, Sam Robertson, he promptly assigned me to the job. "You can keep an eye on that movement and see if anything comes of it," he said.

General de Gaulle's headquarters were in St. Stephen's House, a shabby old building on the Victoria Embankment which was on loan from the British government. The headquarters were bare and almost empty of furniture. A glum-looking sailor told me that the general was away and nobody knew when he would be back.

I had learned that many thousands of French soldiers and sailors had been rescued at Dunkirk; those who had not been taken back to France immediately to fight again were in British hospitals and camps. I visited one hospital to talk to some of the wounded about General de Gaulle. Some soldiers simply turned their faces away and would not talk to me. Others wanted only to talk about going home to find out if their families were still alive. Others spoke admiringly of General de Gaulle and were impatient to get well and join him. "It's a ruse," they told me confidently. "It must be. Maréchal Pétain would never surrender. He saved France at Verdun. He has sent de Gaulle out for some secret purpose. Maybe to gain time. Maybe to get our armies from the colonies." There were many theories, but none of the men could accept that the armistice request was genuine.

More anxious than ever to get an interview with the general, I went to see Geneviève Tabouis. In no time a meeting was arranged.

Beyond my reporter's instinct, my main reason for wanting to see General de Gaulle in the flesh and hear what he had to say was not to satisfy the curiosity of Canadian Press readers. I had the temerity to think that I had a right to size him up personally and decide whether or not I thought he was worthy of those millions of betrayed people, those two-and-a-half million war prisoners and those bewildered grief-stricken boys in the hospitals. I wanted to be reassured that he stood for the values I had learned to admire and respect in France. I wanted to judge for myself whether this country, which I loved only second to my own, and its people now living in purgatory were about to be betrayed again. Was de Gaulle a genuine patriot, dedicated solely to his compatriots, his country and freedom? Or was he a young general grabbing an opportunity to make a name for himself at the expense of his trampled country, a "man on the make" looking for personal glorification? I was young enough to think that I could make my own assessment.

As I entered the room, General de Gaulle rose to his feet. I was surprised by his great height, his grave and thoughtful mien and the warmth of his keen eyes. As he welcomed me, his voice was soft and his manner touched with old-world courtesy. I was instantly impressed with his air of tranquil confidence. Perhaps my questions were simplistic, but I wanted to know what had happened in France militarily. Why had France fallen so quickly? Why had everyone been so unprepared? Why had the people not been told what to expect? I spoke with all the passion of youth and the conviction I held about the people I had known and had seen dragging themselves through Paris and along the roads outside the city.

A map of France lay on de Gaulle's desk. He took out a large sheet of paper. Patiently, quietly, he explained what had happened, drawing lines on the paper and indicating places on the map. The French and British had been prepared to fight the First World War over again. He told me about the books he had written on mechanized warfare; he explained how the Germans had built their armoured divisions, their tanks and launched their blitzkrieg. They had done the obvious — they had smashed around the end of the Maginot Line, cutting through Holland, Belgium and northern France with long, steel fingers. These columns, led by swiftly moving motorcycle squads, had deliberately, and certainly for the first time in history on such a massive scale, used civilian populations as a weapon.

The only time a bitter note crept into his voice was when he mentioned the use the Germans had made of his books on mechanized warfare. I had never heard of them. Now, he said, he intended to put his theories into practice. The Free French Legion under his command would be mechanized. "It will have three branches, air,

THE FALL OF FRANCE

land and sea, complete with modern weapons," he said. "It will fight under the French flag. Answers to our call are coming from all over the world because this will be a fighting force for France, not a political one."

"Will your army be equipped by and integrated into the British forces?" I asked, wondering just how the remnant of the French army, without equipment, without uniforms, could operate.

Arrangements had been made with Winston Churchill and the British government, he told me. At the beginning of the war the French and British governments had decided that no money would be exchanged until after the war. Each country would supply the other as needed and accounts would be settled later. "We already have considerable credits against which the British government will allow us to draw. They were created by supplies we sent to Britain the first year, mainly foodstuffs. The British will arm and clothe our soldiers."

The general explained that the force would not become a part of the British army but would be a solely French army at the side of its allies. "This is of first importance for the people in France," he said. "It must be seen as an army representing France." The propaganda in France described the Free French and General de Gaulle as mercenaries "in the pay of the British." "The French people must not be led to believe they have been betrayed a second time," de Gaulle told me. "They must feel and believe that the army I will lead is genuinely *their* army. After such humiliation, something to restore their pride and confidence is vital."

I spoke of my feelings of guilt at leaving France.

"No, you were right," General de Gaulle said. "You can do much in freedom. You would have been interned and would have been useless for your own country and your desire to help."

I felt better, watching the strong face with its high forehead and large nose. He continued to speak quietly and I dared not interrupt. Finally he said, "When fighting a war, in the last analysis it is a question of conviction and will. In mechanized warfare it is also a question of the size of the territory the war is being fought over. Were France as large as Russia, this would not have happened. But from the German border to the Channel, a fast car can cross it in less than six hours."

"If the Germans invade England, how long do you think it could take them to force capitulation?" I asked.

"Invade England!" he exclaimed. "Mon enfant, the Germans will never invade England. The Channel is a better tank trap than the Maginot Line. Churchill will never capitulate. The people of England have seen what has happened and now they know what to do. Also they are like the people of France. They do not understand defeat. Fortunately they have leadership which reflects them. Have no fear, the war is only beginning."

As he continued to describe the situation I began to see de Gaulle as a man of vision. I asked him what he thought about the present lack of movement. Why had not the Germans attacked London? Did he think the British could withstand the bombing after losing so many planes and so much materiel in northern France?

He looked at me. I was fascinated by his eyelids, which were like little hoods; under them his eyes gleamed steadily. "Don't worry Mademoiselle. *They* haven't figured out a way to cross the Channel." A smile twitched his lips. "And they won't."

Silence for a moment. Then General de Gaulle said, "Mademoiselle, remember the war has only begun. Yes, we have lost the first battle, but it's the last battle that counts — that one we will win. Before this war is over France will again have an army fighting beside Britain, and your Canadians."

I was convinced. Then I asked, "Is there a place for me in your volunteer army?"

"Hélas," he said, "so far I haven't even one tank. I haven't an ambulance you could drive. I have only the remnants of an army that was taken off at Dunkirk, and those brave young people and others who are escaping daily from France. Some others are coming from our free colonies. Some parts of the navy, merchant ships and our Channel fishing fleet are arriving. But organization is only beginning. You will help us more if you will write the truth of what has happened to the people of France, as you saw it yourself. If you will explain the purpose of the promise I have made to build a French army, and explain that French men and women, though defeated militarily, will not stop fighting. Before the war is over ours will be a real army. We intend to be present at the liberation of our country."

One morning my CP assignment was to interview some of the parents of British children being sent to Canada for safety. Since both men and women were mobilized in the armed services, factories, land army and home defence, the problem of looking after young children had to be solved. Many were sent to country villages and towns to elderly relatives or friends. Then someone had the idea that families in Canada might be willing to take them in. The plan was welcomed enthusiastically on both sides; thousands of Canadian families offered their homes. In Ottawa Dr. George Davidson was in charge of receiving the children; more than 5,000 of them eventually crossed the Atlantic. My task was to find out something about the background of the children and the motivations of the parents prepared to let them go.

Among the homes I visited were several in Manchester and Liverpool. I found myself in dusty drab streets without any greenery except gaunt geraniums behind windows. Smog hung over the buildings. Families lived on small incomes from the factories or busy ancillary shops building war materiel. I knocked on the doors at the addresses I had been given, usually around mealtime. In most of these shabby homes I found tired-eyed women in scrupulously clean kitchens. Mothers and fathers who happened to be home for lunch looked at me with trusting eyes and gave frank reasons for deciding to send one or more of their children to Canada.

"Are you worried about their safety?" I asked.

Sometimes the answer was yes. Liverpool and Manchester were obvious targets. But more often, to my surprise, a mother or father would say, "Canada. It will be a better life for them out there. If we don't survive at least the children will have a chance in that great land. Who knows? It's an opportunity we never had."

Sometimes a man would say wistfully, "I always wanted to try my luck in Canada, or Australia. Maybe after the war..."

Next I went to see one of the ships leave with a cargo of children. I watched with mixed feelings and a large lump in my throat. The pain of parting was obvious, but few parents allowed themselves tears. Once, just as the gangway was about to be removed, a boy, perhaps eight years old, suddenly broke from the children crowding the ship's railings and dashed down to the quay shouting, "I won't go, Mum. I'm going to stay and fight the Germans." There was a sudden hush and then wild cheers. As the ship moved away the eyes of parents and children clung together as long as they could distinguish one another.

Evenings I spent with friends, usually other Canadians, discussing the war situation. Again, the same questions. Why had not the Germans pressed their advantage? Why no massive bombing of London? German broadcasts had promised it, and it had to come. Rumour said hundreds of barges and ships were massed along the French coast. What were they waiting for? Were they trying to negotiate secretly with the British? Lord Haw-Haw, speaking from Berlin, urged the British to accept the inevitable. The British and Germans were "cousins" and would create a "New Europe" together. "The trouble is the Germans can't swim," people wise-cracked. Meanwhile we went on taking our three-inch "blitz baths," discovering unexpected acquaintances and groping our way through the rigorously blacked-out streets.

A stir of excitement arose when the newspapers announced that the British government intended to tax books. Public indignation almost swept the war news off the front pages. Authors, book publishers, librarians and booksellers called a huge meeting to protest, chaired by J.B. Priestley. The meeting turned into an enormous street crowd. "Tax on books! Never! Not in Britain. What are we fighting for?" — that was the message and it kindled thunderous applause. The British government hastily denied any such intention.

One morning in mid-August Sam Robertson told me that I was to travel back to Canada with one of the children's ships. "The plan has caught the imagination," he said. "Thousands of requests and offers of homes are coming in from all over Canada. CP wants you to go along and write about the crossing and how the kids are taking it. You should be ready to leave in a week or ten days. Better be prepared because you won't get more than a day's notice."

I did not want to go. Imagine being anywhere except London! How could I leave? It seemed like running away a second time. What could I do in Canada? Poor Sam had to listen to every argument I could think of.

"Look, you work for CP so you don't have a choice," he argued. "Once you do these stories you can probably come back on a troop ship. As a journalist you shouldn't have trouble."

"But what about the ban on civilians leaving Canada?" I objected.

"Oh, you'll make it. The army is bringing over auxiliary forces. Besides Canadian Press can fix it. Don't worry."

I went around to Carlton Gardens, the new headquarters of General de Gaulle. Now it looked like a full-fledged military command. A smartly uniformed young officer took in my request. Once more General de Gaulle received me. I explained that I was returning to Canada but hoped to be back soon. He thanked me for the stories I had written and asked me to look up Elisabeth de Miribel, who had been his secretary for six weeks when he had arrived in London. She had gone to Canada where she had a mission explaining to Canadians, especially in Quebec, what the Free French Movement represented. He had been informed that Vichy propaganda and appeals in the name of Maréchal Pétain were pouring into Quebec. It was the same propaganda that had been let loose in France; the Free French were being described as criminals, deserters, traitors and mercenaries "in the pay of the British."

"The truth must be known in Canada," he said. "Mlle de Miribel is the daughter of the French general who mobilized France in the First World War. She is trustworthy and has some knowledge of English but no experience as a journalist. If you wish to help us, then help her. Try to explain to your compatriots that our objective is the same as yours, and to save the honour of France."

He smiled suddenly and said, "I have something for you, since you volunteered for service." He handed me a letter stating that I had been made an Honorary Brigadier in the Free French Auxiliary Forces. "Now you are one of us," he said.

Around the 25th of August a messenger arrived at my door with a ticket voucher and instructions about my departure. I was forbidden to say goodbye to friends or even colleagues. Soon a hand-delivered message arrived instructing me to report to the Scala Theatre at 3 p.m. that afternoon with my baggage in hand.

At the Scala were other Canadians and more kept arriving. On the way there I had taken a last look at London, beautiful, busy, vibrant and the only place in the world I wanted to be. How could I bear to be so far from the action? From the theatre we were transported to the train station where we climbed aboard a coach, still not knowing where we were going. Our only instruction was not to speak to anyone outside our own compartment. It was a long ride and several times we had to wait on sidings. Someone said, "We must be on our way to Scotland. I recognize the stations even without their names." It grew dark. After midnight we reached our destination, Prestwick, only to hear a rumour that London had received its first bombing and parts of the old city were on fire. Flashing through our minds were vivid pictures of Warsaw in rubble, a Rotterdam flattened. The waiting-room was filled with desperate people, each trying to use a telephone or send telegrams to find out what had happened. After what seemed interminable hours of waiting a harried station official told us it was not true. We left to board our ship wondering what to believe.

Once on the ship it became evident that the children had boarded earlier and were fast asleep in their cabins. There were several hundred of them. During the crossing I and other Canadians were kept busy answering questions that popped into the children's minds. Would they see Indians? Were there any bears or bison near Toronto? Could they go to see them? How could they get to ranches and become cowboys? After the first day or so of tears and unwillingness to talk to anyone, the children began to look forward to the adventure as eagerly as any explorer. The histories of the children were all much the same — father in the services or a factory, mother driving a bus or an ambulance, nursing or working in a factory. On the whole, they were well-behaved; sometimes homesick, they were comforted by the women accompanying them. There was great excitement as we passed another convoy on its way to Britain. On another day the children excitedly watched a whale blowing fountains of water in the air and an iceberg towering in the distance as we approached the shores of Canada.

The first glimpse of land brought whoops of excitement. Sailing into Halifax harbour, we saw hundreds of people awaiting the ship. City organizations and individuals were ready. Picking up their hand luggage, the children trooped off, some still weeping but the majority staring around with bright eyes, exuding curiosity. Watching them go, I asked myself how long it would be before, if ever, they would see their parents and their homeland again.

Andy Merkel, chief of the Canadian Press bureau in Halifax, met me with a telegram telling me to report to the Ottawa bureau. At lunch I met his sixteen-year-old daughter Mary Liz and her fiancé, Charles Lynch, a young, then very slim, reporter. I happened upon a vehement argument between father and daughter. Mary Liz was making a strong case for an immediate marriage to Charles. "You married Mother when *she* was only sixteen, so what have you got to say to that?" she argued. Andy glanced at me and said nothing.

On the train to Ottawa several cars carried British children. Interested in their first impressions, I asked what they thought of Canada. One solemn little boy staring out the window answered seriously, "It's a very untidy country. All the telephone poles and most of the fences are crooked."

Then we lost a youngster. Mrs. Tremaine, in charge of him and ten others, was frantic after she had hurried back and forth the length of the train and found no sign of him. "Do you think he could have got off the train at that last stop?" she asked me.

"I don't think so. Let's get the conductor to check the men's washrooms. We can check the ladies'."

A moment later Mrs. Tremaine came back clutching the culprit. "I found him in the toilet," she panted. "He was on his knees and his head was in the bowl. When I asked him what he was doing, he said he was watching Canada go by."

PART TWO

In Canada
with the Free French

eight

As soon as I arrived in Ottawa in early September, my mother sent the first letters I was to receive from France. They had come via the United States. Some were addressed to my brother Max in Idaho; others to Americans in New York, Washington and California who were unknown to me.

I learned that the husbands of two friends had been killed in the brief war in May and June. Other friends had been wounded, killed or were prisoners-of-war. Faced with a million-and-a-half prisoners, the Germans decently observed the Geneva Convention. Those they could not immediately imprison in Germany were confined in military camps in France under German guard. There is an old soldier's adage, "If you are to escape, do it at once while everything is in confusion." Several of my friends did just that.

Irène's first letter was written at the end of June 1940: "I write through Max. I hope he can tell me if you are alive (he must write to me through Claude, in Cannes), and if you reached Canada. Your cable to Hélène that you were in London brought us such joy. No word of my brother, or Paul, or Albert. No word of Hélène's mother or my aunt...."

The letter also contained this chilling description of the occupation of Bordeaux: "No words can describe a pain so intense that it freezes the marrow. I feel dead, but my eyes are open. The people on the streets have the same fixed, dead faces that I see in my own mirror. There is something so inhuman about brute force; such an assault on the emotions and the mind that only by remaining frozen is it possible to go on living without feeling alive...."

"It happened today. I saw, in spite of myself, the parading of this army as it marched around all the main concentric boulevards in the centre of the city — in both directions — as if they thought of it as entertainment. It lasted forty minutes. It was to show us their might. No one was allowed to cross a street or move on. I was in a tram. We were stopped. I could not get out so I decided to really look at them and tell you what it is like.

"We were stopped by helmeted soldiers, using manual traffic disques like the police use in German cities. They ordered the people, some of them shamelessly curious, to align themselves along the sidewalks. I observed this army very closely. It was as though I was not there, that I was the eye of a camera, with no more feeling. I had seen this army in Germany, in the cinema and the news theatres, so I knew it well: 'Entry into Vienna,' 'Entry into Prague,' 'Entry into Warsaw,' 'Entry into Oslo,' and now Bordeaux — hallucinating — a reason to scream! This time in the flesh. It's such an ugly, such a monstrous army. The 'materiel' is massive, quantities enormous, the 'floats' interminable, and always all engines looking brand new, but with no 'line,' no esthetic beauty. All are heavy, ill-shaped, snub, squat and a horrible colour. No 'art' (if one may use that word), no refinement — no *style!* Nothing to redeem its sinister menace. Very painful to the eyes, the dominant sensations heaviness and ugliness, but certainly solid and capable of long usage; efficient, technically powerful and in excellent condition; equipped with everything needed. The rhythm of these armoured vehicles very, very rapid, sixty to eighty kilometres an hour in the centre of the city, without reducing speed or having difficulties at corners — all at the same speed.

"The terror of it is that it is something so abstract, so malevolent and scientific. The soldiers are of lead. No, steel! All seem the same height, movement mechanical, the goose step, frozen in their respective attitudes. Standing or sitting, ramrod straight. No human movement. No looking toward the people, no curiosity or mobility in the faces — faces only partially visible under those metal helmets. One sees strong jaws thrust forward, making them one with their machines — assimilated! I remember Huxley, 'all is machine and geometry.'

"Still these same men have had their brothers, comrades, companions killed en masse in Belgium and northern France. And after? Where is the pity? I'm sure they don't think of them as individuals, only as mechanized bodies, part of a greater body. And it is a calculation that they are here, soiling our city, deafening the people with the noise of their motors.

"The people with me in the tram were at the end of their nerves. Myself — my head was spinning. On the streets, though under German police observation, many covered their eyes, their ears while others cried and gave bitter sighs, echoed in the tram. And the remarks...

"'They drive, generously using our gasoline,' a woman sitting near me said bitterly.

"We were told the Germans were poor, the country lacked everything. We were told the Germans were living their last quarter hour, and had to improvise everything. We have been betrayed...

"In the news cinemas they said the German tanks were made of wood; they only had tanks for training....

"Why? Why? Why?

"I watched them scowling and muttering angrily, furious at having been betrayed, duped, victims, like myself, of this formidable *bourrage de crâne* [brain-washing] ....

"Oh you cannot know, you cannot imagine how we have been betrayed... yet there are some who have accepted cigarettes! The mindless, the greedy... are they really aware of what has happened to us...?"

Betrayal. It was the theme of so many letters in the early days of the occupation. Today, rereading some of them, I cannot help but ache.

Other letters, from Hélène, Madeleine, Andrée and Suzette, echoed Irène's. "I am sending this letter via Frances Hart in New York," Hélène had written on July 1, 1940. "I know she will send it because she was so kind to Suzette and me before our ship sailed. I can't tell you what we are feeling. I have no word of mother, who is somewhere in the unoccupied zone, and the Kommandantur refuses to let me go to look for her. I cannot send letters home to see if she is there. I spend my days going from bureau to bureau trying to get a *laissez-passer* — it is more difficult to cross the demarcation line than the Himalayas. The superhuman patience of the refugees is beyond belief and the general consequences very great, the total asphyxiation of the country. The total helplessness of the French government at Vichy to obtain the slightest aid.... The Kommandantur had me pushed out of the office brutally when I asked to send a telegram to mother. I can't bear to think of her despair...."

In her letter to me, Andrée quoted a few lines from a letter she had received from one of her friends in the army: "The sky was filled with Italian and German planes and I saw only 4 Allied ones during the whole day. It was magnificent weather and 'ces messieurs' could

operate in complete tranquility. In combat they arrive in carriers while
we and our comrades from England carry seventy pounds on our
backs — gun, mask, flashlight, maps, jacket, raincoat, rations, water-
bottle and other equipment. We should have been put in jump-suits
like the Germans who move with such ease .... Up to the Marne the
Germans took almost no prisoners...."

A letter some weeks later from Madeleine told me that she and her
parents had escaped to Oran, Algeria, where they had a summer
home. She was in despair about Albert. She had received only one
note and then silence. She quoted a few lines Albert had written: "We
did not know what to do so we went on fighting until June 29th. We
heard some of the military in high places waited at their posts to
collect their month's pay. This gives you an idea of the disgusting
mentality of some — thank God not all — of the leaders. We are
nauseated and ashamed...." Another letter from Madeleine written in
August told me Albert was a prisoner in Germany.

Two other letters came in 1940. One was from Hélène who wrote
about her philosophy students at the lycée. "My students must be
protected from the worst aspects. I have asked them to hide books
written by German or French writers who speak of freedom — even
some by Goethe. And especially English language books must not be
found. I remind them our minds are free and in them we must keep
the great freedoms we have achieved over the centuries. We must
remember they are more precious than our lives ... they must be kept
intact for the day when France is herself again. How else, Glad, can I
fight?"

And again from Madeleine: "I do not know what courage is. What I
feel at times and what allows me to overcome my crises of terrible
despair is not courage. It is some sort of vague hope that Albert is alive,
a prisoner, somewhere...."

In all I have almost two hundred letters written between June 18,
1940, and the end of December 1942 (when the Germans occupied all
of France). Every one of these letters represented a risk to someone's
life. I realized as these letters came along, week by week, that every
minute of freedom I had must be put to use.

For some reason Canadian Press head office in Toronto had overlooked informing the Ottawa bureau that I was joining its staff. Andy
Carnegie, the superintendent, politely welcomed me to Ottawa and
asked me about my plans. "Why, to start work whenever you say," I
replied.

"You've been assigned here? Well, well. Maybe we'd better go out for coffee and talk it over. What would you like to do?"

We agreed that I would cover the parliamentary committees on veteran's affairs and agriculture, writing feature stories about the Canadian war effort. My salary would be $100 a month and I would keep the right to freelance for magazines. Also, thanks to Lois Wheeler, National Secretary of the Women's Canadian Clubs, I already had a number of requests for talks about what I had seen in France.

Canadian Press agreed to let me do a coast-to-coast tour later, in December, as well as give talks to service clubs and other organizations in Ottawa and elsewhere. Burning to tell everybody about the French tragedy, about the Free French and the wonderful way Britain was responding to the Nazi challenge, I accepted any and every invitation. Before July 1941 I had given more than 100 talks to organizations of all kinds, from the Canadian Institute of International Affairs to schools in small towns and the Women's Institutes in rural areas. All wanted the same subject. What had happened in France?

My job had hardly begun in Ottawa when Beatrice Belcourt, Public Relations Officer for Radio-Canada, asked me to give a talk on the French-language network. I was overjoyed at the opportunity. Beatrice was an intelligent, energetic, and truly charming woman who fully understood what was at stake in the war, and was sympathetic to the aims of General de Gaulle. This talk led to an invitation to tea at the French Legation with the new minister, René Ristelhueber, and his wife.

The political situation was still so confused that I had not questioned Ristelhueber's role or why the Canadian government had continued relations with the Vichy "government." Was there a secret understanding with Maréchal Pétain? Was something going on behind the scenes among Pétain, Winston Churchill and General de Gaulle? It was a view widely held both inside and outside France.

The External Affairs library revealed that Ristelhueber had been appointed to Canada a few months before the Franco-German armistice. At sixty-three, he was serving in his last post, after a long and honourable diplomatic career. Over tea I answered his anxious questions. He and his wife were obviously grief-stricken when I described the last weeks in France and the spirit of the throngs of people I had encountered on the roads.

Asked to give a talk at the Legation to the small French colony and other guests, I accepted and discovered that Princess Alice, wife of the

Governor General, would be present. I not only described the last, tragic days in France, but quite innocently expanded on the hope engendered by General de Gaulle and the pride of those wounded French soldiers at the Foch monument in London. It never occurred to me that there could be division among Frenchmen free to carry on the war.

A few days later Princess Alice invited about seventy-five French-speaking women to Government House. She described an Anglo-French Committee she had headed in England to aid refugees in both wars. She planned now to create an affiliate in Canada. I was asked to give a few details of what I had seen in London, particularly about the hundreds of youngsters in the care of Lady Peel's committee. Help was needed. A committee was formed. Princess Alice accepted the presidency; Mme Ristelhueber and Mother Superior St. Thomas d'Aquinas of the Jeanne d'Arc convent became vice-presidents; Mme Thibodeau Rinfrét, wife of a distinguished Supreme Court judge, was named secretary.

René Ristelhueber was the first to take an active part in raising money to send to London. Posted in China for many years, he could speak Chinese, so he gave a hilarious lecture entitled "How to learn Chinese in one hour."

My most vivid memory of that time is the intensity with which we lived. History was being written so fast it was impossible to grasp where we were going. The speed of communication heightened the tension. Every morning we wakened apprehensive. What had happened during the night? During the Battle of Britain we were glued to the radio, following the London blitz, quaking with fear that the city and people should be expected to withstand the thousands and thousands of explosives and fire bombs that rained down upon them. But they did, and we were buoyed by their dogged courage.

Our days raced on, laden with ominous events: the Italians in Libya menaced Egypt; battles began in North Africa; the Japanese occupied Indo-China, then a French colony; Germany, Japan and Italy signed a tripartite pact of mutual aid; Italy invaded Greece; British troops landed in Crete; German planes bombed Coventry and Birmingham; Admiral Darlan was nominated to succeed Maréchal Pétain. Darlan held the offices of Foreign Minister and Minister of the Interior (responsible for police activities against the budding Resistance movements). Summoned to Hitler's headquarters in Berchtesgaden, he gave in to Hitler's demand that German planes and ships be allowed to refuel in Syria, a French protectorate, thus opening a back door against the British in Egypt and Palestine, and threatening the Suez Canal. Germany conquered Greece and took Crete. On June 21, 1941, Germany broke the Friendship Pact and invaded Russia.

And what did we have to cheer us? The success of the heroic RAF in Britain; for not only London, but ports, factory and industrial towns as well as ancient cities had come up smiling, if somewhat grimly. A headline in a morning paper, after the first murderous raid lit the skies of the burning city, set the mood of the people: "London Can Take It!"

At sea the German submarines were taking great bites out of the convoys in the Atlantic and later the Murmansk sea lanes. The loss of so much shipping meant a serious depletion of men, materiel and foodstuffs for Britain. More alarming for the Free French was confirmation of a report that Maréchal Pétain and Premier Pierre Laval had promised that Vichy would give Germany full economic co-operation. The last doubt was gone. Vichy was indeed a German puppet.

On my six-week Canadian Club speaking tour in December 1940 and January 1941 (which also included speeches to university and high school students and service clubs), I found Canadians consumed with the desire to participate in the war effort. At the same time, there seemed to be little awareness that our whole future was at stake. Should Britain fall, Germany would have the whole of highly indus-trialized Europe as a base from which, in time, to attack North America. I wanted to shriek, "Wake up, for God's sake, it *could* happen!" At one dinner, half of my dinner-plate was covered with a sizzling, one-inch steak and perhaps a hundred pounds of half-eaten steaks were carried back to the kitchen. The sight strangled me. I had visions of the rigidly spare rationing in England and the growing hunger on the Continent as the cattle, sheep, pigs, fowl, fruit, grain and wine flowed into Germany from all the occupied countries.

At the time rationing was being discussed in Parliament. It was more difficult than it looked. Canadians had never carried identity cards of any kind; few even had passports. To distribute ration books it became obvious that identification cards were necessary. The uproar in Parlia-ment over identification cards was echoed in every city and town. Canadians were outraged at the idea of being obliged to carry a card giving personal information. The notion of attaching a photograph stiffened opposition even more. Grudgingly, insulted citizens finally accepted a small paper with a few vital statistics noted, an official number and a signature — but no photograph. The only time I ever heard of anyone using it was to get a liquor ration book.

Cheese, eggs, butter, chocolate, sugar, cigarettes, booze and gasoline were on the restricted list. The quota was one forty-ounce bottle of whiskey or other alcoholic beverage per month per person. Few persons west of Quebec drank wine. Since no photograph decorated the flimsy identity slip, people bought for one another and non-drinking friends lent their books so extra stocks could be accumulated for parties. The system was as full of holes as a fish net.

To save materials, long dresses for evening were out for the duration of the war. Rationing of nylon stockings was the greatest hardship for females. A charge-account customer of long standing was on a list to receive a pair whenever they were available. As a newcomer to Ottawa, I did not stand a chance. I never once bought a pair of nylons in the city until 1945. Fortunately my mother was an "old customer" with a charge account in Victoria and could send an occasional pair. In summer we tinted our legs. Some women even managed the acrobatics required to draw a seam up the back of each leg.

When the Canadian government asked people to ration cheese voluntarily for Britain, consumption dropped 90 per cent in ten days. The Minister of Agriculture expressed gratitude but said that people did not need to stop eating cheese altogether — 60 per cent was enough.

While I was bugging Canadian Press about arranging my return to London, I was writing follow-up stories about the British children in Canada. In the winter of 1940-41 in spite of the word "children" appearing in large letters in English and German on each side of the vessel, a German torpedo sent a shipload of British children to the bottom of the Atlantic. No more children were sent to Canada. A few weeks later, Sam Robertson, our London bureau chief, was lost at sea. I was then told flatly that I could not return to London.

People were pouring into Ottawa from all parts of Canada to fill war jobs. The YWCA was filled with western girls arriving with one slim suitcase, thrilled to have a job in Ottawa, and thrilled at the prospect of buying a new dress after the long years of depression. One day Andy Carnegie called me into his office. "Here's one for you," he said. "Two Prairie regiments are here and the brass plan a dance at Lansdowne Park for Saturday night. They've asked us to find 400 Prairie girls, preferably from Saskatchewan." He grinned. "You're always beefing about war jobs — try this one. Got to keep the boys happy."

"But how? I hardly know Ottawa yet myself."

"Call the Bank of Canada, government departments, personnel. Call Charlotte Whitton. She'll know." (Charlotte Whitton was a well-known social worker at the time; later she became mayor of Ottawa.)

I spent hours on the telephone and, miracle of miracles, more than 400 Prairie girls turned up, many of them from Saskatchewan.

The committee on veterans' affairs produced some interesting stories, one of which nearly cost me my job. I had inquired if the meetings were "off the record." The deputy minister assured me they were not. Consequently, I faithfully reported a discussion on how venereal disease was being controlled in the Forces.

The committee chairman called Andy Carnegie, complaining angrily and demanding that I be fired, or taken off veterans' affairs reporting. Andy refused. Had the subject of venereal disease been discussed? Yes. Were the facts as reported wrong? "No, but the story is not in the public interest," was the reply.

"Depends on your point of view," said Andy. "The public has to face the facts and should be glad to know what is being done to preserve the health of the soldiers. If you bar her from the committee meetings we won't report them at all."

nine

General de Gaulle's request that I help Elisabeth de Miribel explain the cause of the Free French to Canadians worried me. I had no idea how to find her. Fortunately, late in March 1941, Beatrice Belcourt of Radio-Canada called to say she had met Elisabeth, who was in town accompanying Admiral Georges d'Argenlieu, a member of General de Gaulle's Free French Council for the Defence of the Empire. Would I like to do an interview?

I discovered that Admiral d'Argenlieu was a monk and head of the Carmel Order. In the First World War he had commanded a battleship and a submarine and had been cited for valour. Mobilized again in 1939, he had been taken prisoner along with other naval officers who had been ordered by Admiral Henri Darlan to surrender to the Germans at Cherbourg. In a convoy transporting prisoners to Germany, some of his companions had created a diversion while he escaped. He told me he had hidden in a field near the coast where a small girl found him. The child realized instantly what she should do. "You're a French soldier escaping, aren't you?" she asked. "Stay there and I'll come for you at dark." That night she took him home where he was given peasant clothing. He then escaped to England and joined the Free French.

At a reception for Admiral d'Argenlieu was a group of French munitions experts who had been working with British experts in England and who had come to Canada to advise the Department of Munitions and Supply. Among them was General Jacques Emile Martin-Prèvel, known in Canada as Colonel Philippe Henri Pierrené, a nom-de-guerre constructed from the names of his four young sons in occupied France. At the time Canada had never built tanks and Colonel Pierrené happened to be an inventor in the field. On behalf of de Gaulle, d'Argenlieu invited Pierrené to act as an "unofficial representative" of the French National Committee to Canada. Meeting him for the first time, I never dreamed I would be working with him within months.

Although my first meeting with Elisabeth de Miribel was brief, we became fast friends. Later, while d'Argenlieu consulted with Canadian officials, we had hours to disscuss Canadian reaction to the Free French. Elisabeth had been instructed by Carlton Gardens to arrange the meetings for d'Argenlieu with the church and federal authorities. The mission had been difficult so she was cheered to hear about my Canadian Club tour, and the enthusiastic and sympathetic reaction of English-language audiences when I described the Free French army rising behind General de Gaulle in London, and about their eager offers to help in any way they could.

Indeed, no one questioned the rightness of de Gaulle's decision to continue the struggle, nor Winston Churchill's recognition of the general as a symbol of France's commitment to continue as an ally. Who could imagine political motivation behind de Gaulle's appeal of June 18, 1940, which had resulted in rallying thousands of men, parts of the navy, merchantmen, the whole Channel fishing fleet and, in time, most of the French colonial empire?

These territories and people who had sided with the Free French had to be protected and administered. The British government recognized this fact in June 1940. By agreement, it accepted de Gaulle's proposals to set up administrative bodies which, the general insisted, were not to be governmental bodies because the Third Republic had not been voted out by the French people and which, like the Free French Movement, would be held accountable for their stewardship to the first democratically elected government after the liberation of France.

The first was the Council for the Defence of the Empire, composed of representatives from various colonies and high-ranking military, diplomatic and educational figures who had joined the Free French. The second was the French National Committee at Carlton Gardens which de Gaulle had set up to handle negotiations and foreign relations with Britain and other countries concerning procurement of arms and materiel, outfitting of his forces, dissemination of information, and international issues.

Elisabeth did not really expect to find any opposition to General de Gaulle in Canada. As the general's secretary in London, she had typed his first, stirring call across the world to Frenchmen and was certainly aware of the cables from two members of the French "colony" in Montreal offering full support and co-operation. For her Canadian mission, she believed there would be ready support.

In August 1940 Elisabeth had been welcomed by relatives in Chicoutimi, Quebec, who offered her a haven for the duration of the war. Almost immediately after arriving, she told me, she realized that she could not carry out her task there. To her urban eyes Chicoutimi was a large village lost in the wilderness. It was far from the means of communication she needed. "But it was in those weeks that I discovered how French-speaking Canadians felt about my mission," she told me, saying then what she repeated later in her book, *La Liberté souffre violence:* "My heart was on fire with the story of our struggle and efforts as I told them about our days in London. There was little reaction. People listened politely and received me with kindness but they treated me a bit like a convalescent in need of rest and fresh air in order to recover and forget. . . .

". . . I discovered the feelings of French-Canadians concerning us were mixed. They didn't like England and were suspicious of an anticlerical France. The conservative and religious aspect of the changes made by the Vichy regime attracted them. Their principal newspapers, *Le Devoir*, of Montreal, and *l'Action Catholique*, of Quebec City, commented with satisfaction on the 'penitent resignation of France' and 'France is punished because she has sinned. . . .' Some even consider the Free French are 'mercenaires', fighting for pay. . . . They esteem and venerate Maréchal Pétain . . . and consider the 'government' at Vichy is the only legitimate one. They said to me 'We ignore de Gaulle as a representative of France, but we serve at the side of Britain to deliver your invaded country. Individually we may admire General de Gaulle's gesture and his military valour, but he doesn't represent France to us'. . . ."

During our first evening together Elisabeth poured out her troubles and disappointments in Montreal. Leaving Chicoutimi, she thought it reasonable to believe that she would find a communciations network in Montreal and a French "colony" to help her. Instead she found the "colony" seething with uncertainty, rivalries, jealousies and personal ambitions. There were about 2,000 French citizens in the city, most of them middle-aged. They were only too anxious to help, but they found themselves being torn between two small groups and bewildered by the choice they were being forced to make. Either they supported the Free French, as was their inclination since they strongly supported the war against Hitler, or they must support Maréchal Pétain, a hero in their eyes, who claimed to be president of a legitimate government in France. It was an almost impossible choice.

The two contenders for the leadership of the "colony" were Dr. Vignal, a physician of excellent reputation, but unpopular because people found him abrupt, opinionated and short-tempered. Although he was a loyal supporter of the Free French, conciliation was hardly his forte.

The other, the Baron de Roumefort, Director of the Credit Foncier, although having pledged his loyalty, lacked conviction about the outcome of the war. Consequently, many of those burning to do something were upset because they saw him as trying to keep his options open in both camps. Elisabeth discovered that the Free French Committee was so involved in this rivalry that little was being done.

Elisabeth was only twenty-four but she was passionately dedicated to the cause of liberating her homeland with honour, and thus created a crisis of considerable proportions among her compatriots with her ardent demands. Every French person, she told them, should forget self and give every ounce of energy, unhesitatingly and unstintingly, to the support of their countrymen free to fight. Because of her representation (although unofficial) of the Free French, both factions in the French "colony" tried to turn her against the other. Disenchanted, Elisabeth turned to the French-Canadians for help.

Tall, raw-boned but with a kind of coltish grace, Elisabeth's best features were her large, intelligent brown eyes and a throaty voice that rang with husky sincerity. She mesmerized her listeners. She had that much overused word "charisma" and could not imagine anyone French not immediately recognizing de Gaulle as the saviour of the honour of France.

Almost penniless, Elisabeth went to the media where her personality and fiery eloquence aroused curiosity and sympathy. A number of enlightened journalists, Jean-Louis Gagnon, Guy Jasmin, Louis Francoeur of Radio-Canada and others helped her with casual work. *Le Canada* and *Le Journal* paid for her stories. CBC gave her time on local stations. At the same time she was appalled by the growing dissension in the French "colony," and suffered all kinds of criticism because she would not take sides.

In Quebec City Elisabeth found more understanding. General and

Mme Georges Vanier, who had returned to Canada immediately after the armistice, took her into their home and gave her the comfort and support she needed. More support came from Mme André Simard, a Frenchwoman married to a Canadian doctor. An indefatigable worker for the Red Cross and other wartime activities, Mme Simard heard General de Gaulle's appeal and immediately began organizing a committee to aid the Free French. Her committee was free of controversy. With the help of Father Georges-Henri Lévesque of the Laval School of Social Sciences, she set about organizing other committees throughout the province.

What disturbed Elisabeth, Mme Simard, the Vaniers and other supporters of the Free French were not only the misconceptions about de Gaulle, but the propaganda being pumped into the province by shortwave from the German-controlled Radio-Paris and Radio-Vichy. Because the United States was neutral, books, documents, leaflets, Vichy-oriented propaganda of all sorts freely entered Canada. It was vicious and the Free French were the target: these young men, some of them in their teens, these professors, officers, diplomats and writers who had answered de Gaulle's call, were described as "soldiers of fortune, traitors and turncoats." Wide publicity was given to the news that de Gaulle had been cashiered from the French army, branded as a traitor by Maréchal Pétain and sentenced to death by a military tribunal.

At the same time Radio-Vichy was giving lengthy stories about how Pétain and his "government" were taking steps to "purify" France right down to the use of cosmetics. French girls and women were told that the fresh, scrubbed, soap-and-water look, domestic duties and modesty would best become them. Skirts had shortened to knee-length just before the war. Now they were forbidden in favour of a mid-calf length. According to Radio-Vichy, the revolution had led France down a false path for more than a century and a half. France was now paying for its frivolity, for forgetting the authority of the church, for its heedless straying from the straight and narrow. The crowning argument was that "this is God's way of bringing France to her knees in contrition and restoring her moral character." This gem was picked up by Sally Solomon, monitor of the shortwave propaganda being beamed into Canada, at the Canadian government's small shortwave station west of Ottawa. Why God had chosen the Nazis to undertake this re-education of France was not explained.

Another shock for Elisabeth was the reaction of French-speaking Canadians to the slightest criticism of Maréchal Pétain. Quebeckers who returned from the First World War considered they had been

led — and indeed they had been — by the great Pétain, glorious hero
of the famous "they shall not pass," at Verdun. Even I had been taught
that at school in Alberta. The veneration for this distinguished old
soldier was almost complete. Besides Canada had a diplomatic representative in Vichy; obviously the Canadian government must trust the
old Maréchal. Were Quebeckers to turn against him when he had
"offered his person" as a sacrifice to save some remnant of French
authority to protect his people? Treachery, let alone bad judgment,
was unthinkable. How many realized that the Maréchal was then
eighty-five years old?

In the meantime, Elisabeth said, the in-fighting in Montreal's
French "colony" threatened to involve Canadians. Many Quebeckers
were mystified as to why both de Gaulle and Maréchal Pétain could
not both be right. It was no time for dissension or a public scandal.
Alarmed, Elisabeth, Mme Simard and others urged that someone be
sent to explain officially the Free French position to church and
government authorities. This was Admiral d'Argenlieu's special mission. Elisabeth had been given the task of arranging interviews in
Quebec with Cardinal Villeneuve and, through the Vaniers, with the
Department of External Affairs in Ottawa.

Elisabeth found sympathetic ears in high places. Norman Robertson, Undersecretary of State for External Affairs, Thomas Stone, an
enthusiastic francophile in charge of French Affairs, Leonard Brockington, special assistant to Prime Minister Mackenzie King, Senator
Cairine Wilson, Secretary of State Pierre-François Casgrain and Sir
Gerald Campbell, British High Commissioner to Canada, were helpful
sympathizers. Although there was no official recognition of the Free
French, they were given a great deal of unofficial encouragement.

In Quebec City Cardinal Villeneuve gave Elisabeth an audience. At
first he was reluctant to be involved, but Elisabeth's earnest and
emotional eloquence won the day. "We fight for Christian civilization
against Hitler's Nazism which has invaded and overwhelmed my
country," she declared. "As Cardinal Verdier, of Paris, said, 'The war is
about the intellectual and moral attitudes created for us by centuries
of Christianity, and which have given human life its moral beauty and
reason d'être.' "

Cardinal Villeneuve promised to receive Admiral d'Argenlieu. After
that he never deviated in his moral support for the Free French
Movement.

I felt that Elisabeth was putting into words exactly how I felt about
the war. I had spent weeks in Germany in 1936, 1937 and 1938; I had

seen the fear in Czechoslovakia during the Sudenten crisis, only a few days before Hitler's troops took over the Sudentanland in a lightning night strike; I had experienced the catastrophe in France. I knew we were fighting for our way of life, our values, our freedoms.

"I am the child of a general and my grandfather was a maréchal* of France," Elisabeth said soberly. "I am the eldest child and we are all girls except the youngest, Patrice. I see my duty as if I were a son. I must devote every moment of my freedom to making the goals of the Free French understood."

We decided that a bilingual press service was a necessity, but how? In the meantime each of us would work in her own language, and keep in touch until we could find a way to create an information service.

Elisabeth spent a lot of time working in Montreal where she had the help of Henri Laugier, an influential French professor who had been invited to establish a Department of Physiology at the University of Montreal. Laugier was often in Ottawa in consultation at the National Research Council. (He was involved in bringing nuclear scientists — some of the Joliot-Curie team — out of occupied France to work in Canada and the United States.) Cécile Bouchard and the Vaniers, as well as news and radio journalists in Quebec, lent a hand. At the end of each exhausting week, items concerning Free French activities were gathered from the papers. We had no money to buy papers so we used the Parliamentary Reading Room where all Canadian newspapers were available. It meant copying articles by hand, then typing and sending them to the French National Committee at Carlton Gardens in London, with our comments.

There were long evenings translating dispatches about the small Free French forces fighting alone or beside the British in North Africa. Reports of a smouldering resistance inside occupied France were being smuggled out to London and sent to us via air. Once we received a copy of *Liberation*, an underground paper, five days after it was printed in Paris. We realized that the fighting spirit had awakened in France.

Meanwhile letters were bringing me tales of hardships, harsh regulations, hunger, the disappearance of neighbours and friends. The winter had been the coldest in memory. "Imagine snow in Paris on April 23rd," wrote Irène. "And we had no heat in the apartment." In the same letter Irène said, "I've received only four letters and two cables

---

*Maréchal Patrice de MacMahon, later president of France.

from you. I can't believe you haven't written more." I had written more, at least one a week, and I was receiving their letters almost every week.

Other letters were a cry of anguish for lost freedom. Obscure references to de Gaulle indicated that people were listening to the BBC. I wanted them to know what I was doing and tried, in amateurish ways, to tell them. I wrote about my "boy friend" Charlie, explaining that he was now in England and was making a lot of friends. Their letters contained sly references and I realized that they had understood. "How's your new boy friend? We're dying to meet him. Give my love to your boy friend," they wrote.

Some letters that arrived in the spring were obviously meant to reassure me. From Irène: "There's a big bully in our neighborhood, but my Grandad has given him a big punch on the moustache!" (Grandad was Russia, moustache was Hitler.)

Marie-Josie Esdouhard, a tiny woman whom we all affectionately called "Le Microbe," wrote in April 1941 describing how she had tried to cross the demarcation line several times and had been turned back. She had wanted to visit her grandfather, her only living relative. "But we keep up our spirits," she wrote. "I must paint you a small picture of our life. Nothing very good about winter, or to cause us to rejoice for next winter. Restrictions come more and more: bread, meat, soap, oil, butter, coffee, wool, a little coal. In spite of it we retain our good humour and the appearance of every new regulation from Vichy brings a sarcastic word and a funny cartoon, which just proves that nothing will stop a French man from laughing and saying he doesn't give a damn, a joke always on his lips. It is our form of courage. Gladie, it is hard and long, but we must be courageous.

"For your amusement I write what a friend who has been in Paris told me. There are almost no buses or taxis. (*They* need the fuel.) A new form of transportation has been invented. The owners of bicycles have built two-wheeled boxes and hitched them behind bicycles. For a few francs it will carry a Parisian somewhere. One sees, for example, dignified gentlemen in these Parisian *pousse-pousse*, reading their papers and lifting their hats to one another as they cross the Place de la Concorde. We would die if we couldn't laugh...."

Later I wrote that I had given up my work with Canadian Press in favour of "marriage." In time my friends understood that I had joined the Free French and congratulations poured in with regrets that they could not attend the "wedding."

Elisabeth usually spent two days mid-week in Montreal, maintaining her connections with her media friends and trying to enlighten some people in the French "colony" who were having second thoughts. The stories of Vichy's economic collaboration with Germany and pictures of Pierre Laval shaking hands with German occupation authorities caused some to think again, though there were others who thought that this was just propaganda.

At the same time there were some of her compatriots who, while not objecting to giving lip service to the Free French cause, were still unwilling to give up a safety line to Vichy (Britian might still lose the war), and they condemned Elisabeth as an interloper. She was a gadfly to their guilty consciences, and the leaders in particular wanted, above everything, to silence or get rid of her.

Having tried and failed to stop or at least have Admiral d'Argenlieu's visit to Quebec under their own aegis, they launched a campaign of calumny, in the form of whispered rumours about Elisabeth. Some members of the "colony" went so far as to link her romantically with Admiral d'Argenlieu, an accusation so outrageous that it boomeranged. Too many people knew that the conduct of both was above reproach. But Elisabeth would return to Ottawa depressed and exhausted.

Occasionally on a summer Sunday we took long walks through the Beechwood cemetery and around an area now known as Manor Park, which at the time was a large wood with a beautiful country trail through it. On one occasion we walked to Chelsea, and another time we took a weekend to walk to Wakefield through the woods and for some hours in a pouring rain. It became so dark that we lost the trail. Then two young men from the National Film Board, equally soaked, met us. All four of us looked like wet rats as we stood there, rain pouring off our noses, and laughing uncontrollably. "We're lost," we gasped. "Do you know the way to Wakefield from here?" Immediately they took us in hand, gave us their flashlight and explicit directions. We gave them some apples.

It was the first time the two young men had heard of Free French "representatives" in Ottawa and eagerly asked questions, which we were only too happy to answer. For fifteen or twenty minutes we stood there, dripping like seals, all of us enthusiastically discussing the war and what we could do about it.

The wife of the hotelkeeper in Wakefield scolded us as though we were children, gave us hot toddies, and an unforgettable stew with dumplings. On these trips and others we took along knapsacks with night clothes, apples and crackers, and the poems of Claudel or Péguy,

Gerard Manley Hopkins, and an old *Oxford Book of Verse* which provided a basis for improving Elisabeth's English pronunciation.

What talks we had about what the new world would be like after the war! This was not a war like any other. This was a struggle between good and evil, between the hard-won values of civilization and freedom and the evils of fascist dictatorship. We hoped to see, after the victory, the world cleansed and aware of true spiritual values that had nothing to do with cosmetics and the length of skirts (the moral yardsticks of Vichy). We scorned the idea that God would use criminals and murderers, like the Nazis, to teach or punish our people. Yet there were people naive enough to believe it. We must find ways to fight this propaganda.

Early in July René Pleven, Commissioner for Colonies in the French National Committee, came for talks with the Canadian government. As a result Colonel Henri Pierrené was accepted as the "Official Delegate" to Canada for the committee, and was authorized to discuss questions of mutual interest with federal government officials. As well, he was given a kind of de facto responsibility for representing the interests of French nationals in Canada. The post was a diplomatic one in all but name.

Before Pleven left, Elisabeth and I spent an afternoon with him discussing the need for an official information service in both languages. We explained the difficulties of our makeshift attempt. He agreed and told us that the clandestine service now operating between France and London was bringing more and more reports on the situation in France — the hardships, the hunger, the brutality of the Gestapo and the growing resistance. There was no means of reproducing the clandestine literature in England. But Canada, with plenty of newsprint and presses in both languages, was the ideal place for the reproduction and distribution of this literature.

Then Mr. Pleven turned to me and said that Elisabeth would have her hands full with Quebec and French-language groups elsewhere. In addition she must help Colonel Pierrené with reports and serve as a liaison with the committee. "But she is not an experienced journalist and there is all of English-speaking Canada," he said. "Someone with such experience and who knows France and the Free French is needed."

Suddenly I knew I was on the spot. "Would you consider the job?" he asked. Leave Canadian Press? I could not give an immediate answer. I promised to continue helping Elisabeth as a volunteer and would help to set up a Free French information service.

During the summer the decision was hanging over me like a cloud.
I consulted several people whose advice I valued and, thinking it over,
they agreed that I should do it. Among the friends whose advice I
sought were Leonard Brockington, special advisor to the Prime Minister, and "Jerry" Riddell in the Department of External Affairs. I also
discussed the dilemma with Colonel Pierrené. He was a thin, graying,
gentle man, whose faded gray-blue eyes were often so filled with pain
that it was difficult to look at him. The defeat of his country, by a force
he believed to be the ultimate evil, humiliated and deeply wounded
him spiritually. He told me that when he had the opportunity to return
to France at the moment of the armistice, it was the hardest decision of
his life. His wife and four young sons were at home in Versailles, in
occupied France; his eldest son was a naval cadet. His decision and
activities might bring unthinkable retaliation.

One morning, while still in a state of flux, my telephone rang at six.
It was Elisabeth. I could hardly understand her, so choked and
changed was her voice. Alarmed, I asked her what was wrong.

"I can't tell you on the phone. Would you mind very much coming
over now? I need to talk."

When I arrived I found her pacing the floor. Her face was extremely
pale and puffy, her eyes like those of a dying deer. Despair was in
every line of her body.

She kept on walking. "I didn't like to call you earlier. I didn't get
back from the Chateau Laurier until nearly four this morning. I don't
know what to do. Should I stay in Canada or go? New York? London? I
don't know, I don't know." Her voice was hoarse.

"What happened? Is it news of your family?"

"It's that man. Last night at about eleven o'clock Colonel Pierrené
called and asked me to go to the Chateau. With him was a man named
Fua. He looked, I don't know, unsavoury and made me shiver. He had
told Colonel Pierrené that the Committee in London had sent him to
remove me from Canada . . . ."

Before Pierrené, Fua told of his own investigations in Montreal
which, he said, he had been asked to do to find out about Elisabeth's
work. Pierrené had said nothing; he just sat and listened while Elisabeth tried to defend herself. The colonel retired finally and then Fua's
accusations became more personal and violent. He questioned her
identity and accused her of making up the story that she had served as
secretary to de Gaulle. Her family? Was not her father a collaborator?
How had she lived without money? What was her relationship with
Admiral d'Argenlieu, with certain newspapermen? Was she just an

ambitious *intrigante* seeking attention? If not, she should realize she was injuring the French cause and leave Canada at once.

"He had a thick briefcase beside him and kept threatening that it contained signed statements resulting from his investigation," Elisabeth said. Fua said that they proved that Elisabeth was a menace to the cause. Perhaps something could be found for her in the United States. If she left quietly so as not to create a scandal, he would use his influence to get her a job. If she refused, he would see to it that she was dismissed.

"And Colonel Pierrené?" I asked.

"I don't understand. He said nothing, just let Fua talk."

Fua said he was returning to Montreal. Elisabeth had until that evening to decide. She could telephone or meet him at the Windsor Hotel in Montreal.

Appalled at the state Elisabeth was in, I suggested that she go to bed. I would get leave and accompany her to Montreal. Later I went to see Colonel Pierrené, who looked extremely pallid and ill. Yes, he was aware of the Montreal situation. His own role was still unofficial from a Canadian point of view and he understood the delicacy of interfering in a situation that might spill over and embroil French-speaking Canadians and the press. Finally, he said, René Ristelhueber was still the "recognized" representative of the Vichy regime. Pierrené was very frank. He told me that he was aware of the falsehoods being spread about Elisabeth and he had written privately to Carlton Gardens. Unofficially he had spoken to certain Canadians and had spent hours trying to decide how the Montreal situation should be handled to prevent an open scandal which could do immense harm to the Free French cause.

I asked him what he thought about Fua's statements and he replied that he knew Elisabeth and he knew there was no truth in the accusations, but Fua must represent someone. Who? In whose interests was someone so anxious to get rid of Elisabeth? He told me that he had allowed Fua to go on talking in order to see how far he would go, what his accusations were. The matter, he assured me, was being discussed with "someone" and he believed it could be settled quietly. "We do not want a public scandal and there is no question of Elisabeth leaving," he finished.

I could see that Colonel Pierrené was sick about the situation and worried about the possibility of the story arousing pubic opinion in Quebec, which could embarrass the federal government. "I said nothing Fua can quote or use," he told me. He asked me to go to

Montreal with Elisabeth if I could get away, and said, "Take care of her." Then he asked me not to repeat a word of our conversation, not even to Elisabeth.

We caught an early train to Montreal, registered at the Windsor and met Cécile Bouchard in her father's suite in the hotel. She planned to go home that night but offered the suite for a meeting-place. Elisabeth went off to see Professor Laugier and Father Ducatillon,* who told her in no uncertain terms that Fua obviously was a Nazi agent and represented Vichy. Elisabeth made one more call, one that she did not reveal to me.

When Elisabeth telephoned Fua, she told him to come to the hotel for her decision. He looked surprised to find Cécile and me there, but he was in no way disconcerted. He was all smiles and oozed confidence. Elisabeth asked him to repeat his accusations before us. I can see him yet, a thin, swarthy little man, with sharp features and overly bright-eyed side glances that made me uneasy. He appeared to be delighted to meet us. "I've been wanting to talk to you," he said to Cécile. "Your opinion would be valuable in my report. Perhaps you could see me tomorrow for a private conversation."

Cécile smiled and said nothing. When Elisabeth said we had been working together disseminating information from Ottawa he was eager to have a private talk with me also.

The conversation consisted of a long list of accusations, interspersed with reassuring offers to find Elisabeth work somewhere else, and barely veiled threats. Elisabeth said nothing but Cécile and I tried to refute. The fat briefcase, to which he regularly referred, sat at his feet like a pandora's box. Cécile said sharply that she knew the people in Montreal he had been talking to, and rather than dedicating their time and energy to the war effort, they were pursuing petty personal ambitions. "The Montreal Free French Committee had many good people but a few are only interested in surviving, whichever way the war goes .... Elisabeth is an unwelcome reminder of their duty instead of their selfish motives," she said.

Meanwhile we kept asking to see the material he carried in the abominable briefcase. He kept saying that he would show it to us, would prove his accusations, and then tacked off on another course, trying to trick us into saying something he could use against her. After an hour of this talk Elisabeth stood up suddenly and said that she was

---

* A French Dominican deeply involved with the clandestine press circulating in the church in France.

going to bed. "I'll give you my answer tomorrow," she told Fua. "I'm too tired tonight to make any decision." She looked dead on her feet.

A few minutes later a friend of Cécile's arrived. Mr. Gagnon was a tall, good-looking man with whom Cécile had planned to spend the evening. Gagnon attempted to take Cécile away, but she said, "Oh, let's stay awhile. Mr. Fua has just come from Europe and has such fascinating things to say about the war. I'd like to hear some more." Fua had interspersed his remarks about Elisabeth with comments about the Free French personnel at Carlton Gardens, the propaganda war in Europe and the destruction the RAF was raining on France. Fua beamed.

As the conversation progressed, Fua became more and more critical of the British war effort. He described de Gaulle as being surrounded by "Jews and Protestants." But he recovered quickly and suggested that de Gaulle was their victim, that he had been taken in by them, and that de Gaulle and Pétain were in communication. He defended the Vichy regime vehemently. His main theme was that 95 per cent of the people in France considered Pétain their saviour, the Vichy regime their legitimate government. He suggested that France had been dragged into the war by Britain, and that Britain was responsible for France's downfall. "Otherwise, France could have made a deal with Germany. Germany did not want to fight France. Britain is not a European country and has led France down a false path to defeat," he told us.

Gagnon posed a question here and there in a way that encouraged and flattered Fua's sense of self-importance. The conversation turned again to propaganda. Fua described himself as an expert in the field and, spurred on by Gagnon's rapt attention, he began attacking the "terrible propaganda campaign Britain was waging over the BBC to the occupied countries, especially France." He charged that Britain was buoying the hopes of the Resistance when it was obvious that it was only a matter of time until Germany would starve the British into submission with its naval blockade. (It was true that almost all the news of the war at sea was bad at that time, and there had been a terrible toll on shipping in the Atlantic.)

At the same time Fua threw in bits of praise for the magnificent courage of the British people. "It's criminal to allow the people to suffer such bombardments and semi-starvation," he declared. The government, Winston Churchill, was responsible.

Cécile and I tried to question him about the flow of propaganda into Quebec from Paris and Vichy. He reiterated over and over that the

Canadian government, dominated by the "English," were sending French-Canadians to their death. Vichy, he said, was only trying to show the true picture to Quebeckers. The argument grew more and more heated while Gagnon sat there with a slight smile, dropping in a word of encouragement now and again. Suddenly Fua said, "You are fools to be deceived by all that British propaganda. It's all lies. The British are about to be destroyed and they want to drag you down with them. General de Gaulle knows a compromise will be needed, and the kind of campaign Elisabeth is engaged in will make it more difficult when the time comes."

That did it. Gagnon in a very quiet voice led Fua on to even more extravagant statements. Then, thanking him for being so frank, Gagnon suggested that Fua had opened his eyes to aspects of the situation he had not considered and his comments deserved some thought. Fua beamed. Then Gagnon and Cécile bid us good night and left.

I was very dissatisfied with the conversation we had had, and was still anxious to see what he carried in that menacing briefcase, so I agreed to continue the talk when Fua suggested that I stay awhile longer. It turned into the longest and most bewildering discussion I ever had in my life. All the time I was trying to get him to open the case and show some of the "evidence" he held against Elisabeth. He kept promising he would show it to me after we discussed and clarified the situation further. In a long dissertation, which I kept interrupting, he insisted there was nothing personal in his accusations; Elisabeth was young and misguided. In Canada we were too far away to assess the situation in Europe; we too were misguided by the British. And we were misinformed about the role of the Free French.

I was mystified and remember asking, "But you say your mission is for the Free French, that you represent General de Gaulle?"

"Yes indeed, but you have not understood the real role the general is preparing for. I cannot say more. You realize in time of war confidentiality is of supreme importance," he answered mysteriously. "His cause is not helped by such over-enthusiasm as Mlle de Miribel displays." He hinted at double games; it was of the utmost importance that Elisabeth leave Canada.

"But what proof have you? I must see the evidence myself," I kept saying.

"Her influence has been disastrous," he went on, ignoring my requests. Once Elisabeth left Quebec, qualified people who "understood" would take over.

Then he said that someone else must take over the Free French information distribution we had begun in Ottawa — an experienced journalist — someone older who "knew Canada." (I have never forgotten that unctuous smile.) Would I consider it?

I could hardly believe my ears. The intention was so brazen I was speechless. Since I was too shocked to answer, he went ahead confidently. I would be handsomely remunerated. (I could have gagged.) He poured on the flattery. "Let me see the 'evidence' you have," I kept repeating. The whole story including his outrageous offer was, as the French say, "cousu de fil blanc."*

I did not know what time it was but daylight was brightening the windows. "You're tired," he said sympathetically. "Let's go down and have something to eat. When we come back I'll show you everything. It will convince you beyond doubt and we can discuss your situation."

I knew now that Elisabeth and I had to find some way to impress the authorities of the danger, and his briefcase no longer interested me. We went out to the elevator. Just as it arrived I started to step in and then stepped back as he stepped in. The doors closed. Something warned me not to appear in the lobby with him, and I turned and ran up the stairs to my room. I was sure Elisabeth would be awake, so I telephoned.

"I couldn't sleep," she told me when I arrived in her room. "I have been turning it over and over in my mind. Perhaps I should leave. I know how anxious they are to get me out, but even so, perhaps I should go. I must not think of myself, I must think of France. It's true. If I were publicly forced to leave Canada — God knows what he has in that briefcase, what lies people have told him — it would create a scandal. I can't do anything to hurt the Movement or the Canadians."

We sat and stared at one another in utter discouragement. Were all the hours and hours we had put into the cause of no use?

"So he wouldn't show you the papers?"

I shook my head. "No. He kept promising but I couldn't stop his talking. He just kept tapping the case with his foot and saying he had the 'evidence,' and he'd show it to me later."

We discussed what the next move should be. Elizabeth was still discouraged but more cheerful when I suggested that we go to General Vanier.

Then the telephone rang. It was Cécile's friend Royal Gagnon, who now identified himself as an RCMP officer. "I just wanted to tell you, Elisabeth, that two of our men picked up Fua as he was about to leave

---

* Sewn with white thread.

the hotel a few minutes ago," Gagnon told her. "We've no doubt about what he is and there will be no more trouble for you. He will be put over the border and never allowed back into Canada."

Elisabeth looked dazed as she told me, and then collapsed on the bed in sheer joy. And I have never felt such a rush of relief.

The outcome restored our faith that truth must triumph. The next day we met Professor Laugier and Father Ducatillon and went to a small but excellent fish restaurant on St. James Street. Laugier had arranged the meal — the whole fish was decorated with small French flags.

ten

T he Montreal episode swept away my last hesitation about joining the Free French. A house had been rented at 448 Daly Avenue, where Colonel Pierrené could live on the ground floor and two floors above were offices for the Free French Information Service. I resigned from Canadian Press and on October 1, 1941, moved into my office, furnished from Johnson's secondhand furniture store: a large oak desk, $10; a rickety typewriter (which I used for twenty-five years), $14; a wooden filing cabinet, $8; a secretarial chair, $5; a few desk items; and a single straight-back chair. Lighting was from a globe hanging from a wire overhead. The other offices were furnished with equal lavishness.

The first staff included Paul Theriault, an experienced Quebec City journalist. A non-conformist, Theriault told me solemnly in fractured English that he had been fired from almost every daily newspaper in Quebec for his mildly anti-clerical views. He was a fiery and enthusiastic recruit. I can still see him as he arrived in Ottawa. Of medium height and very slim, with lively brown eyes brimming with mischief and scepticism, a thin dark face and an ironic twist to his mouth, he had a smile that would light a dark room. We went for walks along the canal while planning the strategy of the new service. He practised his stumbling English and would break down occasionally crying, "Plizz, parlez français. I'm broking down to find dos words in Hinglish. Plizz!" Other members included a young French girl, Blanche Boëtte, Corinne de la Durantaye, a bilingual secretary, and Aline Lacroix, a typist.

On my first afternoon we held a press reception to open formally La

Maison France Libre and the Service d'Information France Libre. The caretaker and his wife hastily prepared sandwiches and we pooled our ration cards to get the necessary beverages. The press turned out en masse and good-naturedly drank the rather watered-down drinks from hired glasses. There was not a stick of furniture in what we passed off as our reception room.

Among the crowd of well-wishers was Percy Philip of the *New York Times*, whom I had welcomed with joy when he had been transferred from Paris to the Parliamentary Press Gallery. He grinned at me as he lifted his glass and said, "Looks as though we are going to watch the war from the sidelines."

Canadian Press carried the story of the opening from coast to coast. If we thought we were busy before, it was nothing compared to the days that followed. Requests poured in from the Free French committees for news, pictures, flags and posters; papers wanted interviews; clubs asked for speakers. Elisabeth, Colonel Pierrené and I took turns on the road, and we were soon joined by Aline Chalufour, a young French lawyer who had escaped from Indo-China.

To get Elisabeth started in English I asked the Canadian Women's Press Club to invite her to speak, explaining that her English was by no means *au point*, but would they consent to be guinea pigs? They accepted with enthusiasm.

Our evenings preparing Elisabeth's first speech in English were hilarious. She simply could not pronounce some words. Hours were spent going over the English text I had translated. The task was to replace every word she could not pronounce. In the end, I blessed the flexibility of the English language. Elisabeth gave a speech that fascinated and convulsed her audience. Her earnest and fiery conviction shone through the jumbled English. Sober Canadians, unused to such eloquent displays of patriotism, cheered and immediately became friends of the cause.

Women were demanding a bigger role in the war effort. With this in mind the Associated Countrywomen of the World held a conference that autumn in Ottawa and invited delegates from the United States. Some twenty Canadian organizations took part, representing the National Council of Women, the Women's Institute, the Catholic Women's League, the IODE and others. Representatives of the Women's Club came from many states as did representatives of the Women's Committee for the Cause and Cure of War in Washington, all of them anxious to know how Canadian women were participating in

the war effort. Elisabeth and I were invited to speak about the Free
French.

For nights on end we rehearsed the speech, changing words, changing sentences, correcting intonations and emphasis, avoiding the
unpronounceable "th" sound. I remember going over to the Connaught restaurant one morning at 3 a.m. to pick up a thermos of coffee
and some sandwiches. We had been giggling almost hysterically with
fatigue over the letter "h" which she found difficult to pronounce in
some places and which gave her English a slight dash of cockney.

The American women, convinced that the United States would be
joining in the war, returned home determined to arouse public opinion through the thousands of women who belonged to the Women's
Clubs in every state. To launch the campaign, they organized a huge
rally in New York. A conference, sponsored by the *New York Times*,
was organized and eight Canadian women, including Elisabeth and I,
were invited to talk about the women's efforts in Canada. For once in
our lives the Canadians were the experts. The group who went
included Senator Cairine Wilson, Phyllis Turner, Corolyn Cox, Mrs.
Edgar Hardy and several others. We did our best to enlighten them.

I remembered how, in Paris, Frank Pickersgill had told me of his
admiration for the French philosopher, Jacques Maritain, whose lec-
tures he had attended at St. Michael's College in Toronto. Maritain was
teaching at Columbia University and was involved with the Free
French. When I met him, I realized why Frank thought so much of this
wise man. During the war he continued to lecture at St. Michael's and I
went to Toronto just to listen to him during a private lunch or dinner.

In New York I discovered from two friends, Mary Jane and Ruth
Loubke, that the famous refugee vessel, *Gripsholm*, was about to arrive
from Europe. On it was Virginia Lane who in Paris had been a bright,
imaginative and witty companion of mine. In the autumn of 1938 she
received a scholarship to a German university. That winter and the
spring of 1939 Virginia came to Paris for an occasional long weekend,
always carrying two old, battered suitcases and dressed for travel like
an impoverished student. As an American on a German scholarship,
Virginia usually got a big smile from the customs officers and a chalk
mark on her unopened bags. She revealed to us that in the cases, sewn
in her underwear, she carried watches, rings and jewelry, which were
deposited in Paris until the arrival of their Jewish owners. For the
return trip her suitcase contained works by German authors forbidden
in Germany. Virginia picked up secondhand copies of banned Ger-

man books as well as used copies of books acceptable to the Nazi regime at the Quai bookstalls in Paris. Ruth and I helped her switch the covers. She returned to Germany, breezing through the customs with her bright smile, and distributed the books among anti-Nazi German students and her Jewish friends. She always referred to her Jewish friends as the "Irish" when she wrote.

We welcomed Virginia on the dock with whoops of joy. She had been working at the American Embassy in Berlin after her scholarship ran out, and she gave us a graphic account of conditions. The picture was sombre. Food was scarce. She told us she had realized what must be happening in France because some days the stores were flooded with French products. Some Germans she knew were terrified of the Russians and thought Hitler's "Operation Barbarossa" mad. They whispered their fears to her, recalling only too vividly Napoleon's disastrous trek. Virginia told us that there had been rumours in Berlin of a second front, but nobody believed it could happen until after the occupation of Britain. Now they had to contemplate fighting on two fronts. "They're scared but they'll fight. They'll do anything for that madman," she affirmed.

A French couple arriving at the same time told us, "Everybody is wearing the Cross of Lorraine under a lapel or beneath a blouse."

Excited, we asked Virginia how we could celebrate her return. "Take me to an ice cream parlour and watch me eat!" she cried as we hugged her.

Where did we go? What does it matter? She ate three huge sundaes and we laughed and all talked at once. We tried to tell her what we were doing, and she told us that she knew some Germans who did not support Hitler but could do nothing about it. Some of her "Irish" friends had disappeared. The synagogues were closed; Jews were being "settled" in the vague "east"; several shops she went to suddenly closed and were boarded up. A week later they opened again with a German smiling behind the counter.

"How do Berliners feel about still no invasion and the way their blitz ended in Britain?"

"Every night we'd listen to the BBC broadcasts and cheer and drink toasts when we got the news of the way the British were holding. The cinemas showed pictures of London burning. It was awful, and yet every night we got those cheery voices over the BBC, "Don't worry, London can take it!"

Towards winter we received regular dispatches based on reports about conditions in France. These were being smuggled out to Lon-

Gladys Arnold in 1942. (Photo by Karsh)

Residence identity card for the Cité Universitaire, Paris, 1938-39.

Canadian Press I.D. card, 1940.

Irène Lézine, 1938.

General Charles de Gaulle in London during the Second World War.

A TOUS LES FRANÇAIS

La France a perdu une bataille!
Mais la France n'a pas perdu la güerre!

Des gouvernants de rencontre ont pu capituler, cédant à la panique, oubliant l'honneur, livrant le pays à la servitude. Cependant, rien n'est perdu!

Rien n'est perdu, parce que cette guerre est une guerre mondiale. Dans l'univers libre, des forces immenses n'ont pas encore donné. Un jour, ces forces écraseront l'ennemi. Il faut que la France, ce jour-là, soit présente à la victoire. Alors, elle retrouvera sa liberté et sa grandeur. Tel est mon but, mon seul but!

Voilà pourquoi je convie tous les Français, où qu'ils se trouvent, à s'unir à moi dans l'action, dans le sacrifice et dans l'espérance.

Notre patrie est en péril de mort.
Luttons tous pour la sauver!

VIVE LA FRANCE !

G. de Gaulle

GÉNÉRAL DE GAULLE

General de Gaulle's historic rallying cry broadcast from London, June 18, 1940. "France has lost a battle. But France has not lost the war .... Our mother country is in mortal peril. Let us fight to save her!"

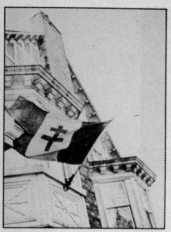

Free French House,
448 Daly Ave., Ottawa.

Elisabeth de Miribel, co-director
with Gladys Arnold of the Free
French Information Service in
Canada. (Photo by Karsh)

Marjorie Gray inside the spartan office of Free French House, Ottawa.
(National Film Board photo)

Colonel Philippe Henri Pierrené, leader of the Free French in Canada, 1941–43, about to make a broadcast to France. Pierrené was a nom de guerre made from the names of his four sons; his real name was General Jacques Emile Martin-Prével.

Commandant Gabriel Bonneau, Delegate of the Free French in Canada, 1943–45. (Photo by Karsh)

The Free French "mobile kitchen" in front of the Chateau Laurier, Ottawa.

Nellita MacNulty and Eve Curie, daughter of the famous French scientist Marie Curie, embarking on a speaking tour of Canada.

General Charles de Gaulle speaks in front of the House of Commons, Ottawa, July 11, 1944. On the left are Canada's Governor General, the Earl of Athlone, and Prime Minister W.L. Mackenzie King. Princess Alice, wife of the Earl of Athlone, is directly behind de Gaulle.

Irène Lézine, 1944.

Gladys Arnold's official letter of introduction for her return to France following the Allied invasion and liberation of Paris.

AMBASSADE DE FRANCE
AU CANADA

Ottawa, le

The Delegate of the French Provisional Government in Canada would be grateful to Allied Authorities for any facilities which may be given to Miss Gladys ARNOLD, chief of the English branch of the French Information Service in Canada.

Miss ARNOLD has been invited by the French Ministry of Foreign Affairs to undertake the study of prevailing conditions in France. Her stay in that country will last approximately two months./.

Ottawa, January 5th 1945.

The Delegate of the French Provisional Government in Canada.

Caen, Normandy, in March 1945 after it was liberated by the Canadians.

Count Jean-Marie de Hautecloque, France' first ambassador to Canada, with his wife and six daughters.

don by clandestine agents. No communication was our continuing torment. Our letters were not getting through and we dared not mention receiving theirs. The only alternative was the ten words via the Red Cross. They were frustrating: "Thinking of you and Irène, Paul, Madeleine, all well, love." And few of these got through.

The prolonged agony led CBC's Beatrice Belcourt to WRUL, a strong Boston shortwave station. Arrangements were made to record five-minute messages by Canadians for transmission to France. We could not forewarn, but we knew that anyone listening would take the messages and spread them.

We knew also that our friends in France were already listening to the BBC and "The Voice of America." The series began with a talk by Beatrice Belcourt, whose ancestors had come to Canada from Normandy in 1648. This was her message.

"My compatriots have volunteered in great numbers. Do not believe those who tell you this war has no meaning for us as French-Canadians. We want to help you. Also I want you to understand how much and why we are heart and soul with Great Britain in the gigantic effort she is making to save you and us. It is our duty to do everything in our power to win the war. The more we understand your plight the more we want to fight. We have kept our traditions, our customs, our language while living happily under the protection of the British flag. You may not know that French-Canadians — keeping in mind that we are only one-fourth of the population — have enrolled proportionally as many soldiers as have our English-speaking compatriots. The latest recruiting figures show that Quebec City has furnished more recruits per capita than has Toronto.

"At this moment there are 80,000 Canadian soldiers, sailors and airmen in England and another 220,000 disseminated elsewhere. Of these only 170,000 defend our own shores....

"Our target for 1942 is 575,000 troops by March and it should be remembered that the entire population of Canada is barely 11,000,000. Soon we expect to have 400 ships and have already established one hundred air-training establishments across Canada. We have sent more than $500,000,000 to Great Britain to help pay for armaments....

"In the next weeks, with the collaboration of WRUL, Boston, you will hear the voices of many Canadians who are giving dedicated work toward the victory that will set you free. These programs will be repeated over and over again...."

From then on the series of talks continued week after week and were repeated many times. It was one bright ray in the dark cloud.

As Christmas 1941 approached, Elisabeth and I were unaware that St. Pierre and Miquelon, two tiny French islands off the coast of Newfoundland, were about to become "the mouse that roared."

In my school days teachers of Canadian history and geography must have missed these bits of foreign territory sitting in the outer reaches of the Gulf of St. Lawrence. Their history was much the same as that of the Newfoundlanders: a community of fishing people had lived on the islands for several hundred years. St. Pierre had been a repair and supply depot for the cod fleet from St. Malo which fished on the Grand Banks. I never heard of the islands until the summer of 1941.

Indeed, I did not realize that French possessions were to be found in strategic locations all over the world. In the Far East, Indo-China; in the Pacific, New Caledonia, Tahiti, the New Hebrides as well as some 300 other small islands; in the Indian Ocean, La Réunion, the Comoras and Madagascar; in the Caribbean, Martinique, Guadaloupe and French Guiana; in Africa, almost half the continent including the protectorates of Tunisia and Morocco; Syria in the Middle East; and in the North Atlantic, St. Pierre and Miquelon.

General de Gaulle was acutely aware of the strategic importance of these territories to the Allies in a global war. His appeal to Frenchmen had rallied the majority of them to the Free French in 1940, bringing millions of people, trained colonial troops, raw materials and food. Among the few which had remained with Vichy were Martinique, Gaudaloupe and St. Pierre and Miquelon.

The Americans, uneasy about these bits of French territory after the collapse of France, arranged with Vichy that the status quo should be maintained, with American co-operation. At about the same time the Pan-American Union of twenty-one American nations met in Havana and decided that there should be "No transfer of sovereignty, possession or control of any territory in the Western Hemisphere held by European powers." Canada was not invited even as an observer.

Earlier the papers had announced that Canada and the United States, in the persons of Prime Minister King and President Roosevelt, had met at Ogdensburg and established the Canada-United States Permanent Joint Board of Defence, composed of equal numbers of members from each country. It was agreed that there should be total confidential exchanges of information on all questions of defence, especially pertaining to the Atlantic coast. Yet Canada was not informed of the United States – Vichy pact.

During the autumn of 1941 we heard rumours about St. Pierre and

Miquelon. There were hints that Vichy had been forced to allow German submarines to refuel there, hints that the shortwave station was giving weather reports to submarines lying in wait offshore for the convoys out of Halifax and St. John's. Some young men from St. Pierre had fled to Newfoundland in order to join the Free French forces. They brought stories that the people of the islands were overwhelmingly in favour of the Free French and had demonstrated on July 14. Families had had their rations of coal and food reduced for showing the Cross of Lorraine and shouting "Vive de Gaulle" before their war memorial. We heard that many feared reprisals against their families under the administration of their governor, Baron de Bournat, who controlled the heavily subsidized food, clothing and fuel supplies. Free French followers in St. John's informed Colonel Pierrené, and both he and Elisabeth discussed it unofficially with friends in the Department of External Affairs. It was a delicate situation and no one had a solution.

An ambivalent situation existed in the United States. The State Department continued full diplomatic relations with Vichy. In spite of President Roosevelt's personal sympathies and actions in favour of the Allied cause, the Free French were persona non grata in Washington. Even at the Canadian border, French de Gaullists were refused entry and treated as renegades. Elisabeth herself was picked up and spent two days in confinement on Ellis Island.

At the same time our Free French colleagues in New York told us that the Free French Movement was as popular in the United States as it was in Canada, and the most important elements of the media, including Walter Lippmann, were outspoken in their support.

This was the situation when we woke on December 7, 1941, to the shock of Pearl Harbour. Now, we thought, the United States will be in the war. Relations with Vichy will be cut and, of course, the Americans will see the Free French for what they are — a fighting ally. To our astonished disappointment, in spite of the fact that Germany and Italy declared war against the United States, a break between Vichy and Washington did not come. Our spirits plunged. We could not understand what sort of game the State Department was playing.

On December 9 we received word that Admiral Emile Muselier had arrived in St. John's, Newfoundland, with the pride of the French navy, the *Surcouf*, the largest and most modern submarine in the world.

As usual Canadian Press and the local papers were after me for pictures, which I could not supply. I sometimes wondered if CP thought I was still working for them. It never occurred to me to give any thought to St. Pierre and Miquelon, although it may have crossed the minds of Colonel Pierrené and Elisabeth.

Thanks to the Halifax Free French Committee which catered to the needs of sailors, I knew that several French crews were serving with Canadians on convoy duty out of St. John's and Halifax. Rear-Admiral Leonard Murray, RCN, was in command in Newfoundland and responsible for the three French corvettes and crews that had come from Britain to serve in the Canadian convoys. We learned that Admiral Muselier was the guest of Rear-Admiral Murray, but did not know at the time that Admiral Murray had agreed to a request that the three French corvettes spend a few days with the *Surcouf* on "manoeuvres" before Muselier returned to England. They would meet in Halifax. This opportunity for the young French crews to meet Muselier and his men, as well as visit the famous *Surcouf*, seemed the most natural thing in the world.

On December 15, 1941, the admiral arrived in Ottawa. Though not tall, Admiral Muselier had a commanding appearance, and we had no trouble visualizing him leading a naval attack. A career officer in his fifties, he was lean, wiry, sun-tanned, with jet black hair and a moustache threaded with white. His black eyes sparkled with enthusiasm.

We took it for granted that Admiral Muselier was in Ottawa to obtain ships and other naval supplies. A friendly reporter with contacts in the Department of National Defence told me confidentially that he had heard that two corvettes had been turned over to Admiral Muselier for the use of more Free French crews who would be joining the Atlantic force on convoy duty. In wartime there is no way to confirm these tips.

The admiral's program of visits with top officials of National Defence, Munitions and Supply, External Affairs and a luncheon at Government House had us speculating about greater recognition for the Free French. On the evening of December 18, a dinner for the admiral was given at the Country Club. The atmosphere was full of excitement. Germany had just declared war on the United States and conversation swirled around its implications.

Admiral Muselier was at his charismatic best that evening. He radiated energy, decisiveness and humour. He reminded me of stories in my childhood about gentlemen pirates in the service of Queen Elizabeth I. He was a fascinating raconteur. When he was asked about his escape from France to Britain, his face lit up as he told the tale. Muselier was in Marseille when he learned of the armistice. Unable to obtain transportation, he remembered the city had a new, very red fire engine. "Like every small boy, I had always dreamed of driving a fire engine. Now I saw my chance." His eyes sparkled. Commandeering the machine and driving along back roads, Muselier arrived in Paris and drove directly to the Ministry of Marine. With the aid of companions he ran a hose into the building and then proceeded to burn documents. Meanwhile his men were carrying out boxes of top secret reports and hiding them in the empty water tank. Back in the driver's seat, he roared out of Paris with his companions ranged professionally along either side of the fire engine. Not one German had made the slightest attempt to find out what it was all about and intercept him. Back in Marseille Muselier gathered together all the merchant and war ships he could find and sailed off to Britain.

The admiral left Ottawa. We took it for granted that he had completed his business with the Canadian government, business we never expected to know anything about since it was wartime.

On Christmas morning I was still sound asleep when my telephone rang. It was someone at Canadian Press. What did I know about Admiral Muselier capturing St. Pierre and Miquelon? I was astounded, delighted and speechless.

"Come on now, you must have known something about it. We've been expecting something ever since Muselier was here," I was told.

"Are you sure it's happened?" I demanded. "How do you know? Have you checked with External Affairs?"

"Couldn't get any of the chiefs. One Indian was home and swore he knew nothing about it. No statement, but he didn't deny that the department was aware of the possibility. It's been discussed."

"I can't tell you anything. I'm sorry, but honestly I don't know a thing."

"The hell you don't! I know damn well you know something. Don't give me that line," he yelled. "Where did he get those corvettes?"

"What corvettes?"

"He picked up three corvettes in Halifax. How did he come to have them? They're all at St. Pierre-Miquelon."

I continued to protest my ignorance but he did not seem to believe me.

Colonel Pierrené and Paul Theriault were already discussing the event when I arrived at Free French House. The telephones were ringing and Pierrené and Paul had each had calls from Montreal and Quebec.

It was a Christmas Day I will never forget. We had no respite from the telephone calls from newspapers across Canada, from New York, from Free French committees and individuals, all expecting us to be able to tell them something. It was hard to convince our callers that we had been kept in the dark too.

The next day Colonel Pierrené got details. The story had already swept the front pages of the newspapers to such a degree that the fall of Hong Kong went unnoticed. Later I felt guilty about that, knowing that more than 2,000 young Canadians had fought and been taken prisoner there by the Japanese.

We gathered all the newspapers we could buy at Ottawa's only international newsstand. The main accounts came from Ira Wolfert of the *New York Times* and in the French press from Jean LeBret, foreign editor of *Le Jour*, in Montreal. Admiral Muselier had invited Ira to accompany the "invasion" and we heard later that Jean had somehow got wind of the impending takeover and had threatened to blow the story if he was not taken along.

On Christmas morning the St. Pierrais had wakened to find the *Surcouf* and three corvettes, the *Mimosa, Alysse* and the *Aconit,* sitting in their harbour. Almost immediately hundreds of Tricolours with the Cross of Lorraine were waving in the windows.

Without the slightest opposition, Admiral Muselier and his officers went ashore to the cheers of a gathering crowd. Governor de Bournat did not resist and was put under house arrest aboard the *Surcouf.*

The next step was to organize a referendum. The choice was simple — which regime did the St. Pierrais want, Vichy or the Free French? To assure fairness in the eyes of the public, Muselier asked Ira Wolfert and Jean LeBret to serve as scrutineers. The population voted 98 per cent for the Free French.

Press and public reaction was overwhelmingly favourable. We were delighted, and chuckled over such editorials as that appearing in the *New York Times*: "The bloodless investiture of these surprised Islands by four little warships was accomplished with a display of style and manners in the best tradition of Alexandre Dumas!"

Reports we received from London were reassuring. "The news of the coup has not met with displeasure" was the formal way it was put. In Ottawa our friends at External Affairs and National Defence frankly expressed their delight that it had come off so well.

In Washington the official reaction was different. What Ira Wolfert called "the nicest Christmas present the world got," in his *Times* article, struck one State Department official as "a hell of a Christmas present," and a Canadian correspondent in Washington wrote that Secretary of State Cordell Hull was "livid with anger."

Every hour brought new developments in this incident which, in the context of the total war, was insignificant, but whose repercussions, diplomatically and politically, were blown up to proportions so far beyond commonsense and so ridiculous that soon the press and public were laughing. The first excess was Cordell Hull's towering anger and his demand that Canada or Britain, or both, *force* those "so-called Free French" out of the islands, and that their control be restored to the Vichy governor, Baron de Bournat.

This brought a fiery reaction from Admiral Muselier, who issued a warning that "should planes or ships of any foreign power approach the islands, without permission, the Free French would be obliged to blow them out of the air or water!" The cartoonists had a field day. Among the best cartoons was one showing Muselier standing with a foot planted on each island and firing at a plane with a nineteenth-century elephant gun. In fact, the island had only half-a-dozen ancient cannons and piles of rusting cannon balls. Two cannons worked, and were used occasionally for firing ceremonial salutes. Later verification proved that the cannon balls were too large for the cannons.

Meanwhile in the United States the reaction was even more dramatic than it had been in Canada. Secretary of State Hull's use of the word "so-called" caused an uproar. Dorothy Thompson's "On the Record," carried in many Canadian papers, described Hull's statement as a "gratuitous insult." Thousands and thousands of Americans wrote letters, sent long lists of names and telegrams addressed to the "so-called Secretary of State" at the "so-called State Department." The switchboards were swamped with irate telephone calls; the protest was always the same — "The people voted democratically for the Free French. They have spoken and the Vichy regime must not be restored against their will."

A friend of a friend of a member of the Free French delegation in Washington told us that Gaston Henry-Haye, the Vichy ambassador to Washington, angrily demanded that the State Department force the islands to return to their old status. He was taken down to a mailing room and shown the piles of mailbags overflowing with correspondence. His guide was reported to have said, "These are from Americans objecting to any move to remove the Free French. Every mail brings more. In the face of such public opinion, what can be done? We are a democracy."

At the first announcement of the takeover I was interested, as a Canadian, to see how the public would react. Editorials, initially, were almost unanimously favourable. Then, after Cordell Hull's reaction, some of our papers began to have doubts, indicating that Washington's pleasure and opinion then was just as inhibiting as it is today. But when American editorialists and public opinion championed Muselier, some Canadian papers switched opinion again. Fortunately, most of our editorialists stuck to their guns. I read and compiled these mountains of clippings, trying to sort out opinion trends common to all, and chuckled over the fickleness of the commentators and the wit of the cartoonists.

At that moment of editorial indecision in some of the Canadian media, support for the Free French came from an unexpected and powerful quarter. Winston Churchill arrived in Ottawa on December 30, 1941, and addressed a gathering in the House of Commons. Elisabeth, Paul and I were in the Press Gallery. We were delighted to discover that protocol had placed Colonel Pierrené (delegate of General de Gaulle) and René Ristelhueber (Minister of Vichy) in the same row among the diplomats of other countries. It could only suggest that the Canadian government accorded them equal status.

Some passages in Mr. Churchill's speech must have made Ristelhueber squirm. Mr. Churchill contemptuously castigated the "men of Vichy" for "truckling" to the "Naazzzees," and expressed admiration for the followers of General de Gaulle, "whose names are being held in increasing respect by nine Frenchmen out of every ten throughout the once happy, smiling land of France." We joined in the cheers.

After the address we attended Churchill's press conference. The prime minister was presented with a handsome astrakhan forage-cap, gift of the press corps. We were all touched by his surprisingly boyish pleasure. In his excitement, he put his cigar, wrong end first, into his mouth and burned his tongue.

Via the grapevine, we learned that Ristelhueber had called on the Canadian prime minister to protest the presence of Pierrené in the diplomatic row for Churchill's address. King, we were told, replied stiffly in words to this effect, "I find it hard to understand why one Frenchman who is serving France in his capacity as diplomat should object to our courtesy in recognizing the patriotism of another Frenchman who believes his action is contributing to the liberation of France."

By now, with the exception of Le Devoir, Le Droit and one or two insignificant sheets in Montreal, the whole of press editorial opinion, French and English, supported the Free French cause. In Washington Hull still fumed. We were to learn later that Prime Minister King had been in Washington on December 27 and had been obliged to listen to a diatribe of accusations: Ottawa, and probably London, had known all along about the affair, had they not? King denied having prior knowledge, and later Admiral Muselier revealed that General de Gaulle had cabled him to proceed "without informing the foreign governments."

Yet Hull would not let the matter drop. He still urged the Canadians to do something. In view of the referendum results, Churchill's remarks and the powerful public support in both countries, King refused. Hull declared that the change contravened agreements made in Havana with the Pan-American Union, and with General George Robert, Governor of Martinique, on behalf of Vichy. This gave King his opening. As far as Canada was concerned, he said, he knew of no agreement that involved Canada in maintaining the status quo of the islands. In fact, he could not see how the Monroe Doctrine was involved; nor was Canada made aware of any agreement between Washington and Vichy concerning St. Pierre and Miquelon. What of the exchange of information agreed to at Ogdensburg? In Canadian eyes, no transfer of sovereignty had taken place. The islands were still French and administered by French. The matter was simply one "to be settled between Frenchmen."

In February 1942, Admiral Muselier, still in St. Pierre, invited Elisabeth to visit the islands to gather information for our service. She made a point of calling at every single home and business, and talked to people about their feelings and the former regime under Comte de Bournat. Eagerly they brought out copies of the clandestine leaflets that had circulated on the islands ever since the armistice. From somewhere they had been able to smuggle in pictures of General de Gaulle and reproduce them; framed copies were displayed on the wall of almost every home. "I kept mine on the back of the calendar, so I only had to turn it over," one woman told her. The Cross of Lorraine had been sewn on French Tricolours so that, when Admiral Muselier arrived, out came hundreds of little flags, all ready to welcome him.

eleven

The following spring my mission was to meet the members of the Free French Committees in cities across Canada and call on newspapers, radio stations and the French departments of the universities. The process opened my eyes to a whole new aspect of Canada.

My first call was at *La Liberté* in St. Boniface, Manitoba, where the editor suggested that we visit one or two of the more than dozen French-speaking villages around Winnipeg. That there were small French-language communities struggling to stay alive culturally on the Prairies took me completely by surprise. I had never encountered a French-speaking person while growing up in Saskatchewan.

In Saskatchewan Father Athol Murray took me to two "Alsatian" villages where the people had come to Canada after the war of 1870. They still spoke German, French and Alsatian as well as English. I also visited Gravelbourg, Saskatchewan, where a French-language university existed. I discovered that there were almost as many committees working in Manitoba as in Quebec. Names like Ste. Claride, Ste. Lina, St. Pierre-Jolys, Ste. Rose-du-lac, Our Lady of Lourdes, Ste. Geneviève, St. Vital, La Rochelle, Toutes-Aides and almost a dozen others reminded me of the villages of France.

In recalling the efforts of those little communites I like to think of Saltel, Manitoba. Saltel is so small it does not appear on the map, but the committee reported that it consisted of four households. Someone there had heard the appeal. Neighbours had been alerted in the sparsely populated district and had come together to form a committee. The people came in battered cars over unpaved roads; in winter they travelled in wagon-boxes on sled-runners drawn by horses. Their first activity to raise money was a card party attended by thirty-five people. They raised $31.75. That small sum joined others coming from remote villages to help provide clothing and Christmas gifts for French refugees in southern England. Having taught in a rural Prairie school in depression times, I saw nothing unusual in the feats of these people. My French co-workers, however, were in awe when they read of the dedication of the people of Saltel and elsewhere.

We were too busy at the time to realize the effort that was being made across the country, but when I look at the map now and see where most of those fifty or more Prairie committees were situated, I feel humbled. In Alberta several committees were in the Athabaska region. Therien, St. Vincent, McRae, Craigmyle, all had less than 100 residents, and were long distances from towns and cities. Yet these communities somehow raised a steady trickle of money, adopted crews of corvettes, and sent money and parcels of knitwear to Halifax.

Larger projects were undertaken. In Winnipeg, for example, money was raised to buy a mobile kitchen. On its way overseas, the kitchen was parked on a traffic island in front of the Chateau Laurier in Ottawa for three days. Passersby bought cups of coffee and made donations. The vehicle was driven by Mrs. Colin W.G. Gibson, wife of the Minister of National Defence for Air, and by the wife of General H.D.G. Crerar, Chief of the General Staff, both in Canadian uniform. Among those serving with the kitchen were Mme Frederic Gilbert-Berthiez in French uniform and Suzanne Cloutier, daughter of the King's Printer. One afternoon the kitchen moved to John Street where it was strategically placed between the National Film Board and the French Legation. All afternoon dozens of employees of the Film Board came out for coffee, shouted "Vive de Gaulle! Vive la France!" and occasionally took a stab at singing "La Marseillaise." We wondered if, behind the curtain of the minister's office, Ristelhueber might be watching and wishing he could join in. It was Bastille Day, July 14, and on the Legation lawn the Tricolour drooped at half-mast.

At exhibitions in the cities and at small town fairs, Free French Committees had stalls and we were asked to provide flags, pins and documentation. In some cities Free French Committees set up blood donor clinics during exhibition weeks. From Carlton Gardens' information services in London we received a large glossy print showing a tank and crew in the North African desert. Across it was painted in white letters "City of Saskatoon." The people of Saskatoon had heard an appeal from London for money to buy arms for the Free French. They had raised the money and sent it to London to buy a tank.

In Montreal where the French "colony" continued to be divided, a large number of members of the committee abandoned those who had paralyzed the work by attempting to serve two masters. They chose de Gaulle.

The committees not only raised money to aid their own work. With great enthusiasm they took part in every kind of local activity, from participating in War Savings Bond drives to donating blood. The amounts of money raised, in a country relatively poor after the long depression and the many years of drought in the West, were impressive.

I encountered ingenious money-raising schemes on visits to committees in the Maritimes and the West. Auction sales, ball games, hockey games, bazaars, booths at country fairs, pot luck suppers, box socials, lotteries, penny-savers (children's banks in which the whole family put all the one-cent pieces they received) were only a few. Packets of French recipes, handwritten or typed on cards and tied with blue, white and red yarn, sold by the hundreds. In our office we all spent many evenings preparing the cards for a Free French garden party in Ottawa. More than a thousand sets were eventually sold at twenty-five cents each.

Under the patronage of Lady Eaton, the Toronto Committee held its first tag day. Windows of Eaton's and Simpson's stores were draped with French flags and posters and inside at every counter was a box for coins. At every corner in downtown Toronto, French and Canadians stood with their trays of pins tied with bits of blue, white and red ribbon. More than 175,000 people bought tags that day and the result was $12,000.

For me the most exciting money-raising event was a benefit concert in Ottawa featuring the world-renowned coloratura soprano, Lily Pons. The diminutive French diva of the Metropolitan Opera, with flowing dark hair and the flashing eyes of the Mediterranean, was an enthusiastic supporter of the Free French. The Capitol Theatre was filled to standing-room only. On the stage General Georges Vanier in uniform stood ramrod straight as he waited to introduce the famous singer. Her entrance was breathtaking. She was dressed in a crinoline-skirted white gown, her only ornament was a wide blue, white and red satin sash looped over one shoulder. Her head thrown back, she burst into "La Marsaillaise" as she swept onto the stage. The audience gasped and sprang to its feet as one, cheering, then humming or singing the words. General Vanier stood at attention, tears glistening in his eyes. By the time she had finished the anthem, there was hardly a dry eye in the house.

We were saddened that summer by the news that the corvettes *Mimosa* and *Alysse*, which had accompanied the submarine *Surcouf* in the liberation of St. Pierre-Miquelon, were lost at sea. Aboard the corvettes were some of the crew from the islands. The youngest, Jean Bourdreau, went down with the *Alysse*. He was not yet eighteen.

In the letters from France the privations came through in cautious paragraphs. From Suzette Provost, written in April 1941: "It's been colder this winter. Our flat is so damp and humid that black patches are on the ceilings and real rivulets on the walls. We were so happy to find a tiny stove that takes one stick of wood at a time and are using it to heat one room. I dream of soap. I dare not describe the dirt. What we can buy is a mixture of lye and sand, or ashes. Everybody is so tired that we neglect ourselves. Maybe it's because we are still a little bit human, but without soap, so little water and nothing new to wear, nobody to exert one's charm for, makes one feel old and shrivelled." (The writer was twenty-four).

Irène never lost her sense of humour, not even in the worst of predicaments. She wrote: "I took your bicycle and rode out into the country to visit a family I know but hadn't seen since... well the grandmother and an old man who used to look after their horses (the horses had been requisitioned) and my friend were there. They had secretly butchered an animal and gave me a huge steak — but how to get it past the guard at the Porte d'Orléans? Don't think I'm terrible. I wrapped it against my body and covered it with a long piece of old sheet they gave me. Then I put on my clothes. When I got to the Porte I was stopped and asked what I had in my basket. I showed a few vegetables. The guards aren't bad and they know we're hungry. It's the others — the G...... Well just then I felt something running down my leg and was horrified to see a red streak. I thought for sure I'd be searched but instead the guard saw it too and turned just as red. He waved at me in a hurry and said 'Passez, passez, Mademoiselle!' Did we laugh when I got home — and was that steak good!"

By 1942 the letters came through with a regularity that would put most post offices to shame. I asked myself so often: How did they get their letters to Geneva, or Lisbon or Marseille?

May 1942, from Irène: "I have just received a small parcel from Switzerland containing some butter, cheese, a sausage and some chocolate. It makes my mouth water but I am quite resolved to keep everything for my next box to my brother (prisoner-of-war) for it is next to impossible to find anything in Paris... We hear by the weather forecasts that we can expect a summer of tempests in the Channel. It's been a very *rainy* spring.... The Bassanos often visit us... they are very thoughtful...."

At first I was puzzled by reference to the Bassanos. By chance I mentioned it to a liaison officer in touch with the Norwegians, Belgains, Free French and others who were training as pilots under the British Commonwealth Air Training Plan. "Bassano?" he said. "There's a big air-training school in Bassano, Alberta." Then I remembered. A letter from my mother during the "phony war" spoke of the Bassano school and I had told Irène and others about it. She and they adopted the word to tell me of the RAF air raids.

Irène, spring 1942: "The weather is so dry now we're hoping for a real rain. It can't come too soon.... We want to wash away all this dirt. [Weather words — rain, storms, clouds — became synonyms for allied air raids; filth, tenants, cowbirds, cuckoos — synonyms for Germans.] The summer should bring us some happy visits from friends...."

I realized after several letters that my friends were hoping for the invasion. There was a thread of euphoria in those letters.

June 2, 1942, from Hélène: "I dream of the lovely lavender soap you gave me for Christmas and wonder when I will ever be able to have a lavender bath again."

June 1942, from Madeleine in Oran, Algeria: "Only two letters since November from Albert.... He is in a new residence farther east, farther away from me. I do not know if he can receive my letters... I told you, dear Glad, I am not the courageous kind of woman.... I have passed my bar exams in Algiers, but what use. I cannot practise now." (Albert had already escaped and been recaptured twice in Germany. By now he was in a camp in western Poland.)

Other members of our staff were receiving similar letters with disguised messages. We learned, however, that our correspondents in France were better at getting their letters out of France than we were in getting ours in. Then we were warned that the Free French Information Service and its personnel had been reported to Vichy. Canada had its Fifth Columnists too.

Our French correspondents took great risks. A letter from Irène told me how she and her friends were looking after a young girl. I knew the girl was Jewish and with Irène's own uncertain status I realized the chances she was taking. Later I learned that until the liberation of Paris, the girl had spent her days in a big wardrobe in a friend's room. Her only exercise was to pace the room at night and sit by the open window in the dark for some fresh air. She never left the apartment and every trace of her presence had to be kept inside the wardrobe.

We received word that a regular underground courier service was in operation between occupied France and London, and that some of the clandestine newspapers circulating in France had actually reached London and been reproduced. The first time I held copies of *Liberation* and *Combat* in my hands I tried to imagine what the printing and circulation must have cost and meant inside France. The papers were hand-set. What astonished me was the content of these two-page papers. "André Philip, well-known leader in the resistance in France, has arrived in London to join General de Gaulle," I read in one. Another mentioned a news report on the BBC. We gathered around these papers excitedly, wondering how they had been produced and by whom. Where did they get the printing presses? Who were the printers? Who did the distribution? Who had taken copies out of France to deliver to London? We got no answers to these questions, but we were informed that a group of French writers and journalists who had escaped to London had set up a little publishing house, called Les Cahiers du Silence (The Paperbacks of Silence), where the original papers were copied. Because we had French press facilities in Canada, copies were sent to us to be reproduced in quantity for distribution in other parts of the world. Some months later the mail brought *Le Silence de la Mer*, the first book published by an underground writer called Vercors. Nothing during that period of the war intrigued us more than how this underground literature we were getting was reproduced and distributed.

As the fourth year of war was looming, a sort of suppressed excitement emanated from letters from Irène, Hélène and Claude. Were we going to invade? We all longed for the day when our armies would set foot in France.

Unhappily, the Dieppe raid on August 19, 1942, was taken at first to be the beginning of the invasion. The terrible news that followed brought French and Canadian members of Free French House even closer. The Dieppe force of 6,000, the vast majority Canadian, included regiments from every province in Canada as well as British and Free French commandos and a few representatives of other occupied countries. Nearly two-thirds of the Canadians were left in France, taken prisoner, wounded or killed. Later a native of Dieppe told me that many people in the city were so sure it was the invasion that they turned on the Germans and eventually paid heavily for it.

Several weeks passed and there were no letters from France. We did not know how much the French people knew about the raid, but the propaganda over Radio-Paris and Radio-Vichy treated it as a victory for "The New Europe" and warned French-speaking Canadians to take heed.

Our office was a pretty sober place those weeks. Then one day I received a letter from Irène from the south of France. Somehow she had crossed the demarcation line. The methodical, thorough checking by the Gestapo was too close, so she had slipped through the line and taken refuge with friends on the Côte d'Azur. Her letters in the next weeks exploded with the joy she felt about the difference between the two zones — the beauty of the Mediterranean countryside, a greater sense of security and, at last, a little more to eat.

But Irène's respite was short. Though a French citizen, her mother needed her in Paris, so Irène returned to take her chances. After that letters from Irène were rare, and I felt sure that my letters were not getting through. Those I did receive were very cautious; the tone revealed the growing repression. The absence of any veiled references to the RAF or conditions in Paris let us know that the situation had become more dangerous.

On November 11, 1942 (was the date a deliberate choice?), we awoke to the news that the German occupation armies had crossed the demarcation line. They moved south rapidly and the fiction of Vichy was fully revealed. In a few days the occupation force was almost to the Mediterranean, setting up military posts and repressive administrations everywhere. The larger part of the French fleet, immobilized since the armistice, lay at anchor at Toulon and Germans were racing towards it. The war had already taken a terrible toll of British shipping and convoys, but it had also depleted the German navy. German submarines had wrecked havoc in the Atlantic but many were destroyed. In German hands the French fleet could be devastating. But the French naval officers and crews were ready. They had wired their vessels and placed their explosives. When the German SS Panzer Corps seized Toulon, it was too late. Admiral Laborde had given the order to scuttle, the hardest order any naval man can give. Three battleships, seven cruisers and sixty-two other craft, including sixteen submarines, went down with some loss of life.

I shall never forget that morning. The first news we got was a brief mention of "considerable loss of life." Colonel Pierrené's face was ashen. I could not meet his eyes. "My son was aboard one of the ships," he said.

No one in our group doubted the outcome of the war, but each day we became more aware of the terrible price victory would exact.

twelve

I n the summer of 1942 I boarded the train for New York and Washington, carrying a small suitcase filled with the underground Resistance literature Elisabeth had gathered in St. Pierre-Miquelon. The Free French Information Service in New York and the Free French delegation in Washington wanted to see it. They were considering reproducing the crudely drawn but often witty cartoons and leaflets that had circulated among the St. Pierrais during the Vichy regime.

I had no problem in New York with Customs officials. When I stepped off the train in Washington a polite official asked me to follow him. Once inside his office he told me to open my suitcase. As soon as he saw the words "St. Pierre-Miquelon" on a document, my luggage and I were conducted into a large empty room and told to wait.

After fifteen minutes of examining a crack and a water mark on the ceiling, I got out a copy of de St.-Exupéry's *Wind, Sand and Stars,* determined to keep my quaking imagination under control. Nearly an hour later two men in uniform arrived and, without a word to me, began going through the papers. Neither one spoke or read French, so they could not understand the material, although they could clearly see that it was all about General de Gaulle. I tried to explain but they waved me aside. Another hour passed.

Finally I asked if I could call the Delegation. When they refused abruptly I began to feel a bit of panic. Was I about to end up like Elisabeth who had spent two nights on Ellis Island in the company of Germans and Italians, thanks to the St. Pierre-Miquelon visa stamped on her passport? After another wait a man in plain clothes appeared. He not only spoke French but had the quiet, courteous manner of a diplomat. He asked my name, where I was born and how it had come about that I was carrying this material. He did not introduce himself and I did not dare ask.

In no time he had the contents of my suitcase spread over the table and began going through it methodically. It was obvious that he was becoming more and more interested, and was even enjoying himself. My anxiety mounted. To break the silence I said hesitantly that I was taking the material to the Free French delegation because they wanted to see it. He nodded and asked a few questions. Before I knew it, I had blurted out that the material was being considered for publication in the United States. He made no comment. Surely he realized that the Free French were fighting on our side. While I ruminated, he simply went on reading. For more than five hours I sat there, stewing about my fate. At the very least I would be deported and never allowed to return.

Finally, he packed everything back neatly and closed the valise. I asked him if there was anything wrong. He just smiled, said not to worry and offered to give me a lift to my destination. It seemed terribly anti-climactic. Getting up my courage, I asked him what he thought of the contents of my suitcase. "Very interesting, very interesting," he answered, straight-faced. "Those St. Pierrais have a good sense of humour."

In September 1942 André Philip, leader of the Christian Socialists in France and the Resistance movement, came to Ottawa. He brought the message that the Resistance movements were now totally united and were secretly training small units in preparation for the day of the invasion. They called themselves the Fighting French of the Interior (FFI) to symbolize their unity with the Free French armed forces *outside* France; the latter were known henceforth as the Fighting French.

On Sunday, November 8, the telephone rang beside my bed. At the other end was Paul Theriault. "Have you heard the news?" he shouted. "The Americans are invading North Africa! They're in Algiers!"

Within an hour almost the whole staff were at Free French House celebrating and answering telephone calls.

We were delighted to learn that Prime Minister Mackenzie King had joined President Roosevelt, Winston Churchill, General de Gaulle and General Giraud (a French general who had escaped from Germany) in explaining the objectives of the invasion and in asking all to co-operate. The next news announced, to our satisfaction, was that the United States and Canada had severed all diplomatic ties with Vichy.

Events were beginning to move very fast. Naturally we jumped to the conclusion that the Free French would take over Algeria and the French protectorates of Tunisia and Morocco. Our French staff and Colonel Pierrené were appalled to find out that the Americans had invited Admiral Jean Darlan, High Commissioner for North Africa and a minister of the Pétain government, to take charge. I tried to remember all I had heard about Darlan. He had been Minister of the Navy in Pétain's "cabinet" and had refused to allow the French fleet to go to Britain in 1940. He had visited Hitler and had allowed the Syrian bases and ports to fall into German hands, pitting Frenchmen against Frenchmen. He had urged Frenchmen to go to work in Germany. Darlan was a traitor and his position in North Africa was a thing of blatant expediency.

Within days Darlan broadcast from Algiers that he was assuming all the powers and responsibilities of the French state. Did not this mean that, after victory, Darlan and his clique expected to represent France and install his own government? Did he not have the blessing of the American State Department? Knowing Admiral Darlan's record, his hatred of Britain, his handshake with Hitler, and the bitter enmity of the Resistance, such a move after liberation could only mean civil war.

In our office morale plummeted. If our group felt betrayed and frustrated, what must the people in France be feeling? Were those who had betrayed France in the first place going to be reinstated after the war? We were receiving more and more evidence from inside France that the people and the Resistance were loyal to the Fighting French. They trusted de Gaulle. If Cordell Hull and others were suspicious that General de Gaulle was "Britain's Man" (no doubt it must have given Winston Churchill occasions for a wry smile), now the State Department had its own "man," Admiral Darlan.

Christmas morning, 1942: the telephone was ringing again. The room was still dark. I lifted the receiver and heard the eternal Canadian Press voice. "Hi, Glad. What have you got in the way of pictures of Admiral Darlan?"

"Why?" I snarled sleepily. "Don't you know it's *Christmas?*" It seemed to me that I spent the war getting up at unearthly hours to find something for the press or radio stations.

"He's been assassinated!"

I was wide awake now.

"We need pictures right away. We work too so don't scream. How soon can you get us something?"

I dressed quickly and started for the office. It was a thirty-minute walk on slippery streets, but quicker than a sluggish street car. It was a morning of crystal trees, deep blue Laurentian hills, crisp snow crunching underfoot, and not a breath of wind. Pictures? We must have some pictures. There was the one the Toronto *Star* published with Admiral Darlan shaking hands with Hitler at Berchtesgaden. Had it been returned? We must have the one of Darlan with Pétain and two German occupation authorities grinning into the camera. Darlan. I had a warm feeling of gratitude towards the assassin, and hoped he had escaped safely.

Were the Free French involved in the assassination? It was hard to convince reporters that we were as much in the dark as they were. Then we learned that the assassin was a twenty-year-old student, Bonnier de la Chapelle. Investigation was unable to connect him with any group, including the Free French. Admiral Darlan's entourage made short work of the affair: Bonnier was quickly tried, convicted and executed. Aware of the evil role Darlan had played, and might have played in the future, our sympathies were all with Bonnier. With Darlan laid to rest we gave a sigh of relief. At least Churchill and the British government had refused to recognize Darlan. My thought was: bully for Churchill!

Bonnier de la Chapelle lies in a grave now marked simply, but deservedly, "Mort pour la France."

Who would follow Darlan in North Africa? This was a crucial decision. It must be someone who would co-operate fully with the Allies. Two liberation routes were open to our armies, through Italy and southern France, or across the Channel. In either case the French Resistance was expecting to play a part. Now the only choice possible to succeed Darlan seemed to be de Gaulle. Would Washington accept him?

As a Canadian, I was deeply involved, feeling that the lives of Canadians depended upon this decision. For the first time I truly appreciated the political aspects of the situation. Obviously, whoever took charge of North Africa would ultimately form the first provisional government in France. In the weird way of international politics, the Americans had originally chosen General Henri Giraud, a soldier of impeccable military honour, to take charge of North Africa once it was liberated. However, when Admiral Darlan, high commissioner in charge of military and civil affairs in North Africa for Vichy, fell into their hands, Giraud was dropped. The State Department still believed that the population of France supported Vichy. Now we hoped that de Gaulle would be accepted.

Our hopes seemed dashed when Giraud was invited back.

Although a military man par excellence, General Giraud insisted that he knew nothing about government or civil administration. A few weeks later, in January 1943, Winston Churchill and President Roosevelt met in Casablanca to plan the invasion and, by Churchill's insistence, both Giraud and de Gaulle were invited. The result was a few months of joint presidency over the French National Committee for Liberation, set up in Algiers in the spring of 1943. When this arrangement proved unworkable, Giraud was put in charge of all military operations, but was ultimately responsible to the French National Committee for Liberation under the presidency of de Gaulle. This body was the equivalent of a provisional government and, in time, would move to Paris. The majority of the members of the committee were Resistance leaders chosen *inside* France, representatives of the colonies that were free, and representatives of the Free French Committees throughout the world. Mme André Simard was chosen to represent French nationals in Canada.

In January Colonel Pierrené received a call to London for new duties. He was looking much happier. After weeks of distress he had received word that his naval cadet son had been ashore when his ship was scuttled.

On Colonel Pierrené's last evening we all dined together at Free French House. We knew he was going to London, but had no idea why or what he would be doing. (It was like that. People came and went and not until after the war, or sometimes never, did we hear what had become of them.) When Pierrené rose to offer a toast to us and our work, he looked closely into our faces. "What will you do when victory comes and you are no longer so passionately involved in this battle for freedom?" he asked. "I'm afraid you may find life dull. My hope for you is that you will find a way to put so much energy and passion into the fight to keep the peace. We have already fought one world war for it. You will find the victory for peace infinitely more difficult." How often I think of his words these days.

Now the Free French Information Services in London and New York began supplying us with articles written by well-known French writers both inside and outside France. The articles were not only stories of people escaping and bringing evidence of what was happening in France and reports from the Resistance movements, but also the first official documents concerned with the quasi-provisional government that would be needed to manage French political affairs until liberation. To disseminate all this material, we launched *France-Canada*, a monthly magazine in separate French and English editions.

The new "delegate" to Canada was Commandant Gabriel Bonneau, a professor, scholar, diplomat and an expert linguist in the Middle Eastern languages. On the day of the French armistice in 1940 he had been Chargé d'Affaires at the French Embassy in Kabul, Afghanistan. Immediately Bonneau consulted with the head of the French cultural services and other staff members, then they all walked across the city square and offered their services to the armed forces of Britain at the British Embassy.

One evening in February 1943 when two of our staff members, Nellita MacNulty and Marguerite de Cominges, were throwing a housewarming party in their new apartment, Elisabeth got a message that Commandant Bonneau was at the Chateau Laurier. She had not had time to warn us, but decided to ask him to come to the party anyway. The living-room was almost bare of furniture; most of the guests were sitting on the floor. Blanche Boëtte and I were in the kitchen breaking thirty eggs into a large, enamel dishpan for scrambled eggs, while Paul Theriault was busily making a mountain of toast. I was about to pour some milk into the egg mixture when Professor Laugier grabbed my arm and objected, "No milk, no milk! A good French omelet is made with water. Here, let me show you."

In the living-room Thomas Stone, in charge of French relations at External Affairs, and his son were both stretched out on the floor with their backs against the wall. They were alternately leading a sing-song of old French ballads — most of them extremely naughty. The pair boasted that they knew more than 300.

The kitchen crew came out carrying plates of scrambled eggs, sliced tomatoes and toast just as Elisabeth ushered Commandant Bonneau into the living-room. Tommy Stone rose to his feet sporting a big grin on his face as Elisabeth mumbled an introduction and the astonished Bonneau realized that he would be paying a formal call on the songster at the Department of External Affairs the next day. This casual crossing of lines between officialdom and "we ordinary folk" in wartime took some getting used to, especially for the protocol-conscious French. I was to witness it many times, for the rules of protocol in French diplomatic circles, indeed even in family circles throughout French life, have a rigidity built out of centuries of tradition.

Bonneau was a slender man of medium height with dark hair, a rather dark complexion and enormous brown eyes that looked soft but which on occasion could pin people to the wall. He had a rather shy smile and the softest male voice I have ever heard. I think we all instantly fell under the spell of his charm, transparent honesty and thoughtful wisdom. Well disciplined himself, he expected the same of us, though he never raised his voice. His every move was measured, but I remember how his inner dynamism always betrayed itself when he came to a staircase and took the steps two and sometimes three at a time.

Shortly after Bonneau's arrival his wife Sylvie and two small sons joined him from Vancouver where they had been living since 1940. Sylvie was a granddaughter of a former Shah of Persia (Iran) and the daughter of a Swedish ambassador; her parents had met at the court of the Czar of Russia. She had the blonde hair and fair skin of the Swedes, the dark eyes of the Middle East, and classical beauty. She had grown up in Monaco and had studied with the Ballet de Monte Carlo. The most memorable evenings at the Bonneau home on Chapel Street were those in which Sylvie danced with Peter Guest, another young ballet dancer and an English naval officer.

Sylvie's journey to Canada had all makings of a saga. After closing the Embassy in Kabul and joining the British, Bonneau had to decide the future of his family. They could not remain in Afghanistan. They got out the atlas to decide where she and the children should go for the duration.

"Somewhere in the British Empire," suggested Sylvie.

"Perhaps one of the dominions?"

They looked at the world map and Sylvie said, "There — Canada. It is closer to France."

Sylvie, her two young sons, a pile of luggage and her symbol of good luck — a miniature, two-wheeled, handsomely decorated Persian donkey-cart — began their journey. After stopping in several ports they arrived in San Francisco. At each stop the older boy asked, "Maman, est-ce-que c'est le Canada?"

Each time she responded, "No, not yet." At last they boarded a train for Vancouver and upon arrival in the cavernous waiting-room, the tired little boy asked plaintively, "Maman, est-ce-que c'est le Canada?"

"Yes, dear, this is Canada. We are here at last."

Wearily he looked up at her. "Maman, est-ce-que tu crois vraiment que cela vaut la peine?"

Commandant Bonneau turned out to be the man who brought accord and harmony to the French "colonies" in Canada. Although our service made every effort to remain outside the camps of opinion among French nationals and their friends, we knew that they existed. Many of these people had not been in France in twenty years or more and, as individualistic as Canadians, they clung to their various con-

ceptions of duty. Bonneau was an excellent choice to issue the
invitation of the French Committee of National Liberation to all
French nationals everywhere asking them to meet together on June
18, the anniversary of de Gaulle's first world-wide appeal for Free
French support. They were asked to "honour the war dead, sing 'The
Marseillaise', and to gather around and devote themselves to the ideal
of liberation of their homeland."

Few events in my life have been more moving than the gathering at
Commandant Bonneau's house in Ottawa that day. Among those
attending were not only the Free French, but also the former Minister
of France, René Ristelhueber, and the personnel of the former Legation who had remained in Canada as representatives of the Vichy
regime. The pleasure of the Canadian government was embodied in
the presence of Norman Robertson, Undersecretary of State, Hume
Wrong, Assistant Undersecretary, and Thomas Stone. The same ceremony was being celebrated in Committees all over the world as well
as in nearly one hundred Committees in Canada.

Yvonne Daumarie telephoned one morning in March 1943 and
alerted us to the arrival of the ultra-modern French battleship *Richelieu* in New York harbour. Several other warships from French colonial
ports were following it. "The Consulate here and our information
offices are being swamped with sailors," she cried. "They are leaving
the *Richelieu* and the other ships and crowding in here demanding to
be sent to Britain at once so they can join the Fighting French navy. We
have no means of sending them. They want to go to Canada. What can
we tell them?"

Bonneau began talking to the French delegation in Washington.
The incident posed delicate diplomatic problems. He told us that the
men refused to serve under officers who had obeyed Vichy and they
would not sit idle in New York for six months while the ships were
being readied for combat duty. What to do?

Meanwhile the sailors were marching through the streets of New
York, eager to tell their stories to anyone who would listen. American
newsmen were frustrated because censorship had been imposed, but
Canadian Press got the story out to Canada. The situation was embar-
rassing. The State Department still had not "recognized" the Free
French. Yet to deny the demand of these hundreds of French sailors
could create a scandal, and probably an angry reaction from the
American people.

I began to get calls from newspapers and radio stations. Our office
was in an uproar. We soon got the background of this sudden and

massive desertion of the French ships in the Brooklyn dockyards. The sailors were talking to anybody and everybody.

In 1940 part of the French fleet, including the newly commissioned *Richelieu*, had been in the port of Dakar, Senegal. The ship's commander had obeyed the orders of his superior, Admiral Darlan, and immobilized the ships. When a British ship carrying de Gaulle went to Dakar to persuade the French commander to come on side, there was an exchange of fire that damaged the *Richelieu*.

After the *Richelieu* incident, all shortwave radios aboard the ships had been confiscated, so the sailors had no means of listening to the BBC's Free-French broadcasts. The only news they got were carefully vetted bulletins from Radio-Vichy via the ship's radio. The sailors said it was dangerous to show any sign of pro-Allied sentiment. Nevertheless news travelled in mysterious ways. They were vaguely aware of de Gaulle and the Fighting French.

For two years the men were inactive, all the while longing to do their part. Some crew members who were considered "safe" were given a few days of leave to visit their families in France. It was enough. Their stories about the Free French, the Resistance and the situation in France swept through the crews. The luckless "safe" men disappeared and the crews learned later that they had been interned. Now with North Africa free and Darlan assassinated, General Giraud had ordered the *Richelieu* and other ships to go to New York for repairs with a view to rejoining the Allies.

Some of the sailors simply took matters into their own hands. They got on trains for Montreal, Toronto and Boston where they crowded into the Free French "consulates." But there were hundreds more, and Washington was anxious to get them out as quickly as possible with a minimum of publicity. Somehow the solution was arranged with the co-operation of the Canadian government and Bonneau. The men were taken by bus to the Canadian border, picked up there and carried on to Halifax.

When Bonneau reached Halifax he found Surcouf House overflowing with sailors exchanging stories with crews from the Free French convoy corvettes. The men had been out of touch with their families for years so Bonneau managed to have brief messages beamed to France. These messages contained diminutives or other signals that could be recognized only by their families. Soon the men were on their way to Britain to swell the naval forces.

thirteen

By summer 1943 the change in the atmosphere was being felt by everyone: at last the winds were blowing in our favour. In Russia the Germans had been beaten at Stalingrad. After nearly two years of stubborn resistance and death by hunger and cold, the citizens of Leningrad saw the seige broken. The Germans were in retreat. In North Africa the combined forces of Britain, the United States and the Fighting French had liberated the coast and were in Sicily and Italy. Instead of "How long is it going to take?" we were asking ourselves "When and where will the invasion start?" Everybody shared the euphoria.

My French colleagues were very restless. Algeria was so much closer to home and they were speculating about the most persuasive arguments they could muster to be recalled to London or Algiers, where they could serve the French Committee of National Liberation and meet the participating leaders from the Resistance. They wanted to be part of the great force preparing to storm the Nazi-held gates.

It appeared to be a good time to take my first holiday in four years. I got on the train and slept my way to Vancouver. The magnificence of the landscape on the way through the islands to Victoria dazzled me and heightened the joyful reunion with my mother, my stepfather and my brother Max, his wife Marjorie and their seven-year-old daughter Noreen. Asked about my work, I insisted that we forget the war and just enjoy the sea and the roses and my mother's wonderful blackberry steam puddings.

In the warm temperatures and sunshine of Vancouver Island, I relaxed for the first time since the Battle of France. Knowing that I loved picnics, my mother packed baskets and we went off to Saxe

Point, Sooke, William Head and beaches not too far from the city. Fishing in Brentwood Bay, with the mountains soaring on the mainland, the sun glinting off the peak of Mount Baker, visiting Butchart Gardens and having tea in that old quarry turned into a paradise of flowers were a complete change from the atmosphere of heroism and pain I had left behind in Free French House. Sometimes we got up early and took breakfast to Mount Douglas park, where bacon and eggs sizzled over the open fireplace and the smell of coffee whetted our appetites.

The previous night's coolness had brought out the fragrance of the towering fir trees; the sun sparkled across the blue straits and the cry of the seagulls announced the passing of the *Princess Marguerite* on its way to Vancouver. The seabirds sped towards the rocky outcroppings at sunset, squabbled, shouldered one another off, and bunched for the night. The fishing boats looked like delicate Japanese prints; in the twilight they moved steadily towards harbours, a fisherman standing near the prow, a light high up on a sailless mast, another to starboard, each mysteriously sharpened against the darkening sky. The tidy homes, green lawns, the flowers, the sedate old automobiles shining with elbow grease, the men in English knickers and the women in tweedy suits and stout boots — all this enabled me to forget for a time the terrible things going on in the world.

One day when we were picnicking at Saxe Point, four young soldiers arrived on motorcycles. One came over to ask where they could get some drinking water. He spoke English with difficulty, his accent was French. My stepfather always carried a gallon jug of water which we kept cool by placing it in the sea and mother offered to share our picnic. Eagerly I inquired in French where they had come from. Their joy when I spoke was pathetic, their astonishment even more so. They could not believe they would ever find anyone west of Montreal able to understand them. All four came from villages along the north shore of the St. Lawrence River and knew almost nothing about Canada beyond Ontario, which in their minds was Toronto. We talked all afternoon. They were homesick and told us they felt lost in the overpowering landscape of British Columbia.

One morning a long distance telephone call from Elisabeth interrupted my holiday. "I'm leaving for Algiers," she cried, her deep voice trembling with anticipation. "I'm so sorry to have to say goodbye like this, but I'm sure it won't be long now until you'll be coming overseas. Think of meeting again in Paris!"

"How did it happen?" I exclaimed enviously.

"A cable from Henri Bonnet. He's in charge of the Information Service and has something for me. I'm so excited, but I'll write from London. I'll tell them what we need for the service, and please carry on here in our right way. Let me know what you need — records, films, more statistics. Canadians like statistics. Think of it. When I get to Algiers I may be able to send messages to my family! I hear the Resistance people take them back and forth. Maybe I could go myself to France . . . ."

My own imagination caught fire. Might I be attached somewhere as a war correspondent or a liaison officer? The invasion had taken a giant step nearer in my mind. The Allies were taking town after town in Sicily. Lots of reporters would be accredited. My head was in a whirl, but I soon came down to earth. There was still so much to do in Canada, and it was only fair that the French nationals should go first.

Elisabeth would be gone when I got back to Ottawa. Gone too would be our discussions about the war, the future, about values, spiritual issues and poetry. The war had revealed for us the inhuman face of fascism. Everyone could understand communism, we thought. Hundreds of books had been written, and its exponents were only too glad to talk about it. But fascism was more subtle, more difficult to pin down. It came in ways the majority of people did not recognize until too late. It was not the ism of the poor. It was the worm that could enter the heart of the wealthy, industrialized nations where bread, shelter and overcoats for everyone were taken for granted. It led to dictatorship, and the dictator was usually the tool of a small, powerful group representing the top economic and military echelons of society. We considered ourselves wiser than the political scientists and economists. We had seen fascism firsthand.

Innocently we thought that the war had separated the patriots from the villains. The ambitious, the greedy, the power-hungry, the traitors had been exposed. They would be punished. The war had also revealed those who could be trusted because they had asked for nothing for themselves; they had offered their lives. We had a vision of a new world; the evil that Hitler had let loose would be destroyed. But the evils lurking in our own societies had been exposed too. They would be destroyed. Clean governments, purged of these elements, would be drawn from the thousands of people who had proven their purity, their worth. They would serve the people, rebuild the ravaged countries and establish a loftier set of values. Simplistic? Naive? Dreamers?

I would miss Elisabeth and all those long discussions. But I knew the anguish she had suffered in being separated from all those she loved, and I knew her dedication to her country. Now she would have some chance of communicating with her family to find out if they were all alive, not deported in reprisal for her activities with the Free French. Now I would get firsthand information about what was going on in Algeria. Elisabeth's departure meant that the war must be entering its last phase.

A few last-minute notes from Elisabeth awaited me in Ottawa. In one she enclosed a two-dollar bill and an apologetic few lines saying she had taken my suntan lotion. Would I send more if she could not get any in Algeria? In another I discovered that she had expected to fly directly from New York, but American officials refused to give her a visa. Her Canadian friends did not let her down. Wearing a Canadian uniform, Elisabeth left for London, via Halifax, in a troop ship.

"I'm so glad I came this way after all," she wrote from London. "I have been able to adjust to the Old World, see former colleagues and my London friends who have behaved marvellously, so calm and courageous. Also, thanks to General Vanier and Ed Ritchie (young diplomat at the Canadian High Commission) I have had a chance to talk to people about our work and the evolution of opinion in Quebec, the importance of unity among French and English speaking Canadians, and how in future we must have good relations between France and Canada."

After Elisabeth arrived in Algiers, her letters reflected shock and despair. "I write on the corner of a table. Material life is extraordinarily difficult. Everything is lacking, no office space, no phones, no transport, no lodging, no facilities, no restaurants, laundry, anything. In the nights the bombardments have given me my baptism of fire. The Americans mean well but they don't understand. They pay any high price and therefore you can't get a place to sleep or eat or work. Everything has to be 'requisitioned.' They don't realize; they have their own luxurious canteens. They don't know the state of us who arrive to work; but they build too many 'commissions' out of Vichy- ites. This is not our fault. The Vichyites have been in place here so long and the Americans still think they represent France.

"Public opinion abroad is not aware, and I am told all the American press correspondents except purely military ones have been sent home to the United States. I am so disappointed and despairing. The people should know the truth. Unfortunately Vichy elements are getting too much help and try to weaken the Resistance so strongly united behind General de Gaulle. The collaborators are afraid for their future once France is free. They fear France might prefer vodka to coca-cola. This is very serious, but true."

Algiers offended Elisabeth's great idealism. "I am so glad you aren't here," she said in one letter. "You would be bitterly disappointed as I am .... Instead of our poor, suffering France and the martyrs and the people, so many think only of their 'positions' and their selfish ambitions...."

While this disillusionment shook me, I think I already understood that, whatever else war does, it does not change human nature other than by preparing a climate in which its darker side can flourish.

After some weeks Elisabeth's letters changed. I felt her delight when she wrote, "General Vanier is here and he has been appointed the first Canadian ambassador to France. I am so happy to see him." In another letter, "I have met some of the Resistance leaders and they are wonderful. They are so pure and utterly selfless. They think only of how we can rebuild our country and cleanse it of those who have collaborated with the Germans to oppress our people. You would have to know how desperately unhappy and morally alone and 'different' I felt to understand my real joy in meeting these people at last. Inside France they have shared a common battle with us. These young resistants who come over from France carrying messages and documents think only of our country's freedom and how we will rebuild a France worthy of her name. There is no place for self when the soul of a nation is in jeopardy...."

Michel Dumont, who had arrived to replace Elisabeth, reminded me that all municipal and departmental officials had been appointed over the past four years by the Vichy regime, which was actually responsible to the German occupation administration. Meanwhile, the people had rallied behind the Resistance, with the exception of a small fraction of collaborators — the fascist-minded, the anti-British and those who suffered anti-communist paranoia. The clandestine National Council of Resistance in France, representing all segments of the population, had representatives now sitting in the quasi-provisional government in Algiers. The Resistance had also infiltrated the Vichy regime; its unknown members were sitting in official services throughout the country.

The Allies, especially the Americans, feared that disorder would follow the liberating armies as they marched across France. The Americans produced a plan and got reluctant participation from the British and Canadians to set up AMGOT.

Michel explained that AMGOT stood for Allied Military Government for Occupied Territories. The idea was to train teams of military officers to follow behind the armies and take over the civil administration of towns and departments as they were liberated, thus preventing chaos and bloodshed. The plan *seemed* reasonable; like so many think-tank plans, however, it did not consider the reaction of the people. "Can you imagine the situation?" Michel asked me. I had lived in France long enough to get the picture. Imagine Colonel Bill Jones of Detroit, Major John Brown of Lethbridge and two or three junior officers entering a French town and taking over the municipal office. Would the local people accept Colonel Jones as their mayor? It could have been funny were it not so ludicrous.

My French colleagues were appalled. How would AMGOT officers know which municipal officials were secret members of the Resistance, and which were Vichy sycophants? "In France," they said, "it will seem that one occupying force has been replaced by another — but worse — this time by our friends whom we were depending upon to set us free! The psychological effect will be disastrous!"

Henri Silvy, a member of the group of young French officers left in St. Pierre and Miquelon to help administer the islands, arrived at our office one day in the winter of 1943. He was on his way to the United States to attend, as an observer, one of the schools set up to train these AMGOT civil servants. He wrote to me: "They are studying French, and are even planning to use special money they've produced instead of our franc!"

When the National Council of Resistance in France got wind of AMGOT it immediately moved to circumvent it. In the brief space of time between the liberation of an area and the arrival of the AMGOT team to take over, the local Resistance movement would arrest the Vichy mayor, if he had not already left town. The municipal duties would be in the hands of Résistants known to the people and in whom they had confidence. Thus it was that fifty-one of the ninety-one departments (counties) of France were liberated by the Resistance itself, and when AMGOT officials arrived, they were welcomed by the smiling new French mayors and councillors. The AMGOT served a real and useful purpose. It offered to help the local authorities restore telephone, sewage, water, postal and transportation services, and its liaison officers brought in fuel, food and medical supplies.

The magnetism of the Free French headquarters in Algiers was becoming irresistible. Aline Chalufour, our young French lawyer, somehow found a way to go to London, hoping her destination would be Algiers. She had been helping with translation, and without her we could not handle the demand for information in English. I telephoned a friend, Naomi Lang, the women's editor of the Calgary *Herald*. I knew Naomi had studied French and had the kind of personality that would fit in. She did not hesitate when I asked her to join us.

Naomi's arrival posed the most difficult problem we had to face in Ottawa — finding accommodation. Thousands of people had come to the city during the war. Ottawa families were crowded together. Anybody with a spare room rented it, but when family members got jobs in Ottawa, boarders were bumped in favour of a relative. I had to move seven times in those four years.

Some of the lodgings offered — at inflated prices — were unbelievably bad. When I had inquired about one place, the landlady took me down to the basement, past the furnace and open coal bin and through a flimsy door into one long, narrow, windowless room. The space under the verandah had been excavated and the hole turned into a bedroom. In a corner of the basement, a thin partition had been erected, and inside was the smallest basin, shower and toilet I had ever seen. I did not take it.

Naomi got settled, as she said, "in a broom closet turned into a bedroom smaller than a nun's cell." Marguerite and Nellita were looking for an apartment and suggested Naomi join them. They found the downstairs of a house on Echo Drive and were overjoyed at their good luck.

Both Marguerite and Nellita had managed ingenious escapes from France. After a year and a half of occupation, Marguerite, who had been born in San Francisco, decided to claim American citizenship, even though her family had returned to France shortly after her birth. The American Embassy agreed, and she was able to get her whole family out. At the time her father was serving in India as a liaison officer with the British forces. When Marguerite came to Ottawa to work with us she was not yet eighteen.

Nellita's story was even more dramatic. Her family home was a converted *abbaye* at Poissy, not far from Paris. At the time of the capitulation Nell, who was very young and carefree, suddenly had to accept living under enemy occupation. "We didn't realize the full implications at first," she told me, "and having relatives in the unoccupied zone, it was a kind of sport to cross the demarcation line in defiance of the Germans."

Nellita's aunt was the wife of a well-known barrister in Toronto, Gordon Taylor. Mrs. Taylor was in France at the time of the armistice visiting her daughter after the birth of her grandchild. Her son-in-law was a French naval officer, and her daughter refused to consider returning to Canada. She was anxious, however, to have her mother return home and, if possible, take the newborn child, Philippe Mengin, with her.

With the insouciance of youth, Nellita offered to help: "Don't worry, I can get you and the baby across the demarcation line and from there it will be possible to go to Vichy and get the necessary papers through the Canadian representative. After all, you are a Canadian citizen and that should get you out." Mrs. Taylor agreed.

With her aunt and baby Philippe, Nell travelled south to a place near the line. On her other trips across she had been helped by Mme _____ who guided her by a little-travelled path still unknown to the German patrol. Leaving her aunt and the child, Nell went into the countryside to find her guide. On the way there she was approached by a man who said, "If you are going to see Mme_____, don't go. It is too dangerous."

"Why? How dangerous?" Nell demanded.

"Take care, Mademoiselle. Mme_____and the others were picked up by the Germans two days ago. The Germans are watching. You cannot go that way."

The man looked like an ordinary French countryman and she decided to tell him her story. He said he could take her to someone who could get her across the line another way if she would trust him. Nell followed him to a farmhouse some distance away. There she met his mother, who had a contract to pick up milk on the other side of the line and bring it back to the occupied zone. Could she get them across somehow in her canvas-covered wagon? She agreed to try. Nell, Mrs. Taylor and the baby would have to be hidden among the rattling, empty milk cans.

"The only thing, what if the baby cries?" the woman asked Nell. "I'm not afraid otherwise. I've been going back and forth every day for a year now. They used to look into the cart at first, but not any more. They're used to me."

Nell's solution was to give the baby a small glass of Dubonnet just before their departure. He fell asleep immediately.

"We crossed the line in safety. When we got there the guards just waved her through as usual and nobody looked inside. The baby slept for hours and I was terrified," Nell told me. "When we got to our destination we couldn't waken the baby and I was so afraid I might have killed him. However, several hours later he wakened, none the worse."

As anticipated, Mrs. Taylor got her papers and was able to proceed to Barcelona with her grandchild and Nellita. There they boarded a ship for New York.

"With my country occupied by the enemy I couldn't just sit around. I got a job in the French department of the University of Toronto and worked with the Free French in my spare time. Alain Savary, the Free French Governor in St. Pierre and Miquelon, asked me to go to the islands. I did ciphering and decoding of cables and messages and any other job I could do to help. Then I was needed here."

Marguerite and Nell came from a similar sheltered, proper background in France. Alberta-born Naomi's delightful sense of humour and charm won them over instantly. Still there were some problems. Naomi had friends in the military; the other girls, friends in the tiny beginning of a diplomatic corps. In both cases, when a party was given the gentlemen brought beverages; the young diplomats were most generous with wine. Bottles seemed to disappear quickly. Naomi thought that Marguerite and Nell seemed to be drinking a lot of wine. On the other hand, Nell and Marguerite were beginning to wonder if Naomi was an alcoholic — her scotch and rye seemed to vanish quickly. Both sides were too polite and embarrassed to mention anything.

At the same time, all three were beginning to think it peculiar that their landlady, who lived upstairs, often had late-night visitors. They never saw the visitors but always heard them clumping up and down the stairs leading to the front door. They also noticed that cab drivers taking them home often winked and sometimes tried to get familiar when they gave their address.

One Sunday afternoon Nell and Marguerite were entertaining friends at tea and were interrupted when the janitor streaked through their living-room and through the kitchen door to the basement, followed by the landlady clad only in a pair of black panties and a bra. The landlady returned holding a bottle. Stopping in the door, she drew herself up majestically and announced to the stunned tea party, "He stole my bottle!"

It became evident what was happening to the combined wine-cellar and liquor cache — their landlady was a boot-legger.

A few days after the tea party Naomi went to Montreal where she received a telegram telling her not to go back to the apartment on Echo Drive. The police had raided it. When her room-mates went home for lunch, they were not allowed to enter. The police were finally persuaded to give them "escorted" privileges to go in and remove their belongings.

The fate of the landlady is unknown.

After Elisabeth left I became vaguely aware that in the more than three years since I had returned to Canada I had not really come home. It was as though something in me had closed off and I was someone else, totally absorbed in my small war effort. Somehow I wanted to get away to London or Algiers because I could not equate Canada and war. Perhaps because I had not lived in eastern Canada before, I felt it to be almost as different from the West as a foreign country. Perhaps it had strengthened my sense of living in limbo. In some strange way my mind had simply shut out the fact that I was living in a real Canada, and that Ottawa was not as alien to me as a city in a foreign land.

Ottawa was an island, a fortress, from where I was conducting a war. The Chateau Laurier and the Parliament Buildings seemed to be unreal, picture postcards. The canal, the magnificent river and the distant Gatineau hills were beautiful, but like paintings or posters, they had no substance, nothing to hang onto. Now I began to realize that my French colleagues at Free French House must feel much as I did, though even more intensely. They were living in a dream landscape, a theatre set. One day the play would finish, the lights on the stage would go down while the lights all over the world would come on. Then we would all go home. Perhaps this helped to bring our little band together.

It had been a long pull. Between speaking engagements trying to alert Canadians to what they might expect, and carrying on our information activities, we had lost a lot of sleep. One after another members of the staff fell by the wayside with colds or flu, and struggled back to the office within a week or ten days, pale, but rested. My turn came in December 1943.

Lotta Hitchmanova of the Unitarian Services, Madame Thiberti, International Labour Office representative (Section for the Protection of Women and Children), and I had dinner together on Christmas Eve. We talked until midnight about how soon after a sucessful invasion could the first food shipments be made. By the time we broke up I could hardly hear what was being said.

At home I took a stiff rum toddy, soda and aspirin and went to bed. In the morning my sinuses and ears were blocked, my head felt as though it had been inflated with a bicycle pump. It looked as though I should call a doctor — my temperature was 103.

The doctor arrived around noon, unshaven, bleary-eyed and looking as though he had slept in a laundry chute. There had been a train wreck at Almonte, a few miles west of Ottawa, around suppertime. He had spent the night, along with other doctors and nurses, caring for the wounded as they were released from the train. His face was pinched and glazed with fatigue. "I'll never forget picking bits of lace and silk along with slivers of glass out of the gashes and cuts, ground into the flesh of the young girls' faces, arms and shoulders. My God!" The doctor was a man of great sensitivity and I felt guilty to have left a message asking him to come.

He checked my ears and chest and had a new drug called sulpha sent over. On his second visit he told me that sulpha had spared me a double mastoid operation. "We almost never have to operate for mastoid any more, thanks to sulpha," he said. "It's almost impossible to show students the operation now; only when we have people from the North or distant rural districts."

A week later, feeling very wobbly, I met Hilda Turner, public relations officer with the CPR in Montreal. One of her jobs was promotion for the luxurious Montebello Lodge in Montebello, Quebec. "You're not fit to go back to work," she said. "Come out to Montebello for a few days as my guest." Unaware that I would mark another turning point in my life, I accepted.

Fortunately my visit coincided with the January thaw. In the mornings I sat, wrapped in blankets, against the south wall of the lodge and drank in the sun. The air was crisp and clear, the sky blue and cloudless, the ground twinkled with sugar-crystal snow. On the edge of a nearby roof icicles dripped diamond drops. My mind held that wonderful emptiness that comes with undiluted pleasure.

In the afternoons I went for walks along the trails through the woods. The evergreen bows were laden with snow and I delighted in the heady fragrance of pine and balsam. Only the pattern of small, animal footprints marked the snow. It was on one of these walks that, for the first time since the Battle of France, my life seemed to come into focus.

I touched the bark of a silver birch. It was real. It was not a theatre set. I picked up a fistful of snow and squeezed it. It was snow and my childhood was in the ball in my hand. I saw that miracle of a world turning blue for just a few minutes before dusk, deepening the shadows, tinting the snow and filling the ruts with that mysterious Laurentian blue light that seems to glow before it fades. Tears filled my eyes. This sudden awakening was so unexpected that I could not believe I had ever been so blind. I was shaken. It was a vision that had substance, a vision that was real. I knew I was home.

When I returned to Ottawa, I saw the city with new eyes. I wished I could be a young child again and see the Chateau Laurier as a castle in fairyland and the Parliament Buildings as royal palaces guarded by red-coated mounties. I walked along the canal to my basement apartment on the Driveway, touching the trees, choosing one beautiful old maple to be my very own, seeing the children in their bright-coloured toques and snowsuits. I saw the pleasant homes surrounded by so much space, lawns and flower beds sleeping beneath the snow. I saw the business section, still dominated by the Peace Tower and church spires, emblems of the spirit, emblems of the people.

At dusk I walked up Parliament Hill, admiring the beauty of the sixteen-sided library and gazed down the Ottawa River, across golden piles of logs to the Gatineau Hills. In the purple twilight I was so thrilled I could hardly contain it. I was *home*. Ottawa was my home as much as any other part of Canada. All of Canada belonged to me and never would I feel an outsider in any part of it. I was grateful that no bombs, no enemies had destroyed this lovely city, as Coventry and Rotterdam and Warsaw and Dresden and hundreds of towns and villages in Europe had been destroyed.

This experience led me to reflect on the reasons for the lack of understanding between eastern and western Canadians, between English- and French-speaking Canadians. It was not a problem of language. Language, I realized, only added another dimension, but one so visible that it easily became a scapegoat. The real problem lay in an inner need that everyone shares — the need for a place that is familiar, a place to call home. I realized that France had solved a problem in Canada for me; France had given me the capability to see my French-speaking compatriots as Canadian as myself, and Quebec every bit as much a part of Canada as any other province.

Now I understood what Sheila MacDonald (sister of Malcolm Mac-Donald, British High Commissioner to Canada at the time) meant when I asked her what had made her such an enthusiastic supporter of the Free French. Was it just that they were allies in the war? "My impression before the war was that the French and English were always sniping at one another," I said. "What makes the difference?"

Sheila thought a moment and then said, "I think it may be because we are both Europeans and find ourselves in North America in a civilization very different from our own. I feel more comfortable with the French than even with my best Canadian and American friends. It isn't something one speaks about. Perhaps it is because we share many of the same attitudes, ways of thinking, values. We are more aware of it now than in peace time. Then we took these things we had in common for granted." She laughed. "We could afford to snipe at one another then. Perhaps we had no need to explain ourselves, we understood a great deal about one another without explanation. In this we are European, even though as French and English we still have great differences."

I had not understood exactly what she meant — but now I knew that the reactions she was speaking of were not intellectual, they were emotional and instinctive responses.

The whole question of bilingualism and mutual understanding of the rich endowment Canadians had in possessing two cultures suddenly became very important to me. If the size of our country with its different needs, ideas and attitudes in the various regions tended to misunderstanding, we still had some common experiences to glue us together. Cultural activities, the arts and languages know no boundaries; they express the soul of a people. They are our limitless horizons. I thought about what we share: the love of the land, the influence of our broad landscapes, the smell of our forests and the grain ripening in the sun, even our enormous size with our freedom to move and live in many landscapes and call all of them our own. I felt this had a great bearing on what being a Canadian means — the need for space, the love of solitude, the desire to be often alone, alone on a river, in the woods, on mountain trails, or just walking across crocus-covered pastures. It is this need to breathe that finds an echo in every Canadian heart and shapes the spirit of the people.

I went back to work a different person. Now I saw my work with the Free French as even more important. I knew that France had given me a great gift. Having lived by then in an almost totally French environment for almost ten years, I thought I understood the heritage of my French-speaking fellow Canadians and why they clung to it so fiercely. I would always be grateful to France, to the example of my French colleagues whose terrible pain and grief over the loss of their country had caused me to reflect and discover exactly who I was. I think I knew that I would not be returning to France to live. What I had to do must be done in Canada. I wanted to help other English-speaking Canadians share my experience.

fourteen

On June 6, 1944, the Allies landed in France. Who will ever forget the shiver of joy that day? The exultation, the trepidation, the relief as the Germans fell back and our armies were on the beaches. The beach names — Juno for the Canadians, Sword and Gold for the British, Utah and Omaha for the Americans. They were landing in Normandy! There was laughter and joy and tears in our offices as our French staff eagerly read out the names, Bernières-sur-Mer, St. Aubin, Bayeux, Courseulles, Arromanches! No doubt this time. The beginning of liberation had finally begun.

On August 25, 1944, the Allied armies, led by the French Army under General Philippe Leclerc, Comte de Hautecloque, entered Paris, which had been liberated by the French Resistance.

A letter from Elisabeth described that historic day:

"This is about the fifth letter I am trying to write to you. Conditions are just impossible for one to settle down and have a few minutes peace. Think of it, I entered Paris behind Leclerc, the dream of dreams! I was in the very next jeep that morning. I was so lucky, I saw the Germans capitulate at 4 p.m. on August 25th at the Gare Montparnasse, where Leclerc's command post was; de Gaulle arrived at 5 p.m. with Konig, d'Argenlieu, Boislambert, Courcel, etc. — all the top ones. He read through the texts and then drove to rue St. Dominique, quite an exciting drive. We were shot at, near St. François.

"I went down the Champs-Elysées in a jeep beside the cortège and was at the Te Deum where we were fired on again in front and inside Notre Dame Cathedral. All this can be told in a few words. It was above all we could have imagined. The atmosphere of feverish joy was just too exciting. The boys of Leclerc were greeted as heroes, but some got killed a few hours after this greeting. All excitement, intoxicating, rapture, yet death and suffering still at the door. This remains true.

"I found my family the very first evening, same address, everybody alive but my uncle de Touchet who was shot in Caen. I was received like the prodigal child, just the 'fatted calf' was missing, but we drank champagne . . . ."

With Paris now free, postal services were re-established, letting loose at once hundreds of thousands of letters and parcels. The first letters I received from Irène, Hélène, Charlotte and Madeleine made me cry with joy and pain. I was touched by their effort to spare me pain. They told me briefly of friends I had lost and their anxiety because they were no longer receiving letters from their prisoner-of-war husbands, brothers or fiancés. They did not dwell on it. Instead the letters overflowed with gratitude for regaining their freedom and descriptions of the liberation. The children of friends had created flags out of scribbler paper and painted them to represent French, British and American flags. I was asked to send a Canadian flag because the children did not know what it looked like.

On August 29th de Gaulle arrived for his first visit to Canada. He was received with deference and enthusiasm. Mackenzie King hardly left his side and his address in front of the Peace Tower drew the largest crowd I had ever seen in Ottawa. His press conference won cheers from the reporters, and in compiling our report we did not find one critical editorial. In Quebec and Montreal the visit was equally successful. Nothing could have been more satisfying to the small band at Free French House. Finally, the Canadian government had given recognition where it was due.

At the end of October a cable came from Georges Bidault, former Resistance leader in France and now Minister of Foreign Affairs in the Provisional Government. I was asked to go to France for several months to observe the conditions and needs of the civilian population, and see for myself how the occupation had left the country and the people. The next day Nellita told me that she was being recalled to Paris and we would be travelling together. She had not seen her family for four years.

By the time transportation arrangements were made and our travel papers were ready it was Christmas. Nell and I left at the end of December, taking with us, in addition to personal luggage, eight or ten canvas duffle-bags as high as my shoulder and packed with necessities friends had given me to distribute in France — powdered milk, cocoa, coffee beans, tea, tinned butter, salmon, aspirin, vitamins, cough medicine, toothpaste and brushes, needles, thread, knitting wool, wool material, snowsuits for children, paper and envelopes, chocolate. The duffle-bags weighed hundreds of pounds and everybody scoffed at our determination to get them to their destination. Nevertheless, we had them moved to the Ottawa station and put on the train for Halifax. Though neither one of us could lift even one of the bags, we were optimistic.

"How do you think you are going to get them aboard ship?" we were asked. "They'll never allow you to take all that as luggage. And then to France? You'll never make it."

But when we arrived in Halifax, Nell and I asked several RCMP to help us take the duffle-bags to the ship. At the ship, the naval officer pushed his cap back, looked dubious, and then called a couple of sailors and told them to stow the duffle-bags somewhere in a dry place. "I don't know how you are going to get them up to London from whichever port we're ordered to dock in, let alone to France," he said. "There aren't any porters now. You'll be on your own." We were delighted with ourselves for having managed to get them this far, and would worry about those problems later.

Our ship was a banana boat. Most of the inside had been torn out and refitted with dormitories to carry troops. The ship also carried a few passengers and the idea was to keep both bananas and passengers cool. It was hardly the ship for crossing the North Atlantic in January!

Our convoy slipped out of Halifax harbour sometime in the night. In the morning all that was visible on the heaving, gray sea was a long line of ships, corvettes patrolling on either side like anxious sheep dogs. A storm that had been hovering on the horizon finally struck and our small ship pitched and rolled. Inevitably, I went to bed after contributing a full meal to the fish. Until the weather cleared a few days later my diet consisted of tea and soda crackers, the only combination of food willing to remain with me.

We were very lucky to have a cabin. Most of the passengers were women: Salvation Army, St. John's Ambulance, Red Cross and CWACS (Canadian Women's Army Corps). They had to share makeshift dormitories even colder than our cabin. The women came from all over Canada and were afraid the war might be over before they got there. A record player played the desperate music of the "Warsaw Concerto" over and over again, conjuring up pictures we had seen in the newsreels of Warsaw burning.

One morning we woke to discover that we were in the English Channel and would be docking in London instead of Liverpool — another duffle-bag problem solved! We also learned that the last two ships of our convoy had been torpedoed just outside Halifax harbour. I wired my mother that I had arrived safely.

Sailors carried our duffle-bags ashore and stowed them in a freight shed on the dock. We knew they would be safe there until we could find a means of getting them over to France. We started happily off for Carlton Gardens and were astounded at the sights along the way. The newsreel pictures we had seen paled before reality; the sight of crumpled buildings and rubble jolted us. Oxford Street looked like a giant comb with most of its teeth broken. A building here and there was standing, the rest were one storey high with temporary roofs or just fenced off. The streets, however, were teeming with people — somehow those millions of tons of stone and rubble had been removed. In back streets we could see how it had been pushed back and hidden from the main thoroughfares.

It was an even greater shock to see how people were going about their business in a normal way, clustered at intersections, gazing in windows where windows still existed, pushing baby carriages. The red buses rolled along merrily; the bobbies directed traffic calmly; a bomb-crumpled curb was edged by a huge patch of new cement. Nell and I stared at one another. She said wryly, "London as usual."

At Carlton Gardens we presented French officials with the problem of finding us a place to stay. It was not an easy assignment. Almost no accommodation could be found in London. At last a woman in the Information Service found us space through a friend who belonged to a women's club. Two military cots in the basement, not far from the furnace, was the best she could do. The cots were narrow and only two or three inches off the floor. Both Nell and I were afraid of rats. However, we wrapped ourselves up in the gray army blankets and slept like dormice. At breakfast everyone was talking about the air raid in the middle of the night. We had not heard a thing.

Someone managed to get a double room for us at Durrant's Hotel, not far from Paddington Station. This old hostel, with its permanent lodgers, was a heaven-sent refuge. Every morning we were amused to see the elderly residents, usually sitting alone, each face hidden by a newspaper propped against a toast rack. On some tables a tiny pot of jelly or jam disappeared when its owner returned upstairs. We managed, after some searching, to buy a little jar of extremely pale strawberry jam to carry back and forth too. Other meals were taken out since our search for transportation to France, including our duffle-bags, could find us anywhere in London at mealtime.

We sallied forth optimistically every morning only to return disappointed. We combed London, followed every lead offered. We haunted the docks looking for someone who might be crossing the Channel, and we were told that every ship leaving had more important things to carry than our cumbersome bags. At Canada House I was delighted to find Mary Harding of Regina. Mary was the love of Canadians on leave. Posted at a counter near the entrance, she took and delivered messages and mail, suggested places to eat, advised on lodgings, and often turned her own apartment over to stranded Canadian service men on leave, who slept on her floor during the day while she was at work. But even Mary could not help us.

Nell and I were downcast and beginning to believe that our scoffing friends in Ottawa were right. At Canada House we made another plea, this time to John Holmes of External Affairs, always a warm supporter of the Free French. No luck, but he offered consolation by taking us to a little French restaurant where we had the best coquille Saint-Jacques I have ever eaten. "Something's happened to the food here," we told our friends. In spite of the severe rationing of all dairy products, eggs, sugar, chocolate, fruit and goodness knows what else, we were given the address of several excellent little restaurants. Gillian, one of my London friends, explained. "You can thank the refugees. The only way some found to make a living was by opening a tiny restaurant. We've learned to eat European food as well as drink good coffee. The good old prime roast beef and Yorkshire pudding is only a memory." In fact, we found excellent restaurants run by Italians, French, Greeks, Belgians and Arabs.

The new London was awesome. Streets and restaurants were a babel of languages. Theatres opened at 6 or 6:30 p.m. and were crowded. Pubs and bars bubbled with laughter and conversation — no longer any inhibitions about speaking to strangers. The black-out at night was filled with giggles, chuckles, fragments of animated conversation, occasional curses and even song. "How has all this come about?" I asked Gillian, my expert on her home town. "People speak to me everywhere, in the tube, at lunch counters, the streets and stores. This morning on the bus everybody seemed to be talking. It was like a party. What happened to all that English reserve?"

"We've been living in the dark for nearly five years. It does wonders for one's inhibitions," she laughed. "I suppose we aren't so shy now."

The morale was high. At noon free concerts by musicians of the calibre of Myra Hess were going on in the National Gallery. The place was freezing; everyone was bundled to the eyes, but not even standing room was available unless you arrived very early. I can still see Dame Myra Hess, wearing a fur coat, her feet in heavy shoes and her blue fingers flying as she sat before the piano.

V-1's, known familiarly as buzz-bombs, put-putted their way across London skies. They were rather slow and the RAF could shoot many down before they reached the city. If one was just overhead, people hesitated: that was the second before the put-put stopped and the bomb dropped. An explosion and the people moved on again, picking up the threads of their conversation as though nothing had happened. The V-2's were more demoralizing. Bigger, swifter, travelling very high, they simply dropped out of the sky and we heard the long sigh of their coming after the explosions. One morning Nell and I were almost blown out of bed by a nearby blast. We discovered later that the bomb had damaged Paddington Station. When we arrived to take the underground it was roped off, the entrance blocked by debris.

No matter how serious a situation, there is always a lighter side. Mr. Collier had been my guardian angel in London when I had first arrived ten years earlier. Now well beyond retirement age, he was still in charge of the *Winnipeg Free Press* office facing Canada House across Trafalgar Square. He had befriended me so many times. He had advised and introduced me to London editors; helped me out of a sticky situation in Italy; managed an invitation to a garden party at Buckingham Palace; let my mother know back in 1940 that I had escaped from France and arrived safely in London. As usual, Mr. Collier tried to help Nell and me find a way to get our duffle-bags to France. Even he failed.

One day I went to lunch at his home in Hampstead Heath. It looked out over the roofs of London. After the meal I heard the sound of the V-1's and Mr. Collier and I went to the window. We could see the slowly cruising buzz-bombs. There were three of them. We waited with bated breath. The silence was broken by Mrs. Collier saying plaintively, "Oh, do close that window, dear. The flies will get in."

After days of frustration, we found our problem mysteriously solved. A way to get our duffle-bags to Paris had been secretly arranged. Someone said, "I can't tell you how they are going, but you may leave any time and you'll have them within a week."

Jubilantly, we hurried off to make final arrangements. We decided to have a look at St. Paul's Cathedral, having heard that the area had been heavily bombed. When we got there we saw that almost all the buildings between St. Paul's and the Thames were in a rubble, with more ruins on the other three sides. In some way the great church looked liberated, in spite of the scaffolding. Inside a contingent of workmen were making repairs. Then we noticed a very well-dressed, middle-aged man, accompanied by a woman in a chic soft leather suit and six girls, ranging from about eighteen down to five or six. As we passed the group in the cathedral I noticed that several of the girls were wearing almost identical coats of a long-haired, reddish-brown fur. The younger ones wore blanket-cloth coats trimmed with the same fur. The family were in animated conversation in French.

Nell poked me and whispered, "It must be Baron de Hautecloque. I heard before we left Ottawa that he had six or seven daughters. I'm sure he's the new French Ambassador to Ottawa. I wonder what they are doing here? I'm going to speak to them."

We turned and Nell spoke. Indeed it was the new French ambassador, first cousin to the famous General Leclerc. He and his family were on their way to Ottawa. We were showered with questions and agreed to meet later.

No doubt Mme de Hautecloque noticed my curious glances at her beautiful kidskin suit and the odd collection of coats on her daughters. Her eyes twinkling, she said, "The Paris couturiers presented me with this suit. They thought I should look well to represent France. Otherwise I'd be wearing a bed cover too."

We all burst out laughing. I had learned something of the ingenuity of Mme de Hautecloque. What to do, faced with moving to Canada in mid-winter and the Paris stores stripped of warm clothing? What to do? Patronizing the black market was absolutely infra dig. But in those days and perhaps today (unless Brigitte Bardot has changed their minds), it was every French girl's ambition to possess a fur comforter for her bed. Undoubtedly the de Hautecloques had them. Three of the coats worn by the de Hautecloque daughters had been made out of comforters, the fur left over used to trim blanket-origin coats for the younger girls.

Mme Madeleine de Hautecloque was an admirable woman. After the French armistice, she took her children to the family château at Bermicourt, not far from Arras and the Channel. The area had been fought over. German launching pads for the V-1's were placed in the area and drew heavy bombing from the RAF. One of the "pads" was in the château grounds, which put the family in grave danger. Nevertheless, Mme de Hautecloque turned her home into a refuge for war victims, the salons and safer underground cellars accommodated wounded civilians. In the months before D-Day, when the V-1 attacks on Britain were at their height, the RAF tried desperately to take out the launching sites. Many people were killed or wounded. Mme de Hautecloque and her older daughters went into the nearby villages and helped to gather up the wounded and the dying lying in the streets. I remarked that it must have been a terrible experience for them, especially such young girls.

"My daughters are not afraid to face blood, and it does not hurt them to see the result of war," she told me grimly. "They know how to take care of the sick and wounded. They must face reality if they are to grow up to be strong women to face the postwar problems."

After the de Hautecloques settled in at the Ottawa Embassy, the girls, whose education also included sewing and cooking, had to take turns in the kitchen a week at a time. They prepared luncheon for their parents whenever there was not an official luncheon. The cook supervised but only with advice. "I wonder what they're going to serve up to me today for lunch?" Baron de Hautecloque murmured to me stoically one day. "I hope it's not another of those tuna fish concoctions."

PART THREE

Liberation

fifteen

The next day, about January 23 or 24, we sailed for France. It was raining and the Channel was at its miserable worst. We emerged at Dieppe too wan to notice much, and boarded the only passenger train running anywhere in France. Nell and I were shocked as we stared out at the desolation of the countryside, towns and blasted stations looming in the dusk. We literally crept over every small bridge.

On the train we ate soup, eggs stuffed with mushrooms, a mixture of vegetables, apples, wine and coffee. The coffee was undrinkable. Still, I thought it must give foreigners a wrong impression — letters I had received told me that my friends had not seen an egg in months. I spoke to the waiter. "My family in Paris doesn't get anything like this to eat," he said. "Here it is possible to get eggs. They are saved for the visitors. Don't believe that this is France today, Mademoiselle."

"We worked fourteen hours a day, seven days a week to get the port cleaned up and this train running," the trainman told us. He looked very proud. "Before the war we had nearly 1,000 first-class carriages, now we have less than 140, all badly used and being repaired. There is so much to be rebuilt. The Allies had to blow up our stations. We understood. It was necessary and we bear no resentment. Without that we would not be free. Many of my comrades died blowing up the engines they had driven for years. Do you know how an engineer feels about his engine? Like a horseman loves his horse. But he blew it all the same, because the Germans were shipping ammunition to the Channel."

At 6 a.m. the Gare du Nord was already filled with people. We would never forget our first impression: hundreds of people "clack-clacking" in wooden-soled shoes, shabby, pinched, sad-eyed. In our warm and comfortable clothing we could not meet their eyes. Everyone seemed to be wearing their entire wardrobes on their backs. The extraordinary combinations of colours were terrible, but evidence of the stark need for warmth. "It's not French!" Nellita kept repeating. "No Frenchwoman would wear such colours together." Her eyes were filled with tears. "What has happened to our poor France?"

My first view of liberated Paris came when we emerged from the metro at the Trocadero station. Below the terrace of the Palais de Chaillot, the city lay still in the grip of what had been the coldest winter of the war. Trees, bare and stark, lined the shining ribbon of the Seine; above the rooftops floated the domes of Sacre Coeur; every street recalled a still life of Utrillo or Pissaro; the delicate dome of Les Invalides gleamed in the morning air which, as always, seemed to be compounded of blue and rose and dusted with powdered silver. High above the Eiffel Tower the Tricolour fluttered free against the pale sky. The sight of it brought a lump to my throat.

To the right and to the left were the Museum of Modern Art and the Museum of Man. I wondered if the beautiful collections of Indian and Eskimo art were still intact. Was the magnificent totem pole from British Columbia still standing proudly at the entrance of the Museum of Man? Leaning on the balustrade, Nell and I looked across the Seine to l'Ecole Militaire, then left to Notre Dame, and saw the city through a thin, silvery mist. Gradually the mist cleared and a bright sun sparkled on the Seine. Both Nell and I found it difficult to find something to say. We were back!

A room had been reserved for me in the Claridge Hotel on the Champs-Elysées. The entire hotel had been requisitioned for the use of the foreign press. The warmest room in the unheated Claridge was the foyer. There body heat, fueled by alcohol, took the chill off as correspondents sat around, glass in hand, sketching their versions of the progress of the war. The bones of the latest Allied moves were picked clean as they pontificated, pointing out, "Now what they should have done..."

Too excited to sleep, I spent the rest of the day paying nostalgic visits to my old haunts. After the terrible damage in London, so much ruin between Dieppe and Paris, I could hardly believe that the streets and buildings I had grown to love were really intact. No, not quite. Though the central city had escaped relatively unscathed, the people had endured four years of occupation — and it took something from their souls. The industrial suburbs were in ruins from the heavy RAF bombing, bombing that Parisians had welcomed. Britons had suffered equally in another way, but had fought in freedom.

The walls everywhere were pitted with machine-gun fire. Notre Dame, the Prefecture, the Concièrgerie — where Marie Antoinette, Robespierre and so many others had languished, awaiting execution — Place St. Michel and the streets of the Latin Quarter were pock-marked with bullet holes. Whole chunks were taken out of the stone. In every street bits of paper were pasted on walls: "Jacques . . . killed here August 25th." "Raoul and Madeleine, age 18 and 20, killed August 24th. Vive la France." Or simply, "Jean, August 25th." More names and dates were printed on sidewalks. Snipers had killed them while they were resisting, for the Parisians themselves had the glory, almost on their own, of liberating their beloved city.

The flower borders of the Tuilerie Gardens were being readied for spring planting. Remembering the beautiful flowers, I spoke to one of the gardeners. He shook his head. "No, not flowers, vegetables to feed the people."

Walking through the streets I had to pinch myself to believe it was true. What a price had been paid! For so long it had seemed the war would never end and we would never be back on the Continent again. But here we were, and the war was still on.

The chairs we used to rent for a few centimes in the Luxembourg Gardens were still there, rusted and looking ready for the scrap heap. They had not had their spring paint for five years. The Boulevard St. Michel had its quota of students, hurrying with hunched shoulders in frayed coats towards the cafés. I was beginning to get used to the clacking of wooden soles. At the metro station, on the corner of the Boulevard St. Michel and rue Gay-Lussac, to my joy I saw a familiar face — the flower woman. Beside her was a man, wrapped in blankets sitting in a wheelchair. She was arranging her flowers. She turned and her eyes searched my face and then she actually threw her arms around me. "Yes, yes, yes, it is! It is Mademoiselle du Canada. The war must truly be over!"

I shared her feeling. She brought all my memories rushing back: the one rose, the one carnation, the bunches of anemones, the Parma violets, however few, she always wrapped in a thin paper, tied with gold string and attached a big gold sticker. She introduced me to her husband as we babbled on excitedly. She carefully replaced a shawl that had slipped from his shoulders, for he was partially paralyzed. And what of her son? A prisoner-of-war and still no news. I asked for a few sprays of mimosa. She took a bundle and, though I protested vigorously, it was in vain. Apologizing that she could no longer wrap them, she wiped the stems with a cloth. It was impossible to pay her. I remembered to take a package of Nescafé, some cigarettes and a bar of soap the next time I passed.

It was only a few steps to the Foyer International. Would Miss Watson and Madame Fournier still be there? They were, and we fell into one another's arms. Over coffee Miss Watson told me about their war adventures. "After you all left I quickly filled the Foyer with French students. Poor girls, they were so delighted to get in — for the cafeteria of course — and we had some heat until the Americans joined the war. The Germans tried to requisition the Foyer several times. I protested. No real trouble the first two years while the United States was neutral. By that time I knew the Gauleiter in this quarter and gave him a cup of decent coffee once in awhile. He wasn't a bad sort. Some might call that collaboration but it wasn't. It was my duty to protect the young girls. Later the Germans tried everything — cutting fuel, electricity, and then threats. But I kept reminding them that the Germans prided themselves on being 'Korrect.' It worked. Thank God I didn't have to deal with the Gestapo.

"Our troubles weren't over. As soon as the French arrived they wanted the Foyer too, but gave up when I explained that even the Germans were too 'compassionate' to turn all these young girls into the street! Well, then the Americans arrived and thought that it was my duty as an American to make the Foyer available. When I told them my story they didn't have the face to insist.

Miss Watson laughed triumphantly, her blue eyes snapping, her stiff white hair standing on end. I could still see her standing four-square in the Foyer entrance as I was about to leave Paris nearly five years earlier when her last words had been, "The whole German army won't get me out of here!"

The reunion with my dear French friends was a mixture of joy and sorrow, for I had to learn of all those who were missing, those who were still prisoners-of-war or in concentration camps, those who had been shot or who had died prematurely from privation. I had to look into those eyes, brimming with love, but dull with sorrow and realization of what human beings can do to one another. I had to see the pale, unhealthy skin, the starch-bloated stomachs of the children, the weary, pinched faces of mothers and friends who veiled their pain to spare me. I went to see Paul's sister Charlotte. Her big black eyes were too large for her face and her two little girls so thin. Her husband had nearly died of tuberculosis. But our happiness at seeing one another again, knowing it meant that France was almost free, could not be dampened.

What a reunion it was. I took some coffee, soap and chocolate that I had carried in my suitcase. How could one forget the delight in the faces of little Annie and Jacqueline? Annie accepted the chocolate with a solemn "Merci." She opened it under the intent gaze of Jacie, and broke off four of the small squares. First she offered one to me — Charlotte signalled to me to take it — then to her mother and sister. She took a piece herself, closed the wrapper and put the bar in a drawer. It made my heart ache. Yes, they had tasted chocolate. Following the French army's entry into Paris, the Americans came, and Annie had stood on the curb waving her homemade flag. A soldier had given her a chocolate bar. Much as they wanted to eat it at once, they doled it out sparingly, one small square per day.

Charlotte brought a bar of "soap" from the kitchen. It looked like a piece of slate, iron gray, gritty, a mixture of sand and lye. "Nothing is white any more," Charlotte said, tears in her eyes. "The sheets, towels, underwear, the children's clothes, all a dirty gray." I asked Annie to bring a bowl of water and an egg-beater. I dropped in a bar of Ivory soap and suggested that she turn the beater. Her astonishment and delight at seeing soap bubbles, the way Jacqueline clapped her hands and crowed almost caused me to break down. Charlotte protested. "Oh, no, no. Don't waste it." Annie cried, "Maman, Maman, it's white! The soap is white! It's so beautiful!" Charlotte took the soap out and carefully dried it, but let the girls play with the soapy water as long as the bubbles were left. Then she said, "Now keep the water for washing tonight." I decided my first parcel after returning home would contain two bubble-pipes. I kept the bar of grit Charlotte had shown to me. I have it still to remind me of what I must never forget.

The morning after my visit Charlotte called. "Glad! Glad!" she gasped, "one more thing I will never forgive the Germans. Last night André and I had our first cup of coffee, real coffee. No longer that awful roasted barley. But can you imagine the worst? We couldn't sleep a wink!"

I found my friends, one after another, at least those who were still in Paris. I had not had a chance to say goodbye to Irène after those nights together on the road in 1940. Now I found her, thin, colourless and looking very ill. Her weakness showed in every line of her body. But in her eyes lurked a spark of her old mischievous humour. Soon she would be bedridden for many months from decalcification of the spine, the result of years of malnutrition. The next year Professor Henri Laugier sent Irène to Canada on a six-month scholarship to study child psychology and to stay with me. She needed the Canadian dairy products to regain her health. Irène Lézine became one of the world authorities on infant psychology. She died in 1985.

I received a ration book and decided to try a different restaurant for lunch every day. I lunched in restaurants in the 16th and 8th arrondissments — the areas of the affluent — and in the 5th, 6th, 7th, 18th and 20th — areas of the working class, students and the very poor. This gave me a cross-section of what food was being served in Paris. There was little difference. Nineteen forty-five was the year of the cauliflower, after three or four rutabaga winters. I do not think I had a lunch or dinner that did not include cauliflower. Occasionally I saw a potato. As spring came I had dandelion salads, beets, turnips, carrots and dried beans or lentils in small quantities — never meat, butter, eggs, or sweets. Dessert was invariably a small yellow apple. By the time I returned to Canada at the end of April I had lost twenty-one pounds.

One night at the little restaurant where I often went for dinner, the owner stopped beside me and whispered, "On Sunday come at nine o'clock for your dinner. You are invited." I was surprised. The restaurant was never open on Sunday. My curiosity was aroused. When I arrived, I recognized other customers who were regulars. Triumphantly, the owner and his wife carried in from the kitchen plates of hot, delectable omelets garnished with water cress. The pleasure in the faces of the customers only reflected that of our hosts. They poured the table wine and we toasted Paris, the Allies, liberty, omelets, and shook hands all around. My ears burned with all the praise I heard for Canada. We were not allowed to pay one franc. The proprietor told me they had gone to the country early in the morning to a village where they had relatives who owned a nearby farm. The fresh bread, eggs and cress had been their gift. The proprietor and his wife had decided to share the bonanza with their faithful customers and me, the guest from Canada. It is now a heartwarming memory.

The warmth of the welcome from friends was genuine: perhaps one reason was that my presence was proof they were free again. At the same time I slowly began to feel that my presence had an element in it that was also painful, almost a subconscious affront. French friends, returning home from exile, have told me that they had the same uneasiness. It could not be defined in words. Gradually I got the impression that somewhere in our relationship there was a block, an area that could not be reached, a corner I could not enter, something that had not been there when I left France. For want of a better description, I felt some sort of barrier closing off a spiritual sensitivity, a protective curtain around a soul that had been "seared." It was as though they had passed through fire, their skin blistered until the surface of the personality was so raw and so excruciatingly sensitized to pain that even a wrong word, a look of sympathy, would make them scream. It seemed to me that even my closest friends instinctively shrank into themselves at the slightest mention of what they had endured.

Unconsciously I began choosing my words carefully, at the same time knowing that I could never be careful enough. I felt that my friends had been waiting to unburden themselves, to ease their pain and blur the sharp edges of their memories. But when I got there they could not. They could not find words to express something that could only be understood by sharing the experience. No matter how much they wanted to unburden their hearts, they could not communicate what the occupation had done to them. Even their own compassion held them back. They wanted to spare me suffering. So there was an invisible barrier which, in time, I accepted.

Realization began one day when I went to one of the Paris stations: a train was expected from Germany, bringing the first group of women from a liberated concentration camp. The platform was crowded with people hoping to find one of their own family among those returning. The train came in slowly, its windows overflowing with flowers. At every station as the train crossed France, people had stood with their arms full of flowers for these women. At each carriage entrance the women began to step out to the platform. Many were still wearing the striped garments of the concentration camp; it looked as though this garment — in February weather — was the only thing they had. Every sort of covering served as shoes; there were no stockings; legs and arms were emaciated. Some of the women had short hair, and some attempt had been made to make it look more presentable. Others had obviously torn a strip off the bottom of their striped shifts and wound it around their heads. We learned later that their heads were shaved. In the camps all heads were shaved on arrival, and as a punishment for the smallest contravention of the rules or out of pure malice, they were shaved over and over again. Nothing is worse for a woman. It strips her of her confidence, her pride, her dignity and her hope. Even the memory of those cringing, hanging heads still fills me with helpless rage.

People in the waiting crowd anxiously scanned the faces, those gray faces, thin and ravaged beyond belief, bodies of skin and bone, and their eyes — enormous eyes. But my greatest shock was the way the women clung together in small groups, refusing to look at the waiting crowd or to search out their families. Even from them, perhaps most of all from them, they wanted to hide. Instinctively the women turned to each other, to those who had shared their martyrdom and who understood.

The woman with whom Irène and I had gone to the station was hoping that her mother and sister would be among those on that train. They were. Irène and I left, unable to watch such a reunion. There are some kinds of grief so great that they kill joy; some kinds of joy unbearable to watch. The mother lived to reach home, but died shortly afterwards.

I discussed this experience with Henri Teitgen, Minister of Information, under whose auspices I was working. He told me that his father had been incarcerated in one of the worst German concentration camps; I think it was Belsen. As a doctor, he had used his professional skills to help his fellow prisoners. According to him, men who had actively resisted in some way had mustered the strength to live. Among those who died quickly were usually men, even very young ones, who did not know why they were there. They were simply taken in a round-up because a German had been shot in the street. They had not drawn together within themselves all their strengths, convictions and determination to survive. Even frail, old men with this determination survived. "But they will not live long, my father says," Mr. Teitgen told me. "In five years most of those who were in the camps will be dead."

When I spoke of the women I saw huddling on the train platform, he said, "That is spiritual survival. The spirit kept them alive to reach home. Their bodies are emptied of all strength and this last effort of the spirit is truly their last. Many of those who came home lived less than a week."

I asked Professor Laugier, our good mentor in Montreal, if he too had felt that strange invisible wall that seemed to surround those who had lived under the occupation. He agreed. He said also that those returning from the work and concentration camps found it impossible to speak of their experiences to their families. "It is quite unnecessary to speak of it," Laugier said. "They know there is nothing to say. They want to close it off somewhere in their minds if they can, and they wish to spare those they love."

I understood in time that my well-fed face and warmly clothed body and my having escaped the heel of the Nazi were not the true reasons why I could not communicate with my friends as I had before the war. The real reason was that I had not shared their experience. There was an area of their lives I could never enter. How much harder it must be for the men and women who had fought "outside" with the Free French to return home and find this barrier to full understanding.

What of our duffle-bags? Within ten days they arrived. Mine came in large wooden packing cases marked "Diplomatic Mail." Nell and I laughed when we heard that they had been accompanied by a courier. In the boxes with my big bags were a dozen or more small parcels addressed to people unknown to me. A day or so later a stream of people came knocking timidly at my door to ask if, by chance, I had a parcel for them. Their smiles of relief when they saw that indeed I did, made me realize again just how much these small parcels of food and woolens meant.

Before the war I had bought blouses in a small boutique on the Champs-Elysées. The woman who owned it and I had often sat and talked. She had dreamed of visiting Canada one day where she thought she might open a shop. Her regret was that she did not speak English. The shop was not far from the Claridge so I walked down to see if she was still there. In the window was a beautiful blouse priced at a thousand francs. A closer look revealed that it was not so beautiful; it was of very cheap rayon, probably worth about two dollars. A number of exquisite perfume bottles on display were filled with pale yellow, faintly pink or green liquid. Beneath each bottle a small sign read "Factice" (artificial). When she saw me it was the reunion with the flower woman all over again. Suddenly I realized that we were chattering excitedly — in English.

"But you're speaking English!" I exclaimed.

"Yes, it was my big war effort," she smiled. "I decided to keep my store open and to learn English some way. I am ready for my English customers when they come back. I knew the Germans would be so mad if they knew I was learning English. It made them mad too that I could keep my store open without any stock. All my shelves were empty. When a German asked for the blouse in the window I would say, 'No, Monsieur, it is the blouse of a friend. I have mended it and she lets me use it for my window.' Also they wanted to buy the perfume and I would say, 'I am sorry, it's only coloured water these days.' They could not understand how I could keep my store open. But I moved into the little storeroom at the back with a small stove, my cot, my cat and my revolver. I studied my English and my friend came nearly every day to help me. She speaks English. We would sit in the store mending for all my old clients, and making over their clothes. You think my English is good?"

She was beaming and I was delighted to compliment her. Indeed, she was ready for her English clients.

In the first days I returned to places where I had acquaintances to find out how they had survived. The old shoemaker who had fixed my one pair of "Red Feather" shoes for nothing because they were for "dancing," looked so much older and smaller. He told me grimly that he had hidden all his good leather to use for his old customers and had made the Germans bring their own leather for repairing their shoes. "I had to do it, Mademoiselle, but if they were going back to Germany, sometimes they told me so. Then I put a nail where I knew it would work through in about a week!"

The bakeries, the pastry shops, the candy stores, so many places were still closed. But the woman I knew at the laundry had lived through the occupation by sewing. "I was sick with my laundry. It is still as gray as smoke, no real soap. I am so ashamed."

To my amazement the woman in black at the cash register of the café at the corner of rue Soufflot where I had gone so often was still there, looking absolutely unchanged. She had always been extremely thin and had sat straight as a ramrod on her stool, her eyes roving over the customers. In the old days, squares of custard, pickled eggs, *chinois* (a variety of currant bun) and croissants would be piled on plates along the counter. Customers chose what they wanted and told her at the cash. But she knew before they got there exactly what had been eaten, and heaven save the customer who tried to cheat her.

When I paid for the hot wine she looked at me sharply and said, "Well, Mademoiselle, so you're back." I don't know whether she was pleased or not, though there might have been a tiny lift at one corner of her mouth.

In the few months since the liberation of Paris, there had been an explosion of new books, papers, theatre, music, concerts. The only restraint on this outpouring was the lack of paper, lack of electricity (still severely rationed) and material for production. Of course there was no heat; all fuel was saved for hospitals, schools and essential services. Cinemas and theatres of all kinds were filled and opened as they did in London at 6 p.m. I tried to go to as many as I could — among them Les Deux Anes, le Théâtre de Dix Heures and my favourite *chansonnier*, the Lapin Agile. At the Comédie Française,

Claudel's *Le Soulier de Satin* was playing to packed houses. The play lasted almost five hours. The theatre was deathly cold. All around me people sat in thin clothing, feet freezing, fingers blue and noses dripping.

On the metro that night I noticed people staring at me. It had happened before. When Irène and I got out I asked her why they were staring at me with such fixed looks. She grinned. "They saw your boots, your fur coat and said to themselves, 'Slut — wonder who's keeping her so she can patronize the black market?'" I was glad when the weather turned warm enough to wear a raincoat.

sixteen

I had carte blanche to go anywhere in France. My interviews were arranged, tickets bought and transportation and accommodation booked as I requested. I once asked Henri Teitgen of the Information Service if he would like me to show my articles to someone in the service. He looked surprised and answered, "No. Write about whatever you see and hear that has a bearing on the welfare of the civilian population. Isn't it this freedom we've been fighting for? All I ask of you is to be honest, not sensational. Write what you believe to be true. There will be bad things as well as good ones. We are human."

Elisabeth, Nellita and I had a happy reunion at Quai d'Orsay. Elisabeth was now in charge of press and public relations for the presidential office. We were all three extremely busy so could meet only occasionally for lunch or dinner. My days were filled with making arrangements to have documents and statistics of all kinds sent to Free French House in Ottawa.

One evening I was invited to Elisabeth's home to meet her parents. Transportation was still very difficult, but Elisabeth's position at Quai d'Orsay gave her "duty" access to the use of an official limousine. She had arranged for a chauffeur to call at about 10 p.m. to take me back to the Claridge, and since the car had to return to her neighbourhood, she decided to accompany me.

The Champs-Elysées was a demonstration of human ingenuity in transportation. Ancient and battered automobiles crawled up the avenue, fueled by coal, wood, straw, and a few, mostly official cars, with that precious commodity — gasoline. In addition there were bicycles, tandems, pedacarts, scooters, a whole variety of rickshaw-type contraptions, and hand-barrows. During the black-out at night the number was reduced but the variety remained.

After slowly crossing the Place de la Concorde in the dark, we turned into the Champs-Elysées and suddenly stopped. In front of us was a wreck of some sort. Elisabeth and I got out and found a high, two-wheeled gig broken down and four young American soldiers jumping out. In front of the gig a horse was lying on its side. Kneeling beside its head, a shabbily dressed old man was alternately crooning softly in French as he rubbed the horse and angrily shaking his fist in the direction of an American military jeep, parked a short distance ahead.

The young soldiers rushed forward. Two squatted beside the old man while the others examined the horse and asked anxious questions. Obviously the old man could not answer. An excited crowd gathered out of nowhere, everyone talking at once. A moment later a young American sergeant arrived from the jeep, while Elisabeth and I joined the other soldiers and asked what had happened. "That jeep swiped the side of the horse," one replied.

Immediately the sergeant began a tirade in English. "My jeep never touched the horse!" he roared officiously. "I'll want your names and company. I'm in charge here!" Then, grabbing the old man by the shoulder, he shouted, "What are you doing out here with this contraption at this time of night?"

The soldiers muttered that they had only hired the gig to drive back to their quarters, while the old man began scolding vehemently in French. The sergeant shook him, bawling, "Speak English, you damned old fool! Speak English!" At that the curious crowd turned angry, moved in closer and began muttering and screaming at the sergeant. Elisabeth stepped in, urging the crowd to be quiet, while the soldiers and I protested to the over-zealous young sergeant.

Telling me to mind my own business, the sergeant began threatening the soldiers with cancelled leaves and other punishments, at which point the four backed off and hastily melted into the park. Then another American, a colonel, joined the crowd. He came straight through to us and we told him when he asked quietly what had happened.

Kneeling beside the old man, the colonel spoke to him softly in French while running his hand over the side of the prostrate animal. Then he got up and examined the horse's legs, body and head. Silently

the crowd watched. "I think we can get him up," he said finally.
"There's a small cut and a bruise on the leg, but it's only a graze I think.
The leg's not broken, but still I'll have a veterinarian examine him
tomorrow. Come on, I'll help you to get him up." The colonel turned
to the crowd and, speaking excellent French, asked for help. In an
instant the horse was standing. The colonel turned to the crowd. "I
think you may leave now. I'm giving my name and address to the
owner and we will have the horse examined tomorrow. The driver
will be compensated for any damage and for his worry." He turned to
the sergeant and said severely, "I want your name and number, and
the name of your superior officer. You are to get in touch with me first
thing in the morning and we'll see about your case. Never forget you
are in France, and these people are friends of the United States. You
are in their country and they are entitled to every respect and courtesy
from you."

The crowd clapped and quickly dispersed. The old man took the
colonel's card, thanked him profusely and promised to meet him the
following morning. As we walked back to the car the colonel accompanied us. He said with some bitterness, "This sort of thing is one of
our worst headaches. One incident like this can undo the efforts of
hundreds of us trying to represent our country properly."

We reached the limousine and the colonel was plainly disconcerted
when he saw the flag and the official plates. He grinned, embarrassed,
and said, "I hope this doesn't become an incident." We laughed and
Elisabeth assured him that she thought the reputation of the United
States was in good hands.

The Institute of Demography was my first official call. I had sought
statistics there before the war and knew their penchant for accuracy.
Apologetically they told me the statistics were only estimations for the
moment. The population of France appeared to have dropped from 42
million to something under 38 million. There were perhaps 2 million
still in Germany. In France there were several million more women
than men. The number of refugees and other aliens — more than 2
million in 1939 — had dropped drastically; they were among the first
to be seized in the occupied zone and sent to work camps in Germany. The birth rate was now much lower than the death rate;
programs to encourage larger families would be needed. Surveys
were under way to discover the general health of the population,
especially the children. First priority would be to restore the nation to
good health.

The Ministry of Agriculture gave me a summary of the food situation. The country had been stripped of most of its sheep, goats, pigs, cattle, horses, fish, fowl, fruit, dairy products, grain and vegetables. A census of what was left on the farms was being taken.

"How soon do you think you will know what the true situation is?" I asked.

The official's expression was sceptical. "That depends. Our French peasants are smart, and living under the occupation only made them a whole lot smarter. Although hundreds of thousands of their animals were requisitioned and sent to Germany, they succeeded in hiding some in spite of the penalty of deportation or death. Now the census-takers are Frenchmen too. They understand our farmers and we hope they will be just as smart. We may get a more accurate figure. At any rate animals may not be slaughtered for meat until the herds are rebuilt. It will take two or three years. Milk must be reserved for children under two years, for the sick and the old. We will have to import powdered milk, but it cannot be a priority."

In the Ministry of Education I had several talks about what had happened during the occupation and what would be necessary to restore the school system. Some saw it as an opportunity for reform: expanding co-education which had been started just before the war; restocking libraries with books confiscated by the Germans; finding ways to house the student body. Fortunately France had been a pioneer in free education, up to and including university, and had a generous scholarship system. These expenses for education would be accepted without a word by the population. Money would be needed to rebuild schools, buy materials, publish textbooks and import paper.

"We cannot expect much of an increase in our budget yet," one official told me. "A large portion always has been devoted to education, but so much is needed to rebuild the country."

I sought out people concerned with rebuilding transportation and the devastated towns and villages. I was amazed to learn that I could not go south; the first transportation restored went from west to east in northern France because of military needs.

"There is hardly a bridge that does not need to be rebuilt," I was told. "If you want to go to Marseille you can go a distance by train, then walk to a river there to wait and be ferried across, probably in a rowboat. Another walk, another piece of railway, another river. It can be done but it will take days.

"There are more than 600 villages and towns to be rebuilt in the Normandy and Brittany area alone. This is not mentioning the cities of

Rouen, Le Havre and others. Some of them are completely destroyed.
There are others, like Oradour-sur-Glane, where every single inhabit-
ant was killed except one small boy who hid in the woods. The
population was 763 persons; the men were shot, the women and
children herded into the church, the doors locked, then they were
machine-gunned through the windows, the church set afire and those
still living burned alive. The town was razed by the German S.S.
troops."

I felt nauseated when I was shown a few terrible pictures. "It wasn't
the only one. Domptail-en-l'air was razed. A tiny peaceful village. Its
fifty-three inhabitants were massacred because someone had shot a
German officer. The same for Martincourt, and Saint-Nizier, burned by
flame-throwers. I could go on . . ." But I had had enough.

At the Ministry of Health I was told of plans to distribute vitamins,
calcium and foods other than meat to build up proteins in the weakened population.

The schools were next on my agenda. It was early March and still
extremely cold for France. Even in the primary classes there was little
or no heat. "The extraordinary thing," one teacher told me, "is the
children did not seem to develop colds though they were hungry and
the classrooms freezing in the winter. In January this year we were
able to have some fuel, giving us a little heat. Whole classes came
down with the grippe. I suppose the germs were there but didn't
develop in the cold. Unfortunately the children are in such a weakened condition that I am afraid many will be left with chronic bronchitis and lung infections. We haven't the food to build them up."

I noticed that on many balconies, even in the most fashionable parts
of the city, there were rabbit hutches. "Yes," said a friend, "that's
occupation. We say that in 1870, when Paris was under seige, Parisians
ate rats, in 1914-1918 seventeen departments of France ate cats, and it
has been rabbits this war. Our diet is improving." Her smile was grim
and I felt ill. "I know how you feel," she said, "but Parisians will eat
anything to save Paris."

Certainly rabbits were being raised everywhere. I asked friends
about it. "The only meat we saw for months at a time was rabbit, if we
raised them," they said. "Rabbit fur was sold in the markets and with it
we could cover a child's wornout coat and make a bonnet and mitts."
One day I was walking through the Bois du Boulogne in the chic 16th
arrondissement and saw an old gentleman wearing a well-cut but
worn black coat and hat. He had a rabbit on a leash and guided it

carefully to spots where the grass was lush. He, at least, did not patronize the black market.

Irène and Hélène were good sources of information about how problems of obtaining clothing were met. I heard many stories but one element was common to almost all. Nearly every household in France at that time contained piles of pure linen sheets, handed down from trousseau to trousseau. During the war these sheets, softened to silky smoothness by years of washing, became underclothing and even dresses. It reminded me of depression days on the prairie where sugar and flour sacks were bleached and sewn together to make sheets or turned into clothing.

Irène introduced me to her friend Jacqueline, a very tall girl looking as elegantly turned out as if there had not been a war. They both laughed at me as they explained her outfit. Jacqueline was wearing a moss green skirt and bolero and a smartly twisted turban with a large pin on one side. The heavy material resembled damask. Under the bolero she wore a creamy blouse with long, full sleeves and high neck; the front had a row of pearl buttons flanked by many rows of tiny pleats. She was carrying a large handbag, the sides made of the same material as her dress. She wore no stockings but on her feet were open-toed, black patent, low-heeled shoes. She carried herself like a model.

"Well," Jacqueline explained, smiling, "my blouse was made out of one of my grandfather's night-shirts. As for my dress and hat — turbans are all the rage — come with me and I will show you." We went into the dining-room. Going to the window she picked up the edge of the curtain which did not reach the window sills. They were the same moss green. "I just took the bottom off the curtains and pasted black paper on the lower part of the windows for the black-out. My purse was shabby so I covered it with the same material. My shoes were my brother's dancing shoes. He's a prisoner but I know he won't mind. They were too big for me but I took them to my shoemaker and he cut the front down and made them open-toed. He lined them with felt. Aren't they elegant?" They were indeed.

General Vanier, our first Ambassador to France, and Mme Vanier lived in temporary quarters not far from the Claridge. They had visited many parts of liberated France; in some places they were the only foreign diplomats permitted to visit. "The Vaniers are different," Henri Teitgen said. "We feel they understand and will be compassionate, even for those who were afraid to do their duty." On one of my visits

General Vanier told me he had met people in their first state of exhilaration after being liberated. They were living in basements and in partly shattered houses. Gargantuan problems faced them in rebuilding their lives. "But in spite of their weakened condition, they are ready to face the job," he said. "One woman said to me, 'I have read a great deal about Canada. We have to be pioneers like the first French who went to Canada were. I am sure their task was even greater than ours.' I am not worried, they will do it."

Mme Vanier visited hospitals, clinics, families in areas where the damage had been most severe. "What touched me so much" she told me, "especially in Normandy where so many Canadians have their roots, and where our own troops fought, was the way people living among the ruins, the wounded in the hospitals, and those who had lost whole families told me over and over again, 'Do not be sorry, Madame, we bear no resentment. It was necessary. It meant our freedom. Nothing is worthwhile without that. The Canadians, the Allies, they are not invaders, they are liberators.'"

The Hotel d'Orsay was the centre for Canadian soldiers on leave. I accompanied Mme Vanier there. It was early morning and soldiers were straggling down to the big dining-room. We went from table to table as they ate their breakfast. Mme Vanier would sit down and talk to each young soldier, take messages, names and home addresses. She promised to write to their mothers, wives or sweethearts, and so she did.

The kiosks in Paris were loaded with one- and two-page newspapers, Paris editions of *The Times* of London and the *Herald-Tribune* of New York. Piles of small books turned out to be copies of the books published secretly during the occupation. Meeting some of the Resistance writers had been on my mind since leaving Canada. My colleagues and I had been so intrigued by the papers smuggled out to us in Ottawa, and especially by several of the small books, like *Le Silence de la Mer* published by Les Editions de Minuit. I wanted to interview some of these people and find out how they had managed. Where did they get the paper and ink and find printers they could trust?

One morning I arrived at the door of an apartment in the rue Vineuse, not far from the Palais de Chaillot. Yvonne Paraf, a vivacious, dark-eyed Frenchwoman, better known by her wartime pseudonym as Mme Desvignes, welcomed me. She had been asked to tell me the story of the Resistance writers.

At first, she said, the best writers in France decided they would not write at all as a form of resistance. "But writers can't stay silent for long," she smiled. "They were soon looking for ways to express themselves, especially as some less than mediocre writers were given space and publicity by collaborating with the Germans. They decided they would not write anything that could be construed as propaganda, but would write as though France wasn't occupied — the books they had been planning to write when they were free."

The first publication, *Pensée libre* in June 1941, contained serious articles by highly respected authors writing under pseudonyms. *Pensée libre* spread hope like fire throughout the writing community. When a second edition was being prepared, the Gestapo swooped down and seized everything, including the two founders, Jacques Decour and Jean Politizer, who were tortured and executed. They had not revealed the names of their writers. Only one manuscript escaped. Fortunately, its author had been late delivering it. It was Vercors' *Le Silence de la Mer*.

Some writers, anxious to continue this underground activity, had urged Vercors (Jean Bruller) to find the means to publish their work. "He got in touch with me and asked if I could find a few trusted friends and use my apartment for sewing the books together," said Mme Desvignes. "It would be impossible to find a bookbinder but a printer and small press was possible. Of course, I accepted."

She told me about the problems they had had in obtaining lead, paper and ink; of the number of times they had had to move from one small press to another; of the risks taken when a printer began to fear that he was becoming suspect and another had to be found; and of the risks in distributing the books and getting them across the demarcation line into unoccupied France.

"It turned out to be easier for us when the whole of France was occupied," she said ironically. "And the lead, it was so heavy. I remember crossing Paris once with two bags tied together and slung over the bar of my bicycle. I had dandelions sticking out of the top of them to make them look like bags of groceries."

As she talked I looked around the small kitchen, with its high shelf above the sink and its worn and chipped pots and pans of white enamel hanging below. Here, on this table, those precious pages of writers determined to be free had been sewn together. How Mme Desvignes and her helpers must have listened for footsteps on the stairs. How they must have wondered if someone, somewhere, had been caught and had not been strong enough to remain silent under torture. Death is one thing, pain is another. How the failure of a messenger to arrive must have caused apprehension. The long waiting, the panic. Many of the books she showed to me were dedicated to poets and writers who died in Nazi hands. In *Le Silence de la Mer* the dedication read: "To the memory of Saint-Pol-Roux — Poet assassinated."

Although Mme Desvignes smiled as she recounted the adventures and answered my questions, her eyes were sad. It was hard to believe, looking at her, that she could have lived all those years under such stress. I asked her if she had ever dreamed that she could be involved in such a dangerous occupation. She smiled again. "Never! I'm really rather timid."

"What was the worst aspect of your task, if I may ask that?"

She thought a moment and then said, "Sewing." The tedium and the sore fingers that went with sewing together the pages of the books, copy after copy, would make it difficult for her to ever use a needle again. This little group of publishers produced forty books, among them manuscripts smuggled *into* France from Jacques Maritain, Julien Green, Henri Bernstein and André Maurois. They were never caught. As I was leaving, Mme Desvignes took a book from a shelf and gave it to me, explaining that it had been published by her team in March 1944. The pseudonym was Minervois; the author's real name was Claude Aveline.

Shortly after visiting Mme Desvignes I got in touch with Germaine Garreau, a teacher in one of the Paris lycées. She had been deeply involved in the Resistance, using her school as her base.

One evening Germaine arranged to have me meet some of the young people who belonged to the Resistance network between Paris and Bourgogne, and of which she was a member. We met at night in one of the classrooms. All were wearing heavy coats because the room was icy. There was one small electric globe; the light was too dim to distinguish the faces. The leader was a young man of twenty, but he had been in the Resistance since his sixteenth birthday. He seemed to me at least ten years older. His closest associate and liaison with London was a tall, broad-shouldered Scot in his late thirties who had been parachuted into France to help the group. I asked Mac how he felt about taking orders from a leader who could almost be his son. "He's not a boy," Mac answered. "He's one of the most intelligent and mature men I have ever met. I'd trust him with my life."

I asked the young leader what he intended to do after the war — go back to school? He shook his head. "I'm too old. Maybe I'll go out to one of the colonies where I can do a man's job."

Mac shook his head. "No, my lad, you won't. You'll go back to school because your country needs men like you more than ever. Men who know what they are fighting for. What's the use of risking your life in the Maquis if it's not to make use of the liberty you've been fighting for? Education is one part of it."

It was a strange evening, sitting around in the classroom in the semi-darkness, these young men in their rough clothing telling hair-raising stories. Theirs were not the faces of youngsters. There was one woman among them — Dominique Aubier, a young writer. I asked them about the haunting song of the Partisans. Did the Maquis really sing it everywhere? Immediately the whole group began to sing in a low voice. I have never since experienced such a sensation; my whole body was infused with their intensity.

Ami! Entends-tu
le vol noir des corbeaux
sur nos plaines?

Friend, can you hear
the dark flight of the crows
o'er our plains?

Ami! Entends-tu
les cris sourds du pays
qu'on enchaîne?

Friend, can you hear
the dull cries
of a country in chains?

Ohé! Partisans,
ouvriers et paysans,
c'est l'alarme!

Hark! Partisans,
workers and peasants!
It is the signal!

Ce soir, l'ennemi
connaîtra le prix du sang
et des larmes...

Tonight, the enemy'll know,
the price of blood
and of tears!

Montez de la mine,
descendez des collines,
camarades.

Come up from the mines,
descend from the hills,
O comrades!

Sortez de la paille
les fusils, la mitraille,
les grenades...

Bring out from the straw,
the guns and the rifles,
bring out the grenades.

Ohé! Les tueurs
à la balle et au couteau,
tuez vite!

Harken, you killers,
with ball and with knife,
kill quickly!

Ohé! Saboteur,
attention à ton fardeau,
dynamite!

Listen, you saboteurs,
take care of your loads,
your explosives!

C'est nous qui brisons
les barreaux des prisons
pour nos frères...

It is we who will smash
the gates of the prisons
of our brothers.

La haine à nos trousses
et la faim qui nous pousse,
la misère...

Hatred is our burden,
and hunger drives us on,
and our misery...

Il y a des pays
où les gens au creux des lits
font des rêves;

There are lands,
where men in soft beds
lie and dream.

Ici, nous, vois-tu,
nous, on marche, et, on tue
ou on crève,

Here, do you see
we march and we kill,
or we die!

Ici, chacun sait
ce qu'il veut, ce qu'il fait,
quand il passe.

Here, each one knows
what he wants, what he must do
when they pass.

Ami, si tu tombes,
un ami sort de l'ombre
à ta place.

Friend, if you fall
A friend from the shadows
takes your place.

Demain, du sang noir
sèchera au grand soleil
sur nos routes.

Tomorrow, black blood
will be drying in the sun
on our roads.

Sifflez, compagnons,
dans la nuit, la Liberté
nous écoute.

Whistle, comrades,
in the night, Liberty
is listening.

Ami! entends-tu
les cris sourds du pays
qu'on enchaîne?

Friend, can you hear
the dark flight of the crows
o'er our plains?

Ami! entends-tu
le vol noir des corbeaux
sur nos plaines?

Friend, can you hear
the dull cries
of a country in chains?

When they finished the song we sat in silence. I could not speak.

seventeen

When I left Canada names like Bernières-sur-Mer, Arromanches, Courseulles, St. Aubin, Bayeux, Tilly-sur-Seules and Caen were still fresh in my mind. These were the towns where bitter fighting had taken the lives of so many, and filled our newspapers and newsreels with such harrowing stories. I made arrangements to spend a few days between Rouen and the Channel coast. A jeep and a driver would be placed at my disposal; I could work out my own itinerary and take as many days as necessary. Through my driver, accommodation would be arranged at fixed points. Shelter was hard to find. It was not a tourist trip.

On the morning of March 17, 1945, I left for Rouen. The train was crowded. The people in my compartment were returning to Le Havre, Rouen and other towns. Some I spoke to had not been home since June 1940. Others had returned to find their homes in ruins so had gone back to Paris to shop for necessities to start life anew.

In my notebook I wrote: "As we travel through this landscape of devastation, we are all gazing out the windows and some of my companions are anxiously wondering aloud what they will find. Will the houses still be standing? One said the whole centre of Le Havre had been flattened and warned people they should have friends or relatives somewhere near the city as there was little or no hotel accommodation. Others refused to believe it. With one exception, every station since leaving Paris has been bombed out. In many places whole quarters of town and villages are in ruins. The people in this compartment have grown silent and I don't wonder. What they see is making them look more and more worried.

"Every factory within sight of the railway is in ruins, windows and nearby houses blasted; in places windows are filled with cardboard, paper, cloth, anything. I see the disbelief in the eyes of my companions and I'm sure I must look the same to them. It is beyond imagination and no one can take in all the ramifications of what we are seeing. No doubt many of these people have endured bombing, but many are probably as ignorant as I am about what a country looks like after the juggernaut of modern war has rolled over it. Services? What of telephones, electricity, water, heat, sewage, medical attention, school? All the services we are accustomed to must be repaired, replaced. It boggles the mind.

"Beauvais is greatly damaged . . . a famous carpet factory appears to be intact.

"Gournay-Ferrière is greatly damaged. Station and all nearby buildings are piles of rubble. The south side of the town is in ruins. A cheese factory is open to the sky. Town after town, devastated, burned. We creep over frail bridges and I wonder how long a country takes to recover from such destruction, not years, maybe generations? Now in some of the fields the first green is showing, trees are budding. In front of that one small station, patched up, someone has set out a brave show of potted red geraniums.

"Along the side of the tracks are great bomb-craters. They remind me of pictures of the moon, each one about ten yards apart. Every bridge, every viaduct is a temporary structure. Passing some fields with crops about an inch high now. Somebody says winter wheat. A few cattle and they look well fed. I remember the official in the Ministry of Agriculture saying it would be several years before they could slaughter for beef. People are shabby, thin, faces pasty or sallow. Their shoes are worn beyond redemption. All look so tired. I wonder what is going on behind those eyes? They look so patient but disillusioned, dull."

I was met at the Rouen station by someone from the mayor's office. My guide was middle-aged, a First World War veteran, and he could not conceal his surprise that a woman reporter had been sent. He took me to the hotel and promised to pick me up soon to take me to the mayor's office.

The offices were in the still-standing part of a half demolished building; the furniture was makeshift. The mayor and his staff were bubbling with optimism. I spent the afternoon touring the city on foot with my guide. The sides of all the streets were lined with bricks piled five feet high and many rows thick. The people were digging the bricks out of the rubble to use them again. Behind the walls of brick were great piles of rubble and brick dust. Whole blocks had been flattened with here and there a fragment of a building or a church standing. I did not see window-glass intact anywhere.

We visited temporary quarters housing clinics set up to look after the injured, the sick, the hungry and homeless, mostly women and children. Schools, hospitals and public buildings had been destroyed. Already, pre-fab shelters had arrived from Canada. Most of the beautiful old quarters around the cathedral were flattened and, although arches were standing, the interior of the cathedral was in ruins. Along both sides of the Seine, the damage was unimaginable. Only their personal losses caused more grief to the people than the destruction of several magnificent old churches. "But we will rebuild them," they said. I started towards the cathedral but my guide stopped me. It was unsafe to approach. One spire pointed skyward.

On the streets I talked to the people. Their voices reflected their determination to rebuild an even more beautiful city. All the stones that could be recovered would be used again. Everyone had lost members of their families; some were still buried under the tons of broken stone. Children were more warmly wrapped than the women whose thin garments and purple skin made me wince in my warm clothing. The lack of soap was evident everywhere. Clothing of whatever colour was faded and grayed; bare legs were dirty, though faces were clean.

After a spare supper with my guide in an unheated and very damp dining-room, I went to bed. The city was in darkness. There was literally nothing to do. I put on a warm dressing-gown and got into bed, spreading my fur coat over me and leaving my woolen beret on my head. One 25-watt light pierced the gloom as I tried to record with stiffened fingers my myriad impressions of the day. Then the light went out.

Breakfast was two chunks of bread with a little apple jam and black ersatz coffee. At the mayor's office I was told that the day was one of celebration — a shipload of food, medicine, essential metals, nails, tools and petrol had arrived from England. It was the first large ship to reach Rouen via the Seine.

In the morning hours I visited more clinics, shelters, churches, a convent and saw the crypt where many bombed-out families were still living and being cared for by the sisters and priests. I heard of the makeshift efforts to keep education going. I saw more pale, half-starved women and children, undernourished nurses, doctors and volunteers working. As we walked through the open streets, with nothing but rubble meeting the eye, I remembered the words of one woman.

"We waited so long and were delirious with joy when we saw the Allies arriving. Some of us were too numb to show it midst so much death. Now it is winter and every morning I come out and see these piles of rubble — nothing but rubble. For how long? When will we have cleared it away and become a city again? Each morning I become more depressed at the sight; I wonder if we can stand it?"

"Yet it was worthwhile?" I asked her.

"Oh yes," she cried. "Without that hope many of us would be dead now — suicide. Don't think we are not grateful, Mademoiselle. It is just, it is just ..."

I looked around. To face the rubble every morning? Could I?

How would we react at home? I tried to imagine Montreal, Toronto, Winnipeg, Vancouver, sixty, seventy, eighty per cent in ruins. Electricity for only a few half-hours a day. Sewers and water mains cut to pieces. No heat. I could not imagine such a scene. Around me I saw people, many ill with anemia, bronchitis and lung infections. "Thank goodness our water supply, though scant, is pure," one nurse said. "At least we don't have to worry about typhoid."

The luncheon I attended at noon with the mayor's party was given in honour of the representative of the United Kingdom. The British representative told the gathering that the people in Britain were concerned about the suffering of French civilians, especially the children. "I am deeply moved to see this city and the spirit of the people. Our common suffering should never be forgotten; and I hope our peoples will be so bound together that they will build a better world together."

The mayor was close to tears. He choked as he answered, "Monsieur, this food, this seed for our farmers, the generosity of the British people will never be forgotten."

The British group and I were taken on a tour of the harbour in a motor boat. There were miles of destruction on either side of the river and so much debris. Hundreds of small boats and barges, hundreds of great cranes had been dynamited; across the harbour entrance a 12,000 ton whaler and three other large ships had been sunk. The quays were shattered; great masses of concrete jammed the river. The mayor explained that Rouen was the port of Paris, and the largest in

France after Marseille. At Rouen the German army with its tanks, guns, and equipment of all kinds had been beaten back to the south bank of the Seine. All the bridges had been blown up so the army and its thousands of vehicles could not cross. They were an easy target for Allied bombers. The German troops just left their equipment and took off. The German occupation force in Rouen itself blew up all the installations on the north side before leaving. More than 500 small craft, floating docks, tenders and a twisted mass of port installations lay at the bottom of the harbour and the Seine. The Germans boasted that it would take at least six months to clear a passage for even small traffic.

"After the Germans left everyone was in despair, thinking it could never be repaired," said the mayor. "Some of the quays date back to the eighteenth century. But our dockers were magnificent. Within three weeks they had refloated the whaler and opened a passage; they began clearing the harbour while small boats brought in supplies. Everyone, the dockers and Rouen volunteers from all walks of life, worked frantically to repair sections of the quays and docks. It will take months to clear it all, and years to replace the quays, but we have a passage now wide enough for large ships. Before the war we were unloading 45,000 to 60,000 tons a day, but now we are unloading 15,000 tons with little means. Half the cranes have been salvaged and are working again. In ten years, I guarantee, we will have the finest harbour in France."

(I visited Rouen again nine years later. The quays were rebuilt. Along the south side of the river, the trains ran under the quay so they were no longer visible. On the north side under the quays were large areas for underground parking. Above, on both sides, were parks, city gardens, flowers and shrubs. "You see, we solved several problems when we rebuilt," my guide said.)

Mr. Wolf, the editor of the principal Rouen newspaper, and his wife were active in the Resistance. He and his wife and children lived through dangerous days. I asked him to tell me what he thought was the worst aspect of the occupation. Unexpectedly he said, "Teaching my children to lie and steal. I tried to explain to them that to lie and steal during the occupation was a patriotic duty — but after the war they must never again lie or steal. We were only using lying and stealing as weapons to save France. My children helped my wife and myself to survive, but I will not know until they are grown up whether or not I succeeded in teaching them the importance of truth and honesty."

"And what experience do you remember as the hardest you had to bear personally?"

Then he laughed. "Believe it or not, living in a tiny room at the bottom of a laundry chute in a hotel. For six weeks my wife and I had to live in this stifling room and always among dirty bedding and linen. Nothing in the world smells worse. But the Gestapo was looking for us. Our friend, the hotel proprietor, saved us."

"And what of the people of Rouen? What are the worst effects?"

"There are few families in Rouen who haven't lost a loved one. The cathedral, the opera house, schools, libraries, the university are all testimonies to civilized times. They represent the spirit. Such destruction cannot help but touch the soul. The people see the areas of the city where they and their families have lived for generations now uninhabitable. Still they carry on, so what can I say? There are thousands of people who suffered the occupation in Europe and whose names we will never know, but who have touched heights of selflessness and heroism incomprehensible to mankind in normal times."

Mr. Wolf talked about the future, about the use of force to try to solve problems, and the utter futility of it. "If we have not learned our lesson this time, then I see no future for mankind. I have seen the progression of weapons between the First and Second World Wars. What will man invent next to destroy himself and his kind? Whatever it is, the world will not survive it."

This conversation was held only five months before nuclear bombs were dropped on Hiroshima and Nagasaki.

Asked about problems, one social worker told me soberly, "Delinquency. Unconsciously the soldiers aggravate the problem. They don't realize the gravity of it when they ask a youngster to procure a bottle of wine or brandy, and pay him to do so. They do not realize girls sometimes sell their bodies because they are hungry or want soap to feel clean. I am sure these young soldiers would blush with shame if they know they were debasing young girls through their human need to still the pangs of hunger." She spoke bitterly. "We are liberated. Thank God for that. We will win the war. But Hitler will have won all the same. He has turned our men into tubercular shadows of themselves in the prison and work camps. He has taught our children to be liars and thieves; our girls to be prostitutes and beggars; our women...We are a proud nation. The Germans could not touch us intellectually, artistically or spiritually — they could only force us to accept evils for survival. We are only now beginning to understand the moral destitution that occupation causes, not to speak of material ruin. Do you realize women sold themselves to feed their children or aged parents?

"Some lie there still under the rubble. Women starved themselves to send parcels of food to their prisoner husbands or sons. Our men were tortured, imprisoned and sent to slave labour camps, if not shot. This wicked work will not come out of our souls for generations. Peace? Disillusionment? After these past four years, can we believe in anything? No nation should be called upon to suffer as we and the other occupied countries have suffered. If the United Nations cannot find a solution this time our curses will not be on the heads of the Germans — but on our own. For what good is it to save our liberty if it is to be used only to lose it again, Mademoiselle? We will not have won the war unless in thirty or forty years from now we can look at the world and see it at peace, our children secure in unthreatened countries. We will not win unless the United Nations succeeds where the League of Nations failed."

It was like unleasing a torrent, for the words rushed out of her as though she had needed to articulate what she had been feeling for a long time. My mind was in a turmoil. What could I say?

What can I say today?

In the Rouen hotel foyer I met Louis who was to be my driver for the next few days. Louis was a thin-faced, sandy-haired young man with the light, amber eyes of northern France. He was polite but silent as we left for Le Havre in his jeep. As usual with young Frenchmen, I thawed him out by talking about Canada, the mounties, the North and the wild animals. The subject is irresistible. He finally told me he had been in the Resistance and then wounded in the second battle of France. I was surprised to find out he was only twenty-two.

Having spent several days in Le Havre before the war, I thought I would recognize the city, but it was a pile of rubble standing about four or five feet high and covering an area about a mile square. On the rise behind the city I saw the broken skeletons of apartment buildings. Nevertheless, the mayor was already enthusiastic about the plans for the new city. The main avenue lay under the rubble. "But we've designed a new one," he told me excitedly, "and it will be as grand as the Champs-Elysées. Perhaps even wider!"

How many had died there? He said they had numbered in the thousands, but no census could be taken. "Our worst problem now is people returning. As you see we have no accommodation for them. We have hundreds of kilometres of electric and telephone wires to replace, water mains and sewers to put in before we can build."

During dinner the mayor told me how citizens had been shot or sent to concentration camps for aiding British commandos, attending burial services for RAF pilots, and giving refuge to some Canadians who had escaped after Dieppe. "Because the war is still on, we don't know how many will come back," he said gravely.

The next day we drove along the coast to the beaches where the British and Canadians had come ashore. Frequently we stopped and walked on the beaches at St. Aubin, Courseulles, Bernières-sur-Mer — names familiar since D-Day. Even though I had seen glimpses in the newsreels, what I saw now was shocking. The beaches had not been touched since the invasion and were littered with abandoned barges, twisted wrecks of tanks and guns, the water still filled with hulks of ships, barges, parts of the artificial harbours the Allies had towed across the Channel to put in place so the armies and equipment could land. Up from beaches along some cliffs were remnants of walls, piles of barbed wire torn aside and now rusting in the sea air. The empty bunkers and blockhouses had walls so thick it was hard to understand how the Germans had been routed. It seemed to me that the bunkers had hardly been touched. Louis said that he had been told that men had thrown themselves on the wire so others could walk over them. I thought of the young men, followed into this hell a few days after by women with their mobile kitchens, first aid stations, mobile hospitals. Enough had survived to liberate, with the aid of the occupied peoples, all Western Europe in the space of months!

Louis asked me if I wanted to go on to Omaha and Utah where the Americans had come ashore. I told him I had seen enough.

It was dark when we drove into Bayeux, and Louis left me at the entrance of a convent. "Arrangements have been made for you to stay here," he said. "You'll be warm and probably the sisters can give you a good meal."

I was welcomed warmly and taken to a tiny cell, bare except for a cot, a chair, a *prie-dieu* and a small chest of drawers. The only colour in the room was a picture of the Sacret Heart above the cot. At a very simple dinner of excellent fish, my hostesses told me that Bayeux had been almost entirely spared. When the Allied troops were approaching, a priest and a small boy bicycled out to meet them and tell them the Germans had evacuated the city. Suspicious, scouts went ahead and found the story true.

The sisters wept as they told me of their joy and relief at the sight of their liberators, and of their admiration for the service women following them. They urged me to see their beautiful cathedral before leaving, and regretted that their prized Bayeux Tapestry was not on view. However, they pressed into my hands a small booklet of pictures telling the story of King Harold II and the battle of Hastings.

Louis picked me up and we drove through the Norman countryside, through towns and villages in various states of ruin. I asked if he could take me to a place called Tilly. It had been mentioned a dozen times by war correspondents on the CBC. He looked puzzled so I wrote it on a piece of paper. "Ah, I see. You mean Tilly-sur-Seules. But there's nothing to see there any more."

"That's why I want to go," I said.

We turned into a sideroad. Green was already covering some of the ravages of war. After a few miles our road broadened out into a flat surface that reminded me of a Regina golf course during the drought. The perfectly flat surface appeared to be composed of fine stone dust. There were shallow tank tracks. "Well, we're here," Louis said. "This is Tilly-sur-Seules." I looked around. It had been fought over for so many days that nothing was left standing. The remnants of the buildings had been rolled flat by tanks and used as a park for military vehicles.

Here several hundred people had carried on their lives, and before them, generations over hundreds of years. In a few weeks it had been wiped from the face of France. We walked around, saying nothing. At the side of the road were scattered some rude crosses, made of pieces of wood tied together, to mark places where civilians or soldiers had been killed. On one was written "Un Canadien" and a number; on another, "Un Allemand"; on still another, "Un Anglais"; and on one "Jacques Gavreau."

As we stood there trying to gather our thoughts and emotions, a boy of ten wheeled up on his bicycle. He wore a heavy, coarsely knit gray sweater and short woolen trousers. He stopped beside us and stared curiously.

"Do you know this place?" I asked.

"Of course, it is my home, Tilly-sur-Seules."

"Were you living here during the fighting?"

"Naturally," he said, then turned and pointed. "Our house was there. It was bombed. We stayed in the basement of the hotel for many days. Some people went away, but most of us stayed in the hotel basement or the crypt of the church."

"How did you get food? Did you save anything from your home?"

"Yes, we saved some things. We hid them in the field under a big canvas."

"But food? What did you eat?"

"The hotel had some food at first and at night we went out and milked the cows. After awhile the hotel was hit and most of it fell down. The priest came and made us all leave. Then the hotel was smashed."

"Did you see the soldiers?"

"Yes, the Germans, and then the British, and then the Germans, and then they went away for good."

"Were there any Canadians?"

"Yes, and some were killed. The doctor has the papers and things."

"Where did you go when you left the hotel?"

"The priest took us to the crypt and then he made us all go to the farms."

"Where are you living now?"

"On a farm, not very far away."

"Were many people killed here? I mean people of the town?"

"Oh yes, a lot. Some wouldn't leave, and there were lots of battles here."

"Could you tell me what your village was like? Could you describe it?"

He turned and walked a short distance. We followed. Then he stopped and closed his eyes. Raising his arm he began to point. "There is the hotel, and next to it is the bakery. There is where Mme _____ lives, and there Mme _____. Over here is the church; there is the meat shop; and there the store. Monsieur le Mayor lives there and next to our house is my friend's house . . . ." Turning slowly he kept pointing and gradually rebuilding the village before our eyes.

Then he stopped and opened his eyes. "Do you think your village will be rebuilt?" I asked.

His eyes widened. "But of course! Already the plans are made. Everything will be just the same as before, but finer. Inside water and everything."

"What of the soldiers buried by the road?"

"I told you. The doctor took the names and papers and sent them somewhere. But he has a record and when the war is over they will be buried in a new cemetery," he answered. Then before I could thank him or do anything for him, he mounted his bicycle and was away, only turning to wave goodbye.

In 1954 I retraced my footsteps. I saw the new Tilly. As the boy had said, the new village was a replica of the old one, except that the building materials were new, and the town's very newness was startling in that ancient landscape. I saw the doctor who had taken charge of the town and its people, and who had kept the names of the dead. His was the only house left standing because it was several kilometres out of town. He smiled at me ruefully and said, "I'm the only person in town who hasn't a new house."

Louis and I moved on from Tilly. I suggested visiting St. Lô, but Louis said soberly, "Only those who are still searching for the dead are allowed in." Even at that distance from the town the sickly sweet smell of death was in the wind.

The next morning we drove to Caen. The Canadians were the main force in liberating the city, which was almost 80 per cent destroyed in the bombing. It was the one city where I hesitated to show my face. The welcome astonished me. "There is no bitterness against us?" I asked.

"There was no way for the Canadians to know most of the Germans had withdrawn. You will find no resentment here. We knew the price of liberty would be high but we were prepared to pay it," the mayor said. "Already we have word from Canada that we will be helped to rebuild our university and Canadians are giving us a library."

I spoke to an old man sitting on a large chunk of rubble at one place. The sun was shining. I thought he was catching the warmth. I asked if he was enjoying the sunshine. He nodded but did not speak. Something about him caused me to hesitate so we moved on. Then my guide said, "That old gentleman's son is a prisoner in Germany; his family, his wife, his daughter-in-law, the children, his sister are sealed below that rubble in the basement. As they have not yet been disinterred and buried, every day he sits there."

eighteen

I returned to Paris on March 23 with a bad cold, physically and emotionally exhausted. The hotel's marble room was still too cold for my Canadian cure — two or three days in bed, plenty of soda, aspirin and comforting hot rum toddies. So I tried the French method — stay on your feet, ignore the running nose and eyes and the hacking cough, drink plenty of hot spiced wine and pretend there is no cold. Eventually, say in six weeks, it will go away.

Many assignments awaited me. After meeting Irène's friend Jacqueline I was able to recognize that women, including my friends, were wearing garments made from bed spreads, curtains, sheets, wall hangings and some exotic creations fashioned from scarves, shawls, saris and treasured materials that had come home with family members who had served in the French colonial empire. Visiting Dior and one or two other fashion establishments, I discovered that Paris's 40,000 seamstresses had found some work during the occupation transforming wardrobes. Jokingly, I said to one designer, "What will you do now? The Americans think New York has become the fashion centre of the world."

Her eyes flashed. "We are not worried. As soon as we can get the materials, you will see who rules the world of fashion!"

Visits to rehabilitation centres yielded lists of names of orphaned children. Thousands of mothers and children were in dire need. Many husbands were dead. Those who were prisoners-of-war or in concentration camps were being liberated and were slowly returning to France. Most were in poor health, and needed dairy products, vitamins and fats, all in short supply. I gathered lists of names and addresses and had others sent to the committees in Canada.

On the day before Good Friday I accepted an invitation to the country where I had spent so many happy holidays before the war. Bourgogne is my favourite area in France, even though it is far from the sea and does not have the dramatic beauty of the Mediterranean. There is always sun or an impression of sun, even on the stormiest days. When the clouds are gray and heavy with rain, then the light seems to rise from the fields. Something in the vegetation — the autumn fields of maise and grain, the masses of wild flowers in the meadows in spring — gives off a golden light.

Still hoarse and sniffling miserably from my cold, I watched the countryside go by from the train window. Here and there the damage was great, especially in the outer industrial areas of Paris. But as we neared my destination the fields were spreading out; the poplars, now a misty yellow-green, seemed to march single-file, marking the roads and canal. At stations the squares of clipped plane trees were sprouting leaves to form summer umbrellas of shade. Wild plums and quince were in blossom.

Tanlay, the village where Mme Compérot and her daughter Hélène lived, had survived, although it had been occupied for several long periods. An occupation force moved in immediately after the armistice. I do not know how many Germans were billeted there over the years, but they were there again during the retreat. I was told the town was finally liberated by the Canadians.

Although the village looked unchanged, I learned that it had been pillaged. Woolen blankets, down comforters, fur spreads, handwoven linens, books — anything the German soldiers had fancied left with them. When forced out by the advancing Allies, they filled every sort of vehicle. The baker's wife told me that one left pushing a neighbour's baby-carriage filled with booty.

During the years I had lived in Europe I had gathered a collection of books I valued. I had left them with Hélène and her mother. Many had been gifts. Some were beautiful art books I had received in Czechoslovakia, Hungary, Austria and Italy from Ministries of Information. I had also left behind manuscripts, letters and notebooks. For some reason these had been taken by the Germans. But others things, especially letters from my mother and friends in Canada, were discarded and scattered in the village streets when the Germans passed through in June 1940. Mme Compérot had then been on her way south, trying to reach her daughter Hélène in Bordeaux. She told me that her personal papers had been scattered in the same way.

In Tanlay there was a tempting table and a warm room after the biting cold of Paris. Bourgogne is one of the richest provinces of France, renowned for its wine, cattle, grain and corn. It had been stripped, but the farmers were smart. They had been more successful than others in finding hiding places for a portion of their products.

Partridge, wild boars and other game roamed the nearby forests. Every village and town had its hunters and guides. Some of these free enterprisers earned a living following the seasons, doing odd jobs for the local people, selling mushrooms, wild fruit, nuts, quince, baskets of tender dandelion leaves, water cress and truffles. These products of the field and forest helped the local people enjoy a much better diet than the Parisians. During Easter week, I must have regained a few pounds. There were fresh eggs, cottage cheese, salads, honey, nuts and some root vegetables to supplement the small bread ration. There was no meat or butter, nothing that required sugar. Among other things, I took Mme Compérot a pound of tea. She was delighted and showed me that she still had a few leaves in the bottom of a canister. "I was determined to make it stretch until the end of the war," she said. "I admit I dried the leaves to make more tea until there was no colour left. The German officer offered to get some for me but I told him I had sufficient."

Several German officers had been billeted in the house. My hostess had no choice, but she was allowed to keep one bedroom, a small storeroom and the kitchen. When they first arrived, the Germans visited the whole house and decided the little room filled with household rejects was useless, although it could be reached by an outside staircase. When the Maquis in the region was organized, this room came to serve a useful purpose. On moonless nights several members met there. Among them was young Jean-Claude Christol, to whom I had given so many English lessons during the summers. There were two windows and the door was kept ajar so they had a means of escape if the Germans below became inquisitive. In the evenings, unwilling to socialize with the Germans, Mme Compérot went to her room. There she could alert her young friends in the storeroom if she heard a step on the inner staircase.

The purpose of the meetings was to examine mail addressed to the Vichy government or any other officials, which had been confiscated by the local post-mistresses. If a letter contained an accusation against anyone or a betrayal of any kind to the German or collaborating officials, it was kept and the name of the sender recorded. Once a month Germaine Garreau bicycled the eighty kilometres from Paris to pick up the letters.

During the day Mme Compérot was obliged to do the cooking, washing, mending and look after the other needs of the officers. Seeing that she was a cultivated woman, they asked if she spoke German. She replied that she had no knowledge of German but did understand English. The senior officer asked her to take her meals with them. She replied, "I am obliged to cook for you, but there is no obligation to sit at the same table."

"Weren't you afraid?" I asked.

She straightened, her eyes severe. "No, I was not. The Germans understand the kind of 'no' I gave to them."

The officer did understand. He then asked if she would be good enough to listen to the broadcasts from the BBC and tell them what was being said about the invasion. Unfortunately for him, he and his fellow officers did not understand English. Delighted, Mme Compérot complied. It was her duty to arrange with the local farmers for fresh milk and other dairy products, bread from the bakery, meat from the butcher. Also the best Burgundy wine was in demand. Her German "guests" were far down the line of command and were determined to make the best of a boring situation — good food, comfortable beds and the prospect of some hunting. Better than the firing line.

Every morning after the BBC broadcast the officer asked impatiently, "And the invasion Madame, the invasion? What have you heard about that? Has the invasion begun?"

"Nothing about the invasion," Mme Compérot would answer, keeping her joy and satisfaction well hidden. "No mention of the invasion today."

Meanwhile, every morning the farm children arrived with fresh dairy products. Mme Compérot exchanged a few harmless remarks with them between whispers of the latest news that she had picked up from the BBC. The news was relayed through the whole community. "How we shook with horror for the people of London, the people in Britain during those terrible air raids. I lived in England for several years and I worried so much about my friends."

When the Germans finally evacuated the region, municipal elections were held and Mme Compérot was elected mayor. It was something that happened in many villages and towns in recognition of the part played and risks taken by elderly men and by women. These municipal officials were called upon to serve as local courts to try citizens charged with collaborating. Because of their war record, the mayors were thought competent to weed out any charges that might be motivated by spite or jealousy. Mme Compérot became a judge.

Only two men in the village came within Mme Compérot's mandate. Both were local citizens by birth, both hunters and guides. Hunting was the love of their life. In spite of local fury and contempt, the hunters could not resist the temptation to hunt and guide, even if it meant hunting and guiding the Germans. As soon as the village was liberated, the whole population denounced the hunters and demanded punishment.

Mme Compérot had known the men all their lives and understood their weakness. They were outdoor men and a long prison term would not do them any good. Although she did not want to confine them, she knew the temper of the village — the men must be punished. She sentenced them to ten years of no hunting. The villagers received the news with glee — it was fitting!

The château in the village was one of the most beautiful in the region. Before the war I had known the chatelaine, Mme de Tanlay, very well. She was in her late seventies when I met her. It was on the second day of my first visit that she arrived, without invitation, just in time for tea. My hostess had explained that it was one of the privileges of the chatelaine of the château to visit at any house in the village at tea time. When she came in she announced, "I heard that you have a visitor from Canada so I came over to meet her."

Mme de Tanlay was a delightful individual with a bright, well-cultivated mind, a witty tongue and a large dose of curiosity. I had enjoyed her stories of life in France when she was a girl in the late nineteenth century, how she had danced with Edward VII on more than one occasion when he visited the Riviera where she was vacationing with her family.

"He was a rogue," she said, her eyes twinkling with mischief. "But handsome, a charmer and a truly kind person. Always had an eye for a pretty girl." She would roll her eyes and glance at me sideways, suggesting naughty things. "He was loved," she said. "Do you know there are dozens of hotels all over Europe named for him? I think fifty-seven in France alone."

I was so happy to know that she had survived the war. She was now in her eighties and so arthritic she could no longer visit people at tea time. I went to see her and found her in a small sitting-room, her foot propped up on a stool, a radio on a stand about ten feet from her armchair. She was wrapped in a heavy dressing-gown with a great shawl over her shoulders. The room was damp and cold. I saw the same pictures, the same beautiful old furniture now dulled by damp and neglect. On top of the radio was a large picture of de Gaulle. It had been cut from a magazine and badly framed.

We embraced. "Did you know the Canadians liberated us this time?" she asked. "But they didn't stay long. Last time the Americans liberated the village and left one or two little Americans here. I don't think the Canadians had time, but we'll see." She laughed, her bright old eyes twinkling. She had not lost a shred of her spirit.

"Tell me everything about the arrival of the Germans and how they treated you," I urged.

"One of the village boys ran here and told me the commandant of the occupying detachment and some of his staff were on their way to the château. They intended to stay here. I put on a wide sash of blue, white and red satin ribbon from my shoulder to the floor, and met them at the door. I forgot to say I pinned on all my husband's medals too. I said, 'You are not welcome but I know you are going to stay here. Don't forget that this château is classified as a national monument. See that no damage is done to it. You will be held responsible. I have my quarters in the right wing. Please do not enter there. You have the rest of the château and it should be ample for you. Good Morning!'"

She chuckled. "With the Germans you have to give them orders. They are a very obedient people. Well the commandant and his men were like little schoolboys and didn't know what to say. The commandant clicked his heels and said, 'As you wish, Madame.'

"They were not bad, especially the commandant, though we almost never spoke. I think he had a domineering grandmother." She chuckled again wickedly. "I was lucky it was not the Gestapo.

"A day or two after his arrival the commandant knocked at my apartment door. A local farm girl was staying with me and opened it. The commandant said, 'May I come in, Madame?'

'Yes, if your business has to do with this village or its people.'

'It is your son, Madame. We had expected...'

'My son? I have no son. I have only a granddaughter and she does not live here.'

'But Madame...'

'I have told you. Now if you have more business...'

"It is the only way," she told me. "You must let them know who is in charge."

Then we settled in for a good talk. "I see you have General de Gaulle's picture," I said. "What do you think of him?"

"Ah, that one. Now there's a man any woman would be glad to call her son. He is my leader, a true son of France. I have listened to the BBC, 'The Voice of America,' the French staiton in Brazzaville. I have followed his career, he and the Free French. He has saved the honour of France."

"And what do you think of Maréchal Pétain?"

I was totally unprepared for her reply. "Henri? I've known Henri Pétain since dancing school when he was in knee pants. We went to the same parties. Vain prig. What he has done to France I will never forgive. Associating with Laval, that pig. God forgive him."

"But what about the First World War? Wasn't he a hero, the hero of Verdun?"

She hesitated. "Yes," she said slowly, "yes, he was. I admired him for that, even though I knew he was a vain little man. I thought he had redeemed himself." Every word dropped separately, reluctantly.

"What do you think will happen to him now?"

Suddenly she sat up straight, her eyes flashing. "Do you know what should be done with him? What I would do with him? I would announce that he is going to parade down the Champs-Elysées so *tout Paris* could be there. Then he would start on foot towards the Arc de Triomphe, and as he walked I would have young men of the Resistance pull off his ribbons, his medals, his buttons, his stripes, one by one until there would be nothing left. I would humiliate him as he has humiliated my beautiful France." Her tone was ferocious, but her blazing eyes filled with tears. "That's what I would do with Henri."

In a few days my cold was gone. Bourgogne meadows were dotted with wild flowers and the great alley of trees meeting over the main road was covered with bright foliage. Nightingales were trilling in full form.

I stopped nearby to see Mme Christol, wife of the Paris architect who back in 1940 had asked me to deliver those dreaded telegrams to soldiers' widows. We all called her Tante Mimi. In her garden was a long shed-like building where great family gatherings were celebrated at a long table. All around the walls of the shed were life-size silhouettes cut from black paper; she always made silhouettes of her friends. The Germans had not bothered to destroy them. I was happy to see my own still in its place.

nineteen

For some weeks I had been hinting at the Information Ministry that I would like to go to Alsace-Lorraine. Its capital city, Strasbourg, had been freed some months earlier by French forces. When I returned from Normandy all arrangements had been made.

My mission was to observe what had happened to the city, the people and the surrounding country of Alsace-Lorraine during the four years of German rule. The French Front, under the command of General de Lattre de Tassigny, was well inside Germany, north of Strasbourg. Just across the Rhine, the Germans still held Kehl and Offenburg.

I hoped to be able to go to General de Lattre's headquarters for an interview and to see a bit of Germany. Not far from Strasbourg was the notorious concentration camp, Struthof. Thousands of people — French, Jewish, European refugees and even Germans and Austrians who opposed the Nazis — had been taken there twice weekly by trainloads. I hoped to visit the camp. Also I wanted to talk to some of the liberated prisoners from military and concentration camps. They were, I had been told, shuffling their way back to France on foot.

A seat had been reserved for me on the train to Strasbourg, now functioning again once a day. When I reached the station platform there was a solid wall of people. The human crush in the corridors of the train was overwhelming. Yet when I showed my reservation ticket to the men pushing to get into the train, they stepped back to let me on the end of the coach and passed my valise hand-over-hand. On the small platform I was standing between carriages that dated back to the

early days of train transportation. The train started to move shortly
after I boarded. An elderly woman carrying a rolled-up blanket and a
big basket was trying to get her foot on the step to climb on. I noted
that the car behind us was empty. Two American soldiers were at the
door, staring through the window at us. As the train moved, the
woman was held in the air by the strong arms of two men. Suddenly
one of the men holding her somehow jumped off and at the same
time managed to swing her into his place. A cheer went up. Meanwhile the people around me on the platform, squeezed into a lump of
human dough, were shaking fists and shouting at the two soldiers in
the car behind. I called out in English, "Open the door and let these
people in. Why is it locked?"

When they heard my English, they unlocked the door and called to
me to join them, thinking I was an American. "No, I'm Canadian," I
answered sharply. "But why are you locking these people out? The car
is empty."

"Orders," they shouted.

"Whose orders?"

"We're picking up a bunch of our guys down the line somewhere
and we have been given orders to keep this car clear for them."

"Well, can't you let in some of the women and children crushed in
this corridor until we reach the town where your buddies are?"

They looked at one another. "Just as long as they promise to get out
when we stop to pick up our bunch," one replied.

I turned to a tall man near me and explained. Rapidly the word was
passed back in French. "They promise," I told the soldiers. "You can
count on it."

Somehow the people seemed to move aside. Children were passed
overhead and women pushed forward and across the platform to the
empty car. Now everybody was smiling and shouting "Vive les Americans." Once the women and children were out of the corridor, it was
possible to pile more bags and boxes into the baggage nets. Along the
corridor people could sit on their valises. In each compartment extra
people were squeezed in. When we eventually picked up the Americans, they good-naturedly doubled up and left a few compartments for
the French overflow. The whole coach was in a hubbub of
appreciation.

After a short distance, our progress grew slower and slower.
Through the night we crept along, stopping often and then creeping
forward again. It was pitch black outside. Inside curtains were drawn;
tiny blue-painted dim bulbs shed a little light. People instantly fell

asleep. I could see the terrible fatigue and the strain in some of the faces nearby fade. It grew warmer and my legs ached. I could not stretch them in any direction. The air became stifling. I could not sleep and thought I would never breathe again. Then I remembered how hundreds of thousands of human beings had been moved to concentration camps in sealed cattle cars, many suffocating, dead on arrival. All the next day we crept along. I understood our stops now, for before crossing every temporary bridge the train paused. The bridges all looked as though they might crumble beneath us. It was more than twenty-four hours before we reached Strasbourg, normally a six-hour run.

I had not had the good sense to take food and drink with me, and it was impossible to buy anything along the way. However, my companions insisted on sharing some bread, wine and more little yellow apples with me. Crossing Alsace-Lorraine, we passed through a devastated landscape of forests. Great, once stately trees had toppled; they looked humiliated. Having seen these beautiful forests before, where trees were cared for like children, I wanted to cry.

At La Maison Rouge a large and comfortable bedroom had been reserved for me. The portly, middle-aged woman, who insisted on carrying my valise, asked if I would like a hot bath. I could not believe my ears. I had not had a real bath since leaving Canada. She led me down the hall to a room as big as a salon and the largest bathtub I have ever seen standing on lion's claw legs. Along one side wall were hot rods holding huge bath towels. She left me. I shed my clothing and luxuriated in the warm water for an hour. I was so relaxed that I wound myself in a fresh hot towel, picked up my clothes, raced for my room, climbed into the feather bed without supper and never moved all night.

The next morning at about ten I was to meet the man who was to be my guide, Monsieur Martin, Director of the Strasbourg Museum. He was a member of a group assessing damage and working out plans for restoring the French character of the city.

Outside the hotel on the common I caught sight of groups of men clustered around benches, lying on the ground, all of them talking. They had recently been released from work camps and a concentration camp. It was my first view of those skeletal figures with the burning eyes and faces lit with the joy of return. Five days earlier they had been liberated by the French army.

They told me that the German guards were petrified with fear when they heard a French army was approaching. No one believed the story.

Still, they moved out about 5,000 workers, shot 150 and abandoned those they did not have time to move. "We couldn't believe our eyes either," one man told me. "We'd heard the Allies were coming but we expected the Americans or the British. When we saw they were French we nearly died with joy."

Monsieur Martin said that tens of thousands of Alsatians were returning home from the interior of France, where they had been taken for safety in 1939. In many cases they found their homes stripped of everything. The authorities were overburdened trying to sort things out. We went for a long walk through the city. Every vestige of French had disappeared, except some hand-lettered signs in some stores and restaurant windows. The city was still under fire from Kehl across the Rhine. Every day a few shells fell on the city. "It's to remind us that they are still there," my guide said.

I talked to people everywhere, policemen, waitresses and others I met when we visited municipal offices, the post office, churches and the National and University Library of Strasbourg. The city had been overrun before the armistice of 1940 and as far as the Germans were concerned, Strasbourg was not an occupied city but an integral part of Germany. Any sign of French rule had to be erased. The National Library was a case in point. It became a German library and all visible signs of French were removed. Twice before, because of war, the almost impossible task of changing the whole library system from French to German (1870-1871) and back from German to French (1918) had required years of work. Fortunately, this time the task had not yet been undertaken.

A young waitress described some of her experiences. One day without thinking she had handed a menu in French to a German officer. He asked her severely if she spoke German. She admitted she did. "Then if ever you use another word of French in this restaurant you will go to prison. You are in Germany now," he said, and tore up the menu. "That's what happened all the time," she said, "a slip of the tongue and sometimes people were never seen again."

"When the German soldiers first came they seemed to think they were liberating us," another woman told me. "They said, 'But you are German by origin, race, blood and you speak German. Why do you persist in saying you are French?'

'Because we are French. Because we love France and her ideas of liberty, and we don't like you and we hate your ideas of oppression and suppression of the individual and of human dignity.'

"The Germans were puzzled and said, 'Well you won't get away with it. Just you wait until the S.S. arrives. Things will be different then.'

"He was right," she said bitterly. "Things were different. The oppression grew heavier all the time. The Germans cannot abide any opposition to their ideas."

Meanwhile the city was methodically stripped. Since thousands of homes were empty, trucks made regular rounds gathering up everything from books to down comforters. "It was organized efficiently," my guide said ironically. "One month pillows, the next linen, the following clothing or kitchenware. They even collected clocks by the thousands, from ordinary alarm clocks to ornate antiques and cuckoo clocks."

We went to the basement of a church. It was half full of children's books that had been Christmas and birthday presents. One was *Alice in Wonderland*; the inscription read, "To dear little Marianne on her eighth birthday, affectionately Aunt Yvonne." The titles included Kipling's Jungle Books and Grimm's *Fairy Tales*. School editions of the classics in German, French and English had inscriptions from fathers to grandmothers. In some way that basement of children's books, representing so many happy family reunions at Christmas or birthdays, chilled me more than the sight of the damaged towns.

Thunderstruck, I asked, "Whatever did they plan to do with them?"

"Distribute them to schools in Germany, even in towns just across the Rhine. On arrival the fly-leaves were removed and the books then distributed. If you go into Germany, visit a village or two and see for yourself. Most are deserted now, the villagers fled east to escape the war. You will find French books, musical instruments, furniture, even kitchen pots and pans."

For three days I visited Strasbourg, gathering a picture of the city under the Hitler regime. I also found the city better stocked than Paris, so I bought supplies for friends — tooth powder, brushes, shampoo, cosmetics, shirts. They were small things, but Paris lacked everything.

On the fourth morning I was looking forward to a whole day of travelling north through Alsace to try to arrange an interview with General de Lattre de Tassigny. His headquarters was some forty kilometres inside the German border at Kandel. We travelled slowly and carefully, the driver trying to keep the jeep in the faint tracks of a vehicle somewhere ahead. Roadsides were still mined. Three times we took detours. We passed through massacred forests and the damaged towns of Vendenheim, Brumath and Haguenau. As we passed fields, I noticed large areas were marked off with white tape. Sometimes the tape stretched along the highway. Between the tapes on narrow lengths of land, women and children were tilling the ground.

"What are the tapes for?" I asked the driver.

"They mark the mine fields. There have been a lot of accidents but the peasants won't stop tilling the land."

Thoughts of T.S. Eliot and his "Wasteland" kept me company. One could almost smell the gun powder in the air.

At Wissembourg we got permission to enter Germany. Inside the border we crossed the Seigfried line. Heavy fortifications, block houses, deep-ditch tank traps; the latter were about six feet deep and ten feet wide and behind them were concrete teeth driven into the ground. There were thick lengths of log also driven in, each with an iron band around the top. Other ditches were filled with water, barriers of tree-trunks and rolls of barbed wire.

Beyond, several villages seemed to be deserted. At Kandel, I was disappointed to discover that General de Lattre was away. However, some of his officers were ready to talk and I enjoyed having lunch with them. One of the general's aides told me that during the previous winter, when the Germans made their sudden counter-offensive (the Battle of the Bulge), there was a question of having the French army retreat from the city of Strasbourg. General Leclerc and General de Lattre refused, arguing that the city would be defended as long as one French soldier remained alive. Thus was the city saved from a second German occupation.

After lunch we drove northward to the German city of Speyer, where we crossed the Rhine. My driver said that we could go no farther, since military operations were going on ahead. So we turned south again on the east side of the Rhine. Again we passed through damaged villages. Most people remained indoors. When we passed young people they turned their heads away, but the older men took off their caps and the women bowed. Not a sign of a Nazi poster or a picture of Hitler anywhere. "There are no Nazis in Germany now," my driver remarked sardonically. "We can't find one who ever voted for or approved of Hitler."

I remembered thinking of all the destruction I had seen from the beaches of Normandy right across France to the Rhine and beyond. And for what? Certainly every freedom-loving person had a stake in stopping the march of Hitler's ideology. But if the nations of the League had really taken their responsibility seriously and united in the defence of peace, would the Second World War have been necessary? I rememberd that the armament-makers, the politicians, the military-minded and the industrialists usually survive wars, and have their property returned to them afterwards.

I asked my driver to stop along the route and we entered several empty houses. It was true, items of all kinds were there, including books with the tell-tale inscriptions removed. French goods of all kinds had been distributed to the owners of these houses. After a time, trying to absorb so much man-made barbarism and ruin, a sort of numbness sets in. Perhaps it is a merciful protection.

We passed many of the liberated as they shuffled along the road. They were thin, ragged and weary, but with the welcome they got once they crossed the bailey bridge near Karlsrube, their shoulders seemed to straighten and their chins lift. At Karlsrube we discovered that prisoners had been kept there in cellars for five days without food. Some of those we spoke to on the road told us they had been liberated at 10 a.m. the morning before. We crossed the bridge and saw a big sign on the French entrance reading "Entrance to Germany here by courtesy of XM249Y3 (U.S.A.)." I did not know what "XM249Y3 (U.S.A)" stood for but it obviously reflected the American sense of humour.

From the bridge into Wissembourg, the road was lined with pots of flowers and banners of welcome. People offered wine and food and hugs to the weary men. I saw women pick up a handful of soil and hold it out. The men kissed it. Others fell on their knees and kissed the ground.

The sun was low in the sky now and my driver warned that we should be off the road before dusk. Passing all those men I wondered where they would sleep. They were coming back in such numbers that it was impossible to shelter them all even though homes, barns and sheds held as many as they could. Most would probably huddle together at the side of the road or in a ditch.

As we made a detour, we learned that bombs and a mine had destroyed a part of the road we had passed over that morning. At one place we saw a long section of road gone. A truck turning out to pass another had touched off a land mine and been blown apart. The driver was wounded, the soldier beside him killed. I shivered.

The following morning we took the road to Colmar and visited some of the towns and villages on the way. As we came over a rise, a village could be seen a short distance ahead. Then, as we approached, I discovered that only the wooden framework of the buildings were standing; all the plaster between those distinctive Alsatian wood-patterns had been blown out. At a distance, the village gave an illusion of being intact; on arrival it turned out to be a skeleton. Only the storks remained. As we passed through, they would fly off their big nests or stand poised on a chimney.

"Our armies are in Germany north of Strasbourg," my driver explained. "But the Germans are still just across the river from the city and these villages are within range of guns." We passed through Benfeld and Erstein, and thought of all the work their residents would face when they came home again. Then we turned off and visited two villages still intact between the low mountains, Ste. Marie and Ribeauville. They are among the most picturesque I have ever seen, and I wondered how they had been spared. Ribeauville lies in a narrow gorge between two mountains and either end is walled in, so we had to enter through a gate. I talked to some of the people in a café. "We've had some broken windows, but that is about all," a woman said. "But the noise has been terrible, year after year. The guns, the explosions, the planes, and all that noise echoing off the mountains. Still we are so fortunate, and we could give homes to our relatives from Benfeld." The lovely little city of Colmar itself had been spared most of the destruction.

We returned late in the afternoon and I spent some time talking to groups of soldiers and prisoners who were gathering in clusters around park benches as they came into the city. I remember one young man in particular. He had a bicycle that looked brand new. I asked him where he had bought it. "Bought it?" he grinned. "I liberated it. This is the third I've had since I got out of that camp. Been exchanging them on the way home. I picked up the first just outside the camp. Every time I saw a German with a better one I made him trade. They're so scared they will do anything. Besides our army occupies the territory now. We're just getting a bit of our own back. They stole thousands of our bicycles."

Another one had a bag with three live chickens in it. "I'm taking them home. They've eaten all our chickens and used to boast to us that there wasn't a chicken alive in France." His eyes gleamed. Most of the men were just skin and bone; clothing, such as it was, was worn to tatters. I made only one effort to ask about their experiences, but it was clear that they did not want to talk about them.

Next morning my guide was ready to drive me to the Struthof concentration camp. As we drove along, he explained how every Tuesday and Friday trainloads of prisoners were brought in from various parts of France, Belgium and Holland; other trains came from Germany. A station was built and the prisoners themselves were forced to cut a road up the side of a mountain to the camp site. The site itself was beautiful. It looked out over the mountains for many miles

in several directions. As we entered the camp, the quarters for the
official German staff were just inside. A large swimming-pool, tennis
courts and landscaped flower beds made it attractive. Now empty, the
living quarters were just as the Germans had left them. There I met a
small delegation of the International Red Cross from Switzerland, also
on an inspection tour.

Their guide explained the history of the camp and then, to our
horror, took a knife and slit open the side of a thick mattress on one of
the beds. It had been stuffed with human hair. There were lamp
shades of human skin, made by prisoners. We were all sick with the
unspeakable inhumanity of it. Then we moved on into the camp.
Long, narrow barracks were tiered down a long slope and on each side
of a central roadway. On each tier between the barracks stood a
primitive gibbet with a dangling rope. We went into several of the
barracks and were silenced by the mute testimony scratched on the
walls. Names, names, names! Sometimes an address or a girl's name.
Sometimes simply "Mother."

It was down this central road that the prisoners walked towards the
barber shop where their hair was removed. We were taken to a shed
and discovered that human hair was piled three feet deep over its
entire floor — straight, curly, long, short, coarse and fine — it was like
a carpet of an infinite number of shades, black, browns, red, honey-
blonde, gray and white. Curls lay there, perhaps those of a young girl.
We stood transfixed.

From there the path led to the gas ovens perched on the edge of a
shallow cliff. Beside them were other buildings. In one were rows
upon rows of terra cotta pots, looking much like ordinary flower pots
with lids. These were the containers for the ashes. The system was to
write to the family and say that "unfortunately" the relative had died.
The body had been cremated and if the family wished to receive the
ashes they would be sent. Attached was a price list for the various sizes
of containers.

Then we entered the crematorium and saw the gas ovens where not
one but several bodies at a time could be pushed in. Outside the
building at the back, the ashes were dumped over the cliff. It was a
long drop, but the ashes reached almost to the top. The doctor
delegated to guide us said that the ashes had been removed from time
to time and spread on the land as fertilizer.

"But what of the individual ashes sent to the families?" someone
asked.

The doctor looked surprised. "I thought you understood. You saw
the ovens. It would be impossible to have individual ashes. When

requests came, ashes were just scooped up and put in a container. There was a stiff fee, too."

Finally we were taken to a room attached to the crematorium. In it were several rows of large meat hooks imbedded in the ceiling. "Those who tried to escape or who may have earned the enmity of a guard were usually the victims here. They were impaled alive on these hooks and left until unconscious and then cremated," the Alsatian doctor explained. I learned later that this was the fate of one of my friends, Frank Pickersgill. By this time the three Red Cross representatives and I could take no more.

Silently we returned to Strasbourg. I went to bed and tried to wipe away the scenes these terrible mute testimonies had conjured up in my mind. I could not.

I left on the train for Paris the next morning. In the compartment I had for companions a middle-aged couple (the husband had been a station agent), a priest, an old woman, and an auburn-haired housewife whose story was both tragic and comic. She was a native of Strasbourg, but during the war she had lived with relatives in southern France. She had come to Strasbourg a few days earlier to see if her house was still intact. She found it badly damaged and was returning to Paris to obtain what she could to restore it.

"Imagine how I felt when I found out the Germans had turned my house into a club!" She was almost weeping with rage. The house was three storeys high. The Germans had bricked in the fireplaces, pulled out most of the partitions and turned the third floor into a gymnasium with a row of four bathrooms and showers on one side. The second floor had become a large library and games room and several small bedrooms with toilets and basins. The main floor had a dining-room, lounges and a cloakroom; in the basement a kitchen and freezer room had been built. Before leaving the Germans had ransacked the place, taking most of the books, pictures, furniture and anything else that appealed to them. "It will take God knows how long to put the place back in shape. And how much money? I'm not even sure it can be done. The floors are in terrible shape." She was wringing her hands, the tears dropping into her lap.

The conversation turned to pillaging. "The Germans were terrible," the old lady said. "Our boys would never do such things. They did not even leave me with one woolen comforter. They are barbarians, barbarians, those Germans. At least we are civilized, our men are civilized."

The priest smiled and said mildly, "In wartime, Madame, young men will do many things they would not do in ordinary times. We must remember war removes all the restraints of social civilization, even Christianity. War releases all those wild instincts it has taken centuries to control. We must not expect too much of them."

The old lady bristled indignantly. "I don't believe our sons would do such things — destroy one's furniture, steal the blankets off the beds and not leave even one, and it wintertime. No respect for the aged. Ransack and steal the food parcels. No, no, I don't believe it."

The priest replied rather sadly, "I hope you are right, Madame, but in wartime, one must be tolerant. Usually the rules of civilized behaviour are the first to go. One never knows."

Soon a number of French soldiers climbed aboard and filled the corridors. There were two seats in our compartment and two fresh-faced young soldiers took them. One barely mumbled a greeting when addressed, but the other was talkative. In minutes he was telling us his adventures and mentioned that he had another comrade in the corridor "sitting on three typewriters."

"Three?" the station agent exclaimed.

The soldier laughed. "Yes. Nobody was in the store in that town. My friend always wanted a typewriter. The store was full of them, all new and in cases. He only took three. They're good ones, Swiss. They probably swiped them from the Swiss. Only trouble is we have to help him to carry them."

There was a gasp from the old lady, "You stole them?"

The young soldier grinned and winked. "Of course not, Madame, not stole, liberated them. Haven't the Germans stolen everything from us?" At this point he pulled up the sleeve of his tunic and revealed several wrist-watches on his arm. "I didn't want a typewriter but in another store I got these. The old man was scared stiff and gave them to me. Of course, I wouldn't have hurt him. Well, serves them right, they've been stealing everything from France during the whole war."

I caught the priest's eye. It was full of amusement. "My son, you shouldn't have done that. However you look at it, it's stealing. I understand how you feel . . . but never do such a thing again."

Though the other soldier had not said anything, they both got up to leave, looking slightly shame-faced.

The old lady looked at me. I knew she was painfully embarrassed and mortified, especially in front of a foreigner, so I murmured "It's war time, and they're so young, only boys . . ."

She sighed and said, "Yes, it's wartime."

twenty

M y stay in France was coming to an end. Mme Vanier and a panel of English-speaking judges were interviewing young girls who had played active parts in the Resistance to assess their English and their ability to speak before an audience. Many requests had come from the United States, Britain and Canada for representatives of the Resistance to speak to organizations and young people about their experiences. Four girls were selected for Canada and I was to take two of them from Ottawa to Victoria. Another member of our staff would take the other two to Quebec and the Maritimes.

My French friends planned an evening gathering. To my joy Albert Vernier had a few days leave from the Front. He had spent most of them in Oran, Algeria, with Madeleine and their baby daughter Anne. Now Albert had two days in Paris. I was astonished at his appearance. The shy and boyish soldier I had last seen holding hands with Madeleine in 1940 had become a mature and thoughtful man. His experiences had aged him more than the five years. We spoke of his young cousin, Jean-Claude Christol, to whom I had given English lessons and who had died in the Maquis before his twentieth birthday. That evening Albert told me his great news. He had been called to headquarters in Paris and told that he was to be posted as a military attaché to the French Embassy in Washington. After a quick trip to the Front to take leave of his senior officer, he would meet Madeleine and the baby in Paris, and they would leave immediately for the United States.

I was delighted. "Ottawa is so close!" I exclaimed. "You'll be able to come up to Ottawa during the summer and I'll certainly go to

Washington to see you. I'm dying to see Madeleine and the baby."
Excitedly we made plans for the future.

Somewhat hesitantly Albert said, "You never answered our letter asking you to be Anne's godmother. Did you get the letter?"

I was puzzled. "I got several letters from Madeleine, and one from you. Several sections were cut out of yours by the censors, but there was no reference to Anne in the bits I got. In fact, I only discovered you were a father when I saw your Aunt Mimi here in Paris."

"We wondered if it was religion, because Madeleine is a Roman Catholic and you're a Protestant, aren't you?"

"What nonsense, as if that would make any difference. I'd be honoured and delighted."

He shook his head and looked embarrassed. "I'm sorry. When we didn't hear from you another of Madeleine's friends asked to be godmother." Then he grinned. "But maybe while we are in Washington you'll get another chance."

Albert left for the Front and I left for London. Some days after I reached Ottawa I got the news that on that brief visit to the Front Albert had been killed.

I embarked for home on a troop ship. Its principal cargo was hundreds of war brides. Some of them had been married for nearly five years and had one or two children. We also carried several hundred women of the St. John's Ambulance corps, Red Cross and some members of the military services. The rest of the passenger list was made up of several hundred Newfoundland lumberjacks who had been working in Britain during the war.

Cruisers and corvettes gave us a wonderful feeling of security as they steamed along beside us. The trip seemed uneventful, though at one point we took a sharp jog north until the faint line of Greenland's coast was visible. As far as we were aware, no German submarines had been spotted.

Life on board was a different story. There were long, bare dormitories intended for troops, each containing twenty two-tiered bunks, each expected to hold at least twenty women and twenty or more children. Each child was fitted with a life-jacket inflated fore and aft, and to each a tiny battery-powered red bulb was attached to make a child visible in the water. The first day or two they were like new toys. Even the smallest toddler enjoyed running on deck or in the corridors and lounges, falling and bouncing back unhurt.

The real problem was lack of water. Along one wall between bunks were several wash basins; fresh water was available for one hour in the morning, half an hour at noon and another hour at night. Sorting out the problem of how twenty women and twenty or more children in each dormitory were to use the basins, and who should have first go, required all the persuasion and tact the stewards could muster. The purser took me aside. "We have shower rooms where two or three dozen men can shower at once — no privacy and it's sea water. If you want to arrange for some of the women to use them in off hours, and post a woman outside the door, it could be arranged. However, it must be at night and not too many at a time. Let's say about one shower each during the trip."

It was a quandary. How could it be arranged? Finally, each dormitory was given the privilege in turn. As usual every sort of argument was put up for being first in line. I shall never forget the sight of that shower room. The showers were spaced at intervals around a very large room, the water running into a sump in the middle. The women went in, ten at a time, some taking their children. It was bedlam, but it did wonders for the morale.

At that time I always carried a copy of the *Canadian Almanac* with me; it answered so many questions. I was soon beseiged by war brides wanting to know everything about Canada, and I made some dreadful discoveries. Some soldiers had overblown the charms and facilities in their houses and home towns. One young woman with two children showed me a snapshot of the Moose Jaw Public Library and explained proudly that it was the residence of her husband's parents. Another told me she was going to be living "just outside Regina." It turned out to be Climax, Saskatchewan, and as far as I knew the branch line train service ran there three times a week from May to October. The most horrific story was that of a young woman who had been raised in London. Her husband had told her that he owned a hunting and fishing camp on Lake Athabasca. "It will be so interesting," she said. "People fly in from all over America."

"Have you ever lived in the country?" I asked.

"Well, no, but I've been to Richmond."

In Halifax the dock was thronged with people waiting to welcome the brides and their children. Some had come a long way and many carried bouquets of flowers. The period of tentative recognitions was moving. Those who failed to find a welcoming face were taken to hotels. Others left for other parts of Canada by train. I could not help thinking about all the different new lives beginning for these young women, and wondering how they would take it.

On the trip back to Ottawa, it was so satisfying to relax and look at the peaceful green countryside, the bright spring skies, the fields and forests and quiet little towns. During a moment on the platform somewhere, I caught the smell of pine and balsam in the fresh, pure air — that fragrance meant Canada to me. I thought how impossible it must be for the people living along the way to visualize what I had seen in London and in France. What words could I use?

On May 7, 1945, the day before the armistice, I stepped off the train in Ottawa. The next day people were celebrating. I did not go out. While overwhelmingly thankful that the war was over in Europe, I had no feeling of celebration in me. I felt numb. In the evening a friend came over and persuaded me to go downtown. Offices and stores had been closed all day and so were most restaurants. The furniture had been removed for safety from the lobby of the Chateau Laurier; its dining-room and cafeteria were closed. Long lines of people were still queued to get into the Connaught, Murray's and a few restaurants that dared stay open. I did not stay long on the streets.

There was something missing. I remembered the feeling in the crowds at the end of the First World War, though I had only been a child then. It was a feeling of jubilation, thankfulness and great hope. It had been the war to end all wars. And Canadians had believed it. Now we knew that the Second World War had not ended war, and no one dared to even think it. Soon, we hoped, the war in the Pacific would be ended, but it would not end war either. We knew of the heavy price we had paid.

I had gone to Europe ten years earlier to find out firsthand about communism and fascism. I had discovered that both meant totalitarian dictatorship, the mortal enemy of a free and democratic society. The importance of V-E Day was that fascism had been defeated. But had it really been defeated? How does one defeat an idea?

In the forty years that have passed, experience has shown me that labels mean little. There are many kinds of regimes that call themselves communist, or are described that way by others. And there are other kinds of regimes that are fascist, or fascism masquerading under the name of democracy. In both cases, they are loosely or tightly woven totalitarian regimes.

Instinctively that V-E Day I was aware that, even though the end had come to another war in Europe, the ideas lived on and we could be challenged again to gather all our individual inner strengths, intelligence and determination in defence of our free and democratic society, our moral and spiritual values, the kind of civilized world we strive for.

I am reminded of a conversation I and some others had in 1975 with the vice-chairman of Wuhan University in China. His whole education had been western — Shanghai missionary schools, universities in the United States, Edinburgh and Paris. He told us that he owed his knowledge of his own country and people to three years of "re-education" as a labourer and teacher in an agricultural commune. From his conversation I carried away three thoughts about the isms I had been so curious about before the war. "Communism is to socialist societies what Utopia represents to democracy — a vision of the perfect society which retreats as one struggles towards it; socialism is inclined to unravel slowly towards a more democratic society; and fascism tightens into a dictatorship that can only be removed by revolution."

"And what of democracy?" someone asked.

"Democracies have to be vigilant," he said.

Other Canadian Lives you'll enjoy reading

Canadian Lives is a paperback reprint series that presents the best in Canadian biography chosen from the lists of Canada's many publishing houses. Here is a selection of titles in the series. Watch for more Canadian Lives every season from Goodread Biographies. Ask for them at your local bookstore.

An Arctic Man by Ernie Lyall
Ernie Lyall's story of 65 years living with the Inuit people in the Arctic. /239 pages/12 photos/$4.95

By Reason of Doubt by Ellen Godfrey
The story of university professor Cyril Belshaw, the mysterious death of his wife, and his trial for murder. /208 pages/12 photos/$4.95

Canadian Nurse in China by Jean Ewen
The story of a remarkable young nurse who travelled in war-torn China with Dr. Norman Bethune. /162 pages/$3.95

Close to the Charisma by Patrick Gossage
A lively, fresh, entertaining insider's view of the people who ran the country during the Trudeau years /288 pages/27 photos/$5.95

The Company Store by John Mellor
The dramatic life of a remarkable and fiery idealist, J.B. McLachlan, and the battle of the Cape Breton coal miners. /400 pages/35 photos/$5.95

Crowfoot:Chief of the Blackfeet by Hugh Dempsey
The fascinating story of the great chief of the Blackfoot nation: a great warrior, diplomat and peacemaker. /240 pages/12 photos/ $5.95

Glen Gould by Geoffrey Payzant
One of Canada's greatest musicians, Glenn Gould rethought the relationship between music, the preformer and the audience. /250 pages/$5.95

Halfbreed by Maria Campbell
The powerfully-told life story of an unforgettable young Metis woman /184 pages/$4.95

Her Excellency Jeanne Sauve by Shirley Woods
The remarkable and inspirational story of the journalist, mother and politician who became Canada's Governor General. /288 pages/58 photos/$5.95

Her Own Woman by Myrna Kotash et al
Profiles of ten contemporary Canadian women, famous and not-so-famous including Barbara Frum, Margaret Atwood, and sports hero Abby Hoffman. /212 pages/9 photos/$4.95

Hey Malarek! by Victor Malarek
A wonderfully written account of a young, street-tough kid, in and out of boys' homes, in trouble with the cops — truly a good read! /241 pages/$4.95

Hugh MacLennan: A writer's life by Elspeth Cameron
The prize-winning biography of one of Canada's greatest novelists. /23 photos/$5.95

The Indomitable Lady Doctors by Carlotta Hacker
Stories of courage, heroism and dedication — the experiences of Canada's pioneering women doctors./171pages /20 photos/$5.95

Letters from a Lady Ranche by Monica Hopkins
The lively, delightfully-written adventures of a young woman who married a homesteader and started a new life in the west.. / 171 pages/$4.95

northern New Mexico because I have always found that I think more clearly in the mountains, on the water, or by field or stream, than in the office. It gave me a chance to think about why Barry had not been elected. When I returned, I wrote him a long, brutally frank letter analyzing the defeat.

I concluded that Barry himself was the reason for the defeat because he was honest and courageous and said exactly what his conscience dictated. People who wanted sugar-coated pills and not facts didn't like this. It was something of an indictment of our body politic, but it appears that a more adroit and less straightforward man would have pleased more voters. Personally, I believe in absolute honesty. I therefore wholeheartedly approved of his approach.

I recommended that we should do everything possible to help President Johnson and assure the success of his administration. Since the nation was in his hands we, as loyal Americans, had to help him to preserve and improve it. I wrote:

> At the same time those of us who believe in the smallest government that can carry out the necessary functions of government, sound fiscal policies, national prestige, and enhanced national security, must continue to strive to educate the people of our great nation to the dangers of socialism and deficit spending, and the importance of national prestige and national morality. Some day we, or our successors, will prevail.

CHAPTER 24

Although, at 65, I looked forward to more leisure time, I still wasn't really ready to sit and ponder the past. I had met V. J. Skutt, CEO of the Mutual of Omaha Insurance Company, in 1958 and been tremendously impressed with him.

The company had been founded by Dr. C. C. Criss in 1909 and presented an award in his name to honor outstanding contributions to health, safety, education, and/or public welfare. The recipient in 1959 was Dr. Thomas A. Dooley, who was doing some wonderful humanitarian work in Southeast Asia. He had lived in our neighborhood in St. Louis. Someone found out about this, and Skutt invited Joe and me to attend that year's C. C. Criss Award ceremony in Omaha.

In 1961, I was asked to fill a vacancy on his board. I checked on the company very carefully before joining it and found that it was truly a first-class organization operating in accordance with the highest legal and ethical standards. However, I did not want to be just a figurehead and agreed to join the board with one stipulation: I would serve only if my efforts would contribute in a meaningful and significant way to the protection, safety, and well-being of the American public. My stipulation was accepted and I subsequently worked on several committees to develop health insurance plans for Mutual's overseas installations and to draft travel insurance for possible spaceflights and astronaut coverage. I saw my role as contributing to the company's expressed mission of helping others to help themselves. I was especially interested in the company's aggressive programs of fostering travel, accident, and health insurance.

In the years following, I served on the boards of eight of Mutual's companies and was given a number of assignments that fitted into my background in aviation and the military. I made several trips overseas when the company was expanding into international markets.

I was determined never to miss a board meeting, and I never did. But on one occasion in 1965, I had to travel to Omaha by dog sled from a camp in the Yukon to civilization, where I rode a Jeep to an airport, and flew in five different types of planes with five changes to get there. Nearly got trapped by weather in Chicago, but made it to Omaha on time. I vowed never to cut it so close again.

In 1968, I turned 72 years old and was past retirement age for most corporations. I thought the time had come for me to move aside for younger men and women. By that time I had retired from the boards of Shell, TRW, and Aerospace Corporation. However, I was asked to remain as a director on the boards of the several Mutual of Omaha companies and agreed to stay as long as I could be useful to each.

When I reached the age where I was considered a very senior citizen, I remembered a promise I had made to Joe in 1913 while we were still in high school. At that time, I had told her that if she would marry me I would take her on a voyage up the beautiful inside passage of Alaska some day. It's a good thing I didn't tell her when I would do this. In 1973, sixty years later, we flew from Los Angeles to Seattle, boarded a ship, and made a leisurely trip to Skagway, Alaska, then took a train to White Horse, Canada, and returned home by air.

I didn't realize how patient Joe had been, waiting for me to carry out my promise. When we boarded the ship and it seemed certain that she was finally going to get her trip to Alaska, she turned to me and said, "Doolittle, you're a man of your word."

After many years of comfortable living in Santa Monica, Joe and I decided in 1978 to move to a retirement community in Carmel, California. Although we had purchased property at Pebble Beach, a few miles away, we decided that the advantages of moving into a facility that would allow us to maintain our privacy, yet have access to meals and medical facilities, should we need or want them, outweighed the problems inherent in designing and building a house to our specifications. We deeded the Pebble Beach property to our son John and his wife, Priscilla.

Meanwhile, the company graciously offered me the opportunity to continue to serve, so I commuted to Los Angeles for the next two years. As anyone knows who tries it, commuting by commercial airline and living in a hotel away from one's family is very wearing. In 1980, the company opened an office for me in nearby Monterey.

In keeping with my theory about gradually lowering one's plateaus of activity as one grows older, I gradually resigned from committees and the directorships of all of Mutual's companies during the 1980s. However, the company elected me as a director emeritus and consultant for the major company in 1985. The year before, Joe and I were greatly honored by being presented with Criss awards. It was a night to be remembered for us. President Ronald Reagan, Dolores and Bob Hope, Florence Henderson, George Gobel, Charlton Heston, and others paid us tribute. I was especially pleased at what Dolores Hope said about Joe:

> As we know, Jimmy has flown millions of miles and for good reasons was away from home and his dear family for ages at a time. He spent 45 years in the air. Joe Doolittle spent 45 years waiting for him to land—at military bases, at civilian airports—and sometimes at the end of a runway that didn't exist until he landed.
>
> Those of us whose husbands also travel learned from her. For years, Joe was the national distributor of patience. But the Doolittles worked out a special arrangement beyond waiting. When Jimmy began setting records for passenger aircraft, Joe became his official passenger. She flew with him on more than one record flight. She didn't crave the honor. She took the job because her husband needed her. She's an amazing lady.

When Delores presented the award to Joe, she added that Joe

had shared her courage with women everywhere and therefore deserved a Criss Award of her own.

I was doubly honored that night.

Several weeks later, the Society of Experimental Test Pilots paid Joe an unusual tribute. For some time, the society has given a scholarship annually in my name to some deserving young engineering student. In 1984, they decided that one should be given in Joe's name to honor her for taking my place and making many of the annual presentations while I was off somewhere on business, hunting, or fishing. It was also a recognition of her as a test pilot's wife who quietly bore the agony of living with the constant threat of widowhood because of her husband's profession. Once more I was honored by the thoughtfulness of those who realized her important role in my life.

As I complete these memoirs, the world is witnessing a tremendous pro-democracy movement in the Soviet-dominated Eastern Bloc countries and in the Soviet Union itself. The Berlin Wall has come down; the small nations of Eastern Europe that had been swallowed up by Communist regimes are throwing off the yoke of totalitarianism; *perestroika* and *glasnost* have become household words and have come to mean political and economic freedom for millions.

It is a time to rejoice for those who are experiencing democracy, many for the first time, but it is not a time for us to become complacent and cut our military strength to a point of weakness. The Soviets have a long history of broken promises; we have a long history of dismantling our military services too soon after a threat subsides. Over the years, we have never properly prepared for demobilization. No one debates that the military forces can be smaller—they can—but any such reduction must be made in accordance with a well-thought-out plan.

No one expected World War II to end so quickly; too little thought had been given to the demobilization process. General Marshall recalled that the "confused and tumultuous" demobilization was very injurious to our military capability. This was proven when we entered the Korean conflict and found our tactical forces without proper radios or adequate photo reconnaissance, and we were unable to deploy our forces quickly to the Far East.

When we withdrew our forces from Vietnam, we promptly reduced our Air Force fighting strength and the number of aircraft in the operational inventory. Flying hours per pilot fell dramatically; Strategic Air Command pilots, for example, flew only two or three times a month, certainly not enough to retain their flying skills.

Research and development and procurement programs have also been cut drastically after each war. Our post-Vietnam malaise produced the "decade of neglect" of the 1970s and invited a period of "Soviet adventurism" that was scaled back only by the buildup during the Reagan administration from 1981 to 1986. In the 1980s, our inability to react strongly to the hostage situation and the invasion of Afghanistan resulted directly from the conscious underfunding of our forces, the inadequate training they received, and the creation of a "hollow force" incapable of protecting our national interests.

As long as the Soviet Union maintains its awesome military forces and other nations, like Iraq, threaten the peace, we must be prepared for possible conflict. It was especially gratifying to observe the wise use of air power in the 1991 war against Iraq, as the air forces of the international coalition fought a tyrant bent on dominating the Middle East. Following the principles of military leadership, properly employing air power, and using highly sophisticated weapon systems, all developed because of our experience during World War II, Korea, and Vietnam, resulted in early air supremacy for the coalition. I think military analysts and historians will record that thousands of American lives were saved because of our preparedness for such an action. Special tribute must be reserved for those decision makers in power during the 1980s who realized the declining state of our military forces and rebuilt them to a high degree of readiness, thus enabling President Bush to take the actions he did with confidence and assurance of a military victory.

We should always pray for peace; to maintain it, we must remain so strong militarily that no nation will dare to attack us. We must always be able to deter an all-out war and be prepared to cope with the small wars that may from time to time be forced upon us. In order to have that capability, we must have the continuous support of science, technology, and industry because over a period of time what we have on hand is going to become obsolete.

It is possible that at some point, the world situation may permit and encourage us to reduce the size of our forces. If so, I hope we can avoid the problems associated with the previous cutbacks, when all seemed peaceful. If the experience of four wars during my adult lifetime gives me any license to dispense advice, it is to remember how unprepared we were before each of those conflicts. We should never allow this to happen again.

Since the calendar and I have turned into the nineties, I have become a member of the thumb-twiddling society. Several years ago, when I was inclined to take on more extracurricular jobs than I could do well, I deliberately cut down on my workload. I found that when you can't do a job well, you don't enjoy doing it. There's no satisfaction in doing a poor job.

One of the privileges of age is the opportunity to sit back and ponder what you've seen and done over the years. In my nine-plus decades, I've formed some views about life and living that I have freely imposed on trusting audiences, both readers and listeners. I have concluded that we were all put on this earth for a purpose. That purpose is to make it, within our capabilities, a better place in which to live. We can do this by painting a picture, writing a poem, building a bridge, protecting the environment, combating prejudice and injustice, providing help to those in need, and in thousands of other ways. The criterion is this: If a man leaves the earth a better place than he found it, then his life has been worthwhile.

The move to Carmel gave me more time for occasional hunting and fishing expeditions with old, dear friends and to take trips with Joe whenever the spirit moved us. Joe, never one to sit idle, continued to write her daily postcards and letters to each of our friends who was ill, either at home or in the hospital. She continued doing this for "my shut-ins" until she could no longer hold a pen.

On December 24, 1988, after a stroke, followed by months of steady physical deterioration, my precious Joe passed away. It was our seventy-first wedding anniversary. She rests forever in Arlington National Cemetery, where I will join her one of these days.

In February 1990, I moved to Pebble Beach, California, where John and Priscilla built their dream house on the property Joe and I had bought in the 1940s. They had a large addition constructed that is now my final residence and office. As I watch the many bird species scramble for position to get the seed I put out each day, I realize my life has gone full cycle. I'm home and I'm content.

Luck has been with me all my life. Fortunately, I was always able to exploit that luck during my flying years and at each turn in my career. The best thing I ever did was to convince Joe that she should marry me; the luckiest thing that ever happened to me was when she finally did. That's why, whenever I'm asked, I say that I would never want to relive my life. I could never be so lucky again.

Thanks, Joe. I couldn't have done it without you.

APPENDIX 1

PROPOSAL FOR THE BOMBING ATTACK ON TOKYO

Subject: B-25 Special Project
To: Commanding General, Army Air Forces

The purpose of this special project is to bomb and fire the industrial center of Japan.

It is anticipated that this not only will cause confusion and impede production but will undoubtedly facilitate operation against Japan in other theaters due to their probable withdrawal of troops for the purpose of defending the home country.

An action of this kind is most desirable now due to the psychological effect on the American public, our allies, and our enemies.

The method contemplated is to bring carrier-borne bombers to within 400 to 500 miles (all distances mentioned will be in statute miles) of the coast of Japan, preferably to the south-southeast. They will then take off from the carrier deck and proceed directly to selected targets in the Tokyo-Yokohama, Nagoya, and Osaka-Kobe areas.

Simultaneous bombings of these areas is contemplated, with the bombers coming in up waterways from the southeast and, after dropping their bombs, returning in the same direction. After clearing the Japanese outside coastline a sufficient distance, a general westerly course will be set for one or more of the following airports in China: Chuchow, Chuchow (Lishui), Yushan, and/or Chienou. Chuchow is about 70 miles inland and 200 miles to the south-southwest of Shanghai.

After refueling, the airplanes will proceed to the strong Chinese air base at Chungking, about 800 miles distant, and from there to such ultimate objective as may, at that time, be indicated.

The greatest nonstop distance that any airplane will have to fly is 2,000 miles.

Eighteen B-25B (North American medium bomber) airplanes will be employed in this raid. Each will carry about 1,100 gallons of gasoline, which assures a range of 2,400 miles at 5,000 feet in still air.

Each bomber will carry two 500-pound demolition bombs and as near as possible to 1,000 pounds of incendiaries. The demolition bombs will be dropped first and then the incendiaries.

The extra gasoline will be carried in a 275-gallon auxiliary leakproof tank in the top of the bomb bay and a 175-gallon flexible rubber tank in the passageway above the bomb bay. It is anticipated that the gasoline from this top tank will be used up and the tank flattened out or rolled up and removed prior to entering the combat zone. This assures that the airplane will be fully operational and minimizes the fire and explosion hazard characteristic of a nearly empty tank.

In all other respects the airplanes are conventional. The work of installing the required additional tankage is being done by Mid-Continent Airlines at Minneapolis. All production and installation work is progressing according to schedule and the 24 airplanes (six spares) should be completely converted by March 15.

Extensive range and performance tests will be conducted on airplane number 1 while the others are being converted. A short period will be required to assemble and give special training to the crews. The training will include teamwork in bombing, gunnery, navigation, flying, short takeoff, and at least one carrier takeoff for each pilot.

If the crews are selected promptly from men familiar with their jobs and the B-25B airplane, the complete unit should be ready for loading on the carrier by April 1.

General operational instructions will be issued just before takeoff from the carrier.

Due to the greater accuracy of daylight bombing, a daylight raid is contemplated. The present concept of the project calls for a night takeoff from the carrier and arrival over objectives at dawn. Rapid refueling at the landing points will permit arrival at Chungking before dark.

A night raid will be made if, due to last-minute information received from our intelligence section or other source, a daylight raid is definitely inadvisable. The night raid should be made on a clear night, moonlight if Japan is blacked out, moonless if it is not.

All available pertinent information regarding targets and defenses will be obtained from A-2, G-2, and other existing sources.

The Navy has already supervised takeoff tests made at Norfolk, Virginia, using B-25B bombers carrying loads of 23,000 pounds, 26,000 pounds, and 29,000 pounds. These tests indicate that no difficulty need be anticipated in taking off from the carrier deck with a gross load of around 31,000 pounds.*

The Navy will be charged with providing a carrier (probably the *Hornet*), with loading and storing the airplanes, and with delivering them to the takeoff position.

The Chemical Warfare Service is designing and preparing special incendiary bomb clusters in order to assure that the maximum amount that limited space permits, up to 1,000 pounds per airplane, may be carried. Forty-eight of these clusters will be ready for shipment from Edgewood Arsenal [Maryland] by March 15.

About 20,000 U.S. gallons of 100-octane aviation gasoline and 600 gallons of lubricating oil will be laid down at Chuchow and associated fields. All other supplies and necessary emergency repair equipment will be carried on the airplanes.

First Lieutenant Harry W. Howze, now with the Air Service Command and formerly with the Standard Oil Company of New Jersey, will be charged with making arrangements for the fuel caches in China. He will work through A-2 and A-4 and with Colonel Claire Chennault, a former Air Corps officer and now aviation advisor to the Chinese government. Colonel Chennault should assign a responsible American or a Chinese who speaks

---

*I did not know until years later that the third airplane had not participated in the trials.

English to physically check and assure that the supplies are in place. This man should also be available to assist the crews in servicing the airplanes. That the supplies are in place can be indicated by suitable radio code signal. Work on placing supplies must start at once.

Shortly before the airplanes arrive, the proper Chinese agencies should be advised that the airplanes are coming soon, but the inference will be that they are flying up from the south in order to stage a raid on Japan from which they plan to return to the same base.

Radio signals from the bombing planes immediately after they drop their bombs may be used to indicate arrival at gassing points some six or seven hours later.

Care must be exercised to see that the Chinese are advised just in time, as any information given to the Chinese may be expected to fall into Japanese hands and a premature notification would be fatal to the project.

An initial study of meteorological conditions indicates that the sooner the raid is made the better will be the prevailing weather conditions. The weather will become increasingly unfavorable after the end of April. Weather was considered largely from the point of view of avoiding morning fog over Tokyo and other targets, low overcast over Chuchow and Chungking, icing, and strong westerly winds.

If possible, daily weather predictions or anticipated weather conditions at Chungking and the coast should be sent, at a specified time, in suitable code, in order to assist the meteorologist on the carrier in analyzing his forecasts.

Lieutenant Colonel J. H. Doolittle, Air Corps, will be in charge of the preparations for and will be in personal command of the project. Other flight personnel will, due to the considerable hazard incident to such a mission, be volunteers.

Each airplane will carry its normal complement of five crew members: pilot, copilot, bombardier-navigator, radio operator, and gunner-mechanic.

One crew member will be a competent meteorologist and one an experienced navigator. All navigators will be trained in celestial navigation.

Two ground liaison officers will be assigned. One will remain on the mainland and the other on the carrier.

At least three crew members will speak Chinese—one on each of the target units.

Should the Soviets be willing to accept delivery of 18 B-25B airplanes, on lease-lend, at Vladivostok, our problem would be greatly simplified and conflict with the Halverson project avoided.

APPENDIX 2

REPORT OF JOHN M. BIRCH

The Chinese officials at Chuhsien told me that outright purchase of a burial plot was prohibited by existing international law, but that Major Y. C. Chen, representing the Chinese air force, would like to present to the U.S. Army Air Corps the free use of a plot for 100 years or so long as the Air Corps wanted it. I thanked them for their kind expressions and asked them to wait until May 5; meanwhile (May 2), I sent the following telegram to the Military Mission:

> COLONEL DOOLITTLE'S INSTRUCTIONS TO BUY PLOT RE-
> CEIVED. MAJOR CHEN CHUHSIEN AIR STATION OFFERING
> PLOT NOT FOR SALE BUT FOR FREE AMERICAN USE.
> SHALL ACCEPT IF NOT OTHERWISE INSTRUCTED BEFORE
> MAY 5. BIRCH.

. . . No contrary instructions came, so I accepted Major Chen's offer on May 5. He offered to supply the labor connected with the burial, and asked me to instruct the workmen. Hindered by constant air raid alarms and air raids, the workmen failed to have the grave and stone ready until May 19, on which date Faktor's body was buried. . . .

As to information gathered: . . . Concerning those who

came down outside of free China—unofficial and uncertain reports locate them as follows: In Siberia, five men, condition and identity unknown here; near Nanchang, five men, probably those of Captain York's plane, two reported dead, two captured, and one rumored to be safe in free China; in Hsiang Shan Bay, five men, two reported dead and three captured, identity unknown to me.

On May 18, a telegram came to Chuhsien from Dr. White at Linhai, just as his party was leaving there for Chuchow (Chuhsien). He expected to reach us at Chuhsien by May 22. On May 20 I wired the Military Mission, asking whether or not I should accompany him to Chungking; at that time I could not anticipate the subsequent change of his route, which kept him from coming by way of Chuhsien. The reply calling me to Chungking reached me on May 23. Also on that date the Chinese air force officers at Wan Tsuen turned over to me a number of personal articles salvaged from the B-25 which crashed near Shuei Chang, Chekiang, these articles to be carried to the Military Mission at Chungking.

The funds I received . . . are untouched; as regards board and lodging, I was the guest of the Chinese air force from April 28 to May 26, 1942.

APPENDIX 3

BOMBING ATTACK ON TOKYO:
POST-RAID CREW SUMMARY

CREW NO. 2: Lieutenant Travis Hoover was the pilot and had followed us all the way to the Japanese coast. His copilot was Lieutenant William N. Fitzhugh; Lieutenant Richard E. Miller, bombardier; Lieutenant Carl R. Wildner, navigator; Sergeant Douglas V. Radney, engineer-gunner. After deviating to his target area and bombing two factory buildings and storehouses, Hoover sighted us again and trailed us west toward the Chinese coast. As with everyone else, they encountered a stiff headwind and didn't think they were going to make it to the mainland. However, the headwind lightened and then, providentially, turned into a nice 25-knot tailwind. We all could tell when the wind shifted by observing the whitecaps on the waves. When the weather worsened, Hoover had to leave us and go his own way. Instead of bailing out when his gas was about gone, Trav elected to belly into a rice paddy. No one was injured; after hiding out and walking for about three days his crew was taken into custody by about 30 armed guerrillas who fed them and bedded them down.

Beginning on April 22, they traveled by boat to Sungyao where they met Tung-sheng Liu, a young English-speaking Chinese engineering student, who had just come through the Japanese lines disguised as a merchant. He guided them by ricksha, bus, train, and on foot to Chuhsien where they met Captain Davey Jones and Lieutenant Everett "Brick" Holstrom. They had remained there to intercept gathering crews. Hoover's crew arrived in Chungking on May 14.*

CREW NO. 3: When Hoover's plane cleared the *Hornet*'s deck, Lieutenant Robert M. "Bob" Gray took off. Their three explosive bombs were dropped on industrial targets; the incendiary landed on a dock area. They experienced some antiaircraft fire but were not hit as far as they knew. Arriving over China, Gray ordered his crew to bail out; Corporal Leland D. Faktor, the gunner on this crew, was the one who was killed. Lieutenant Charles J. Ozuk, navigator, injured a leg on landing; and Lieutenant Jacob E. "Shorty" Manch, copilot, cut himself with his knife trying to make a water bag out of his parachute's rubber cushion. Bob Gray and Sergeant Aden Jones, the rear gunner, were not injured; all four made their way to Chuhsien with the help of friendly Chinese.

CREW NO. 4: Pilot of this crew was Lieutenant Everett W. "Brick" Holstrom; his copilot was Lieutenant Lucian N. Youngblood. Shortly after takeoff, Corporal Bert M. Jordan, the rear gunner, reported that the gun turret was out of commission. This meant they had no defense against enemy fighters except the .30-caliber gun in the nose. They made landfall south of Tokyo and were fired on by four Japanese fighters. When the fighters appeared, Holstrom explained what he did:

"I told the navigator (Lieutenant Harry McCool) to tell Corporal (Robert J.) Stephens, the bombardier, to try to use his nose gun. I had given him (McCool) previous instructions to have Stephens salvo the bombs if we were intercepted, so the bombs were salvoed [into Tokyo Bay] from about 75 feet."

This crew also bailed out over China when their gas ran out. McCool was injured slightly when he landed on a steep slope.

CREW NO. 5: Captain David M. "Davey" Jones piloted this

---

*After the war, Liu came to the States and received his doctorate in aeronautical engineering from the University of Minnesota in 1947. He became a citizen in 1954 and was employed by the Air Force as an aeronautical engineer at Wright-Patterson Air Force Base, in Ohio, until his retirement.

plane. Lieutenant Ross R. Wilder was copilot; Lieutenant Denver V. Truelove, bombardier; and Lieutenant Eugene F. McGurl, navigator. Corporal Joseph W. Manske, the gunner, had tried to top off the tanks at the last minute before takeoff, but because the carrier was in "battle condition," the fuel supply had been turned off. Consequently, the tanks were not full. After bombing an oil storage tank, a power plant, and a large manufacturing facility, they escaped. This crew bailed out and joined up next day. No one was injured.

CREW NO. 6: The pilot of this crew was Lieutenant Dean E. Hallmark, a husky six-footer. Copilot was Lieutenant Robert J. Meder; Lieutenant Chase J. Nielsen was navigator; Sergeant Donald E. Fitzmaurice, engineer-gunner; Corporal William J. Dieter, bombardier. Their target was a large steel mill in northeast Tokyo. They escaped without being intercepted. When they got close to China and were nearly out of gas, Hallmark elected to ditch the B-25 close to the beach. The landing was very hard. Hallmark was cut and bruised and, with some difficulty, made it to shore where he was joined by Meder and Nielsen. Dieter and Fitzmaurice were badly injured and drowned. Assisted by friendly Chinese, the surviving trio buried the bodies. They were later apprehended by Japanese soldiers and became prisoners of war.

The Japanese slaughtered many of the Chinese who helped this crew and others. We did not know what happened to these men until the war was over.

CREW NO. 7: This crew's story has been widely told in a book and motion picture under the title of *Thirty Seconds Over Tokyo*. Written by the pilot, Lieutenant Ted W. Lawson, with Bob Considine, Lawson tells of his crew's experience from takeoff to eventual recuperation from injuries received when they ditched after bombing factories in Japan's capital city. Lawson, his copilot, Lieutenant Dean Davenport; Lieutenant Charles L. McClure, navigator; and Lieutenant Robert S. Clever, bombardier, all badly hurt, somehow made it to shore. Corporal David J. Thatcher, the gunner, was unhurt. He assisted the others and prevented their being captured. He stayed with them until they began their recovery at a hospital run by Chinese doctors and English missionaries.

Lawson, the most seriously injured of the crew, nearly died. He was saved after Lieutenant T. R. "Doc" White, the gunner on the fifteenth plane, caught up with them. It was very fortuitous that the only physician on the raid was near enough to render assistance. Doc had to amputate Ted's leg to save his life; in the process Doc gave him two pints of his own blood. The second donation made Doc awfully woozy for several days and could have caused him serious problems. I later made sure that Dave Thatcher and Doc White received the Silver Star for their gallantry and dedication to their crews at great risk to themselves.

CREW NO. 8: Captain Edward J. "Ski" York piloted this plane. His copilot was Lieutenant Robert G. Emmens; Lieutenant Nolan A. Herndon, navigator-bombardier; Sergeant David W. Pohl, gunner; and Sergeant Theodore H. Laban, engineer. Apparently, their plane had been dogged by engine problems from the days at Sacramento when the ground crews there fiddled with the carburetors. Both engines burned fuel excessively, which was all too evident on the run into their target area. After they dropped their bombs, York had to make a difficult command decision. They could not make it if they followed the escape route south and then across the China Sea to the mainland. Making a forced landing in Japan was unthinkable. York believed the only option was to head for Soviet territory and, against orders, headed in that direction. They landed at a field near Vladivostok and naively hoped to refuel and be on their way to Chungking.

Although the State Department had been negotiating with the Soviets to allow us to land there after bombing Japan right up until our departure from Alameda, permission was never granted. In their view, they had good reason. Totally engaged in a war with Nazi Germany in the west, they could not afford to have to battle the Japanese in the east. The Soviets declared their neutrality. To preserve this status, York, his crew, and their B-25 had to be interned. Although the Soviets were our allies, these men were virtual prisoners for the next 14 months, until they escaped into Persia (now Iran). For many months, the Soviet government sent us monthly bills for 30,000 rubles for their keep. For some time afterward, I received irate telephone calls from Secretary of the Treasury Henry Morgenthau each time a bill arrived from the Soviet embassy. I recommended he ignore them. I assume he did.

CREW NO. 9: Lieutenant Harold F. "Doc" Watson piloted this plane. His crew dropped their eggs on the Tokyo Gas and Electric Co., on the shore of Tokyo Bay, south of the city. His crew consisted of copilot Lieutenant James M. Parker; Sergeant Wayne M. Bissell, bombardier; Lieutenant Thomas C. Griffin, navigator; and Sergeant Eldred V. Scott, engineer-gunner. As did most of the others, they bailed out in the darkness and rain; Watson was the only one injured and had to be carried to Hengyang by Chinese porters. He was picked up there and eventually evacuated to the States. In the wake of this crew's escape, Japanese forces killed thousands of Chinese peasants for assisting the Americans. It was later estimated that 250,000 innocent Chinese paid with their lives for helping us.

CREW NO. 10: Lieutenant Richard O. "Dick" Joyce's main target was the Japan Special Steel Co., located in southern Tokyo. A secondary target was a nearby precision-instrument factory. Both were hit. Joyce's copilot was Lieutenant J. Royden Stork; Lieutenant Horace E. "Sally" Crouch, navigator-bombardier; Sergeant George E. Larkin, gunner; and Sergeant Edwin W. Horton, engineer-gunner. This plane encountered heavy ack-ack fire but escaped without damage. As Horton received the order from Joyce to bail out the rear hatch of the aircraft, he replied, "Here I go. Thanks, sir, for a swell ride." None of this crew had any serious injuries.

CREW NO. 11: Captain C. Ross Greening headed this crew; with Lieutenant Kenneth E. Reddy, copilot; Lieutenant Frank A. Kappeler, navigator; Sergeant William L. Birch, bombardier; and Sergeant Melvin J. Gardner, engineer-gunner. Their targets were the docks, oil refineries, and warehouses between Tokyo and Yokohama. Intercepted and fired on by enemy fighters, they dropped all four bombs on a large refinery and tank farm, which immediately exploded. When the weather worsened upon arrival over the Chinese coast, Greening elected to have his crew bail out. All did successfully, although Reddy suffered a slight concussion when he hit. He carried a piece of rock in his scalp for several days until he received treatment in Chuhsien.

CREW NO. 12: Lieutenant William M. "Bill" Bower headed this crew. His copilot was Lieutenant Thadd H. Blanton; Lieutenant William R. Pound, navigator; Sergeant Omer A. Duquette, engineer-gunner; and Sergeant Waldo J. Bither, bombardier. When they arrived over Japan, they were trailed by Japanese fighters but not fired on. Barrage balloons had been erected over their target—the Yokohama dockyards—so they dropped one demolition on the Ogura refinery, two on factories, and the incendiary on a large warehouse.

This crew also bailed out; Sergeant Duquette broke a bone in his foot on landing. The Chinese made sedan chairs out of parachute harnesses and carried this crew to a joinup with Dick Joyce's crew.

Sergeant Bither had a serious problem before the bailout. As he made his way from the nose of the B-25 toward the flight deck, he inadvertently sprung his parachute open and had to repack it in the crawlway. Of all the men on the raid, he was the only one who had ever had any training in parachute packing. When I asked him years later if he was worried about it opening, he replied, "Well, I was a little concerned, but if it didn't open, I didn't have anybody to blame but myself."

CREW NO. 13: Being the thirteenth B-25 off the carrier didn't bother this crew. It was piloted by Lieutenant Edgar E. McElroy; copilot was Lieutenant Richard A. Knobloch; Lieutenant Clayton J. Campbell, navigator; Sergeant Robert C. Bourgeois, bombardier; and Sergeant Adam R. Williams, engineer-gunner. After bombing ships in dry dock and nearby workshops at Yokohama, this crew bailed out successfully. They were rounded up by Chinese guerrillas and proceeded on ponies and sedan chairs to Poyang, a city of about 300,000, where they were greeted and feted by hundreds of townspeople. Banners fluttered from windows; a large one read: WELCOME BRAVE AMERICAN FLYERS. FIRST TO BOMB TOKIO. UNITED STATES AND CHINA RULE THE PACIFIC.

CREW NO. 14: My deputy, Major John A. "Jack" Hilger was the pilot of this aircraft. His copilot was Lieutenant Jack A. Sims; Lieutenant James H. "Herb" Macia, navigator-bombardier; Sergeant Jacob Eierman, engineer; and Sergeant Edwin V. Bain, gunner. Their target was a military barracks, an oil and gas works, and the Mitsubishi aircraft facility in Nagoya. They were all hit with precision, especially the last.

This crew bailed out successfully and made their way to Chuchow in two days. Hilger told me later, "I was never so glad to see anyone in my life as I was to see Jones, Greening, Bower, and all their crew members. It was like a homecoming and we were all as happy as kids. There's nothing like a familiar face in a foreign country.'' He was certainly right.

CREW NO. 15: The target assigned to this plane was located in Kobe, part of an industrial complex southwest of Tokyo. It was piloted by Lieutenant Donald G. Smith; Lieutenant Griffith P. Williams, copilot; Lieutenant Howard A. Sessler, navigator; Sergeant Edward J. Saylor, engineer-gunner; and Lieutenant (Dr.) Thomas R. ''Doc'' White, gunner and physician. This crew elected to ditch in the ocean off the coast; fortunately, no one was hurt. However, Doc White lost his medical supplies when their life raft overturned in the rough surf. The crew traveled for several days on a Chinese junk, successfully evading Japanese search parties.

As they progressed toward Chuchow, they learned that Lawson and his crew were injured and headed toward a hospital at Linhai. Smith decided to detour to see if they could help out. When they arrived, Doc found that Lawson, Davenport, McClure, and Clever were in no shape to travel. He elected to stay with them while the other members of Smith's crew and Dave Thatcher of Lawson's crew went on to Chuchow.

CREW NO. 16: This crew was earmarked for trouble from the beginning. The pilot was Lieutenant William G. ''Bill'' Farrow; copilot was Lieutenant Robert L. Hite; Lieutenant George Barr, navigator; Corporal Jacob DeShazer, bombardier; and Sergeant Harold A. Spatz, engineer-gunner. Just after Farrow started the engines, a sailor slipped into the spinning left propeller and his left arm was cut off. He was quickly carried away by his buddies.

Last off the carrier, Farrow followed two other planes to their target area in Nagoya. While under attack by fighters, they bombed oil storage tanks and an aircraft factory. They arrived over the Chinese coast at dusk in rain showers and climbed on top of the overcast. As they plodded on and the gas gauges neared the empty mark, there was a break in the overcast and Barr identified the city lights below as Nanchang. Although they knew the city was occupied by the Japanese, they had no choice and bailed out. All were quickly captured. We knew nothing more about what happened to these five men until after the war.

CAREER SUMMARY

U.S. Army Air Service and Air Corps, 1917–1930
Major, U.S. Army Air Corps Reserve, 1930–1940
Major, U.S. Army Air Corps, 1940
Lieutenant Colonel, 1942
Brigadier General, 1942
Major General, 1942
Lieutenant General, 1944
General, 1985
Commanding General, 12th Air Force, North Africa, 1942
Commanding General, 15th Air Force, Italy, 1943
Commanding General, 8th Air Force, England, 1944
Commanding General, 8th Air Force, Okinawa, 1945
Vice President, Shell Union Oil Company, 1946–1947
Director, Shell Union Oil Company, 1946–1967
Chairman of the Board, Space Technology Laboratories, 1959–1962
Director, Space Technology Laboratories, 1959–1963
Director, Thompson-Ramo-Wooldridge Company, 1961–1969
Consultant, TRW Systems, 1962–1965
Director, Mutual of Omaha Insurance Co., 1961–1986
Director Emeritus and Consultant, Mutual of Omaha Insurance Co., 1986–
Trustee, Aerospace Corporation, 1963–1969
Vice Chairman, Board of Trustees, and Chairman of Executive Committee, Aerospace Corporation, 1965–1969

Director, United Benefit Life Insurance Company of Omaha, 1964–1980

Director, Tele-Trip Company, 1966–1980

Director, Companion Life Insurance Company of New York, 1968–1980

Director, Mutual of Omaha Growth & Income Funds, 1968–1980

MILITARY DECORATIONS

Medal of Honor

Distinguished Service Medal, with Oak Leaf Cluster

Silver Star

Distinguished Flying Cross, with two Oak Leaf Clusters

Bronze Star

Air Medal, with three Oak Leaf Clusters

Order of the Condor (Bolivia)

Yon-Hwei, Class III (China)

Knight Commander, Order of the Bath (Great Britain)

Grand Officer of the Légion d'Honneur and Croix de Guerre, with Palm (France)

Grand Order of the Crown, with Palm, and Croix de Guerre with Palm (Belgium)

Grand Commander (Poland)

Abdon Calderon, First Class (Ecuador)

EDUCATION

Manual Arts High School, Los Angeles, California

Los Angeles Junior College, 1916–1917

University of California, Bachelor of Arts, 1922

Massachusetts Institute of Technology, Master of Science, 1924, and Doctor of Science, 1925

HONORARY DEGREES

University of California, Doctor of Laws

University of Michigan, Doctor of Engineering

Clarkson College of Technology, Doctor of Science

Brooklyn Polytechnic Institute, Doctor of Engineering
Waynesburg College, Doctor of Military Science
Northland College, Doctor of Laws
University of Alaska, Doctor of Science
Pennsylvania Military College, Doctor of Science

HONORS AND AWARDS

Schneider Marine Cup, 1925
Mackay Trophy, 1925
Spirit of St. Louis Award, 1929
Harmon Trophy, Ligue des Aviateurs, 1930
Bendix Trophy, 1931
Thompson Trophy, 1932
Guggenheim Trophy, 1942
International Harmon Trophy, 1940, 1949
Wright Brothers Trophy, 1953
Fédération Aéronautique Internationale Gold Medal, 1954
Silver Quill, 1959
International Aerospace Hall of Fame, San Diego, California, 1966
Aviation Hall of Fame, Dayton, Ohio, 1967
Thomas D. White National Defense Award, 1967
Horatio Alger Award, 1972
Conservation Hall of Fame, 1973
Wings of Man Award, Society of Experimental Test Pilots, 1973
Bishop Wright Air Industry Award, 1975
Sylvanus Thayer Award, U.S. Military Academy, 1983
C. C. Criss Award, 1984
Motorsports Hall of Fame Award, 1989
Grand Cross of Honour, Supreme Council of Scottish Rite, 1989
Presidential Medal of Freedom, 1989

APPOINTMENTS

Member, Army Air Corps Investigating Committee (Baker Board), 1934
Chairman, Secretary of War's Board on Officer/Enlisted Men Relationships, 1946
Member, Joint Congressional Aviation Policy Board, 1948

Advisor, Committee on National Security Organization, 1948
Chairman, President's Airport Commission, 1952
Chairman, 50th Anniversary of Powered Flight, 1953
Chairman, President's Task Group on Air Inspection, Stassen Disarmament Committee, 1955
Chairman, Air Force Scientific Advisory Board, 1955–1958
Member, President's Foreign Intelligence Advisory Board, 1955–1965
Chairman, National Advisory Committee for Aeronautics, 1956–1958
Member, Advisory Board, National Air Museum, Smithsonian Institution, 1956–1965
Member, Defense Science Board, 1957–1958
Member, President's Science Advisory Committee, 1957–1958
Member, National Aeronautics and Space Council, 1958
Member, Plowshare Committee of the Atomic Energy Commission, 1959–1972
Member, National Institutes of Health Study, 1963–1965
Member, Air Force Space Systems Advisory Group, 1963–1967

ASSOCIATIONS

Honorary Fellow, American Institute of Aeronautics and Astronautics
Fellow, Royal Aeronautical Society
Fellow, American Astronautical Society
Member, American Petroleum Institute
Member, Society of Automotive Engineers
Founding President and Member, Air Force Association
Member, National Aeronautic Association
Member, Order of Daedalians
Member, Explorers Club

AVIATION "FIRSTS"

First cross-continental crossing in less than 24 hours, 1922
First to execute outside loop, 1927
First "blind" flight, 1929
First cross-continental crossing in less than 12 hours, 1932

BIBLIOGRAPHY

Arnold, Henry H., *Global Mission*. New York: Harper and Brothers, 1949.

Coffey, Thomas M., *Hap*. New York: The Viking Press, 1982.

Copp, DeWitt S., *Forged in Fire*. New York: Doubleday & Co., 1980.

Copp, DeWitt S., *A Few Great Captains*. New York: Doubleday & Co., 1982.

Cray, Ed, *General of the Army: George C. Marshall, Soldier and Statesman*. New York: W. W. Norton & Co., 1990.

Freeman, Roger A., *The Mighty Eighth: A History of the U.S. 8th Army Air Force*. Garden City, N.Y.: Doubleday & Co., 1970.

Frisbee, John L., ed., *Makers of the United States Air Force*. Washington, D.C.: Office of Air Force History, U.S. Air Force, 1987.

Glines, Carroll V., *Doolittle's Tokyo Raiders*. Princeton, N.J.: D. Van Nostrand Co., 1964.

Glines, Carroll V., *Four Came Home*. Princeton, N.J.: D. Van Nostrand Co., 1966.

Glines, Carroll V., *The Compact History of the United States Air Force*. New York: Hawthorn Books, 1973.

Glines, Carroll V., *The Doolittle Raid: America's Daring First Strike Against Japan*. New York: Orion Books, 1988.

Goldberg, Alfred, ed., *A History of the United States Air Force, 1907–1957*. Princeton, N.J.: D. Van Nostrand Co., 1957.

Gorn, Michael H., *Harnessing the Genie*. Washington, D.C.: Office of Air Force History, U.S. Air Force, 1988.

Hallion, Richard P., *Legacy of Flight: The Guggenheim Contribution to American Aviation*. Seattle, Wa.: University of Washington Press, 1977.

Hallion, Richard P., *Test Pilots*. Washington, D.C.: Smithsonian Institution Press, 1988.

Hansell, Haywood S., Jr., *The Air Plan That Defeated Hitler*. Atlanta, Ga.: Higgins-McArthur/Longino & Porter, 1972.

Johnson, Bruce, *The Man with 2 Hats*. New York: Carlton Press, 1968.

Maurer, Maurer, *Aviation in the U.S. Army, 1919–1939*. Washington, D.C.: Office of Air Force History, U.S. Air Force, 1987.

Meilinger, Philip S., *Hoyt S. Vandenberg*. Bloomington, In.: Indiana University Press, 1989.

Mets, David R., *Master of Airpower: General Carl A. Spaatz*. Novato, Ca.: Presidio Press, 1988.

Parton, James, *"Air Force Spoken Here."* Bethesda, Md.: Adler & Adler, 1986.

Straubel, James H., *Crusade for Airpower*. Washington, D.C.: Aerospace Education Foundation, 1982.

INDEX

Note: Certain kinds of information are grouped under the following headings: Aircraft instruments; Airfields and air bases; Airplanes; Air shows, meets, and races; Military units; Ships of the U.S. Navy. The abbreviation "JD" (referring to James H. "Jimmy" Doolittle) is alphabetized as if spelled "Doolittle, James H. 'Jimmy.' " Other names appearing first name first in subheadings are also alphabetized by last name. An italic n attached to a page number means that the reference is to a footnote.

523

Louis 'David' Riel: Prophet of the New World
by T. Flanagan
A sympathetic portrayal of a great Metis leader — a man too often dismissed by historians as mad. /215 pages/$4.95

Ma Murray by Georgina Keddell
The outspoken newspaperwoman who became a legend in her own time. /301 pages/12 photos/$5.95

Newsworthy: The Lives of Media Women
by Susan Crean
Informal, entertaining, fun-to-read profiles of women in the media — and how they got to where they are today. /368 pages/35 photos/$5.95

Our Nell: A Scrapbook Biography of Nellie McClung
by Candace Savage
The story of Nellie McClung, politician, writer, and vigorous advocate of women's rights. /203 pages /51 pho_tos /$5.95

Pauline: A Biography of Pauline Johnson by Betty Keller
The story of a beautiful, talented, romantic woman of the Victorian era who dazzled Canadians in her role as a Mohawk princess-poet. /352 pages/34 photos/$5.95

The Prince and His Lady by Mollie Gillen
The love story of Edward, Duke of Kent, and his French mistress, and their years in Quebec and Halifax. /282 pages /27 photos/$5.95

Richard Hatfield: The Seventeen Year Saga
by Richard Starr
The story of one of Canada's most colourful and controversial figures - the successes and the scanddals. /262 pages/ 8 photos /$5.95

Something Hidden: Wilder Penfield by Jefferson Lewis
The life of the world-famous Canadian surgeon and scientist who explored the hidden mysteries of the brain — and the mind. /311 pages/22 photos/$5.95

Sons and Seals by Guy Wright
The true adventures of a young student who goes on a seal hunt with a crew of 32 Newfoundlanders. /160 pages /20 photos /$4.95

Stanley Knowles by Susan Mann Trofimenkoff
An informal, affectionate profile of a remarkable Canadian politician who served as a backbench member for 40 years. /240 pages/12 photos/$5.95

Ticket to Hell by A. Robert Prouse
A young Canadian's story of three years in a German prisoner-of-war camp — told with warmth, humour and honesty. /161 pages/50 photos/$4.95

Tomorrow is School by Don Sawyer
The adventure of two young teachers in an isolated Newfoundland outport./205 pages/12 photos/$4.95

The Wheel of Things: L. M. Montgomery
by Mollie Gillen
The remarkable and tragic life story of the woman who created Canada's best-loved heroine, Anne of Green Gables. /200 pages/32 photos/$4.95

Wife Of... by Sondra Gotlieb
An irreverent, often hilarious portrait of Washington's powerful and important people by the wife of Canada's U.S. Ambassador. /208 pages/$4.95